Praise for
TOREY HAYDEN

Books by Torey Hayden

TOREY HAYDEN

TWILIGHT CHILDREN

THREE VOICES NO ONE HEARD UNTIL A THERAPIST LISTENED

AVON BOOKS
An Imprint of HarperCollins*Publishers*

AVON BOOKS
An Imprint of HarperCollins*Publishers*
10 East 53rd Street
New York, New York 10022-5299

First Avon Books paperback printing: March 2006
First William Morrow hardcover printing: March 2005

Avon Trademark Reg. U.S. Pat. Off. and in Other Countries, Marca
Registrada, Hecho en U.S.A.
HarperCollins® is a trademark of HarperCollins Publishers Inc.

Printed in the U.S.A.

10 9 8 7 6 5 4 3 2 1

TWILIGHT CHILDREN

Chapter

1

$\mathcal{S}$he was a small, fine-boned girl with a pointed pixie chin and unusually distinct cheekbones. Her hair was a soft black, straight and shoulder length, but it had been rather raffishly cut, as if perhaps done by another child. Her eyes, however, defined her face. Enormous, protruding slightly, and fluidly dark, like shadowed water, they overpowered her other features. She wasn't what I would call a pretty girl, but she was striking in a faintly unreal way, so that when she lifted her hand to push hair back from her face, I half expected to see elfin ears.

"Hello," I said and pulled out the chair at the table.

She hunched forward, hands down between her knees so that her chin was almost on the tabletop. Her eyes, however, remained on me. She smiled in a manner that was rather self-conscious, yet friendly enough.

"What's your name?" I asked.

"Cassandra."

Ah, a mythical name. It fit the fairy-tale looks.

"How old you are, Cassandra?"

"Nine."

"My name's Torey, and you and I are going to be working together each day." I pulled out a chair adjacent to hers and sat down. "Can you tell me why you've come to the unit?"

Her dark eyes locked on mine, and for a moment or two she stared intently, as if she expected to find the answer there. Then she shook her head faintly. "No."

"What about your mom? What did she tell you about why you were coming here?"

"I don't remember."

"Okay," I said. I bent down and opened my box of materials. Taking out plain paper and a smaller cardboard box, I laid them on the table. "Most of the children I work with come to the unit because they have problems that make them feel bad. Sometimes, for example, they have problems in their family. Maybe someone in the family is really unhappy and it makes them do hurtful things. Maybe there's been a divorce. Maybe there's lots of fighting at home. For some of the children who come here, it's other things. Maybe they've been in an accident or a really scary situation, or they've been very ill. Some have been treated or touched in a way that felt wrong, or people tried to make them keep secrets that hurt. And sometimes . . . sometimes kids don't even know the reason they have troubles. They just feel angry or worried or scared all the time. So these are some of the reasons children come to the unit."

Cassandra watched me with unusual intensity, as if she were really trying to take in what I was saying, trying to absorb it, almost. Nonetheless, there was an oddly blank quality to her stare, almost as if she were listening so carefully not for the content of what I was saying but rather because I was speaking to her in a foreign language she didn't quite understand.

"Hearing about reasons for other children coming to the unit," I said, "do you think any of those describe you?"

"I don't know."

"Okay. Well, I'll share with you some of the things other people have told me about you. You can then say if you think they are true or not.

"Your mom, for instance, tells me that you had a scary thing happen to you when you were five. She says that she is divorced from your dad and that you and your sister were supposed to live with her and not see him. Then one day your dad came to school and had you get into his car, even though that was against the rules. He drove off with you and wouldn't bring you back, and he wouldn't phone your mom to tell her that you were safe, and he wouldn't let you phone your mom. She says you were gone a long time—about two years—and during the time you were with your dad, some very scary things happened to you. Is that right?"

Cassandra nodded. Her demeanor was pleasant, cheerful even, as if I'd said no more than "Your mom says you are in third grade."

"Your teacher tells me that you like school, that you can be very enthusiastic about what is happening in class. She says you are quite a smart girl and can do really well sometimes."

Cassandra smiled.

"But she also tells me that at other times you have lots of problems. You can get very angry and have a hard time following the rules. Occasionally when you are at school, you get *very* upset and then you stop talking. Mrs. Baker says there are sometimes days and days when you don't want to say anything to anyone, and this makes it difficult to do your work in class. But she tells me while these are bad problems, they aren't the biggest problem. She says the biggest problem is that you very often don't tell the truth. You make up stories about people that get them into trouble, and you often talk about things that aren't really happening at all."

I paused. "What do you think? Do *you* think these things have caused trouble for you?"

Cassandra shrugged. It came off as almost a comical gesture, the way she did it. She brought her shoulders way up and rolled her eyes in an exaggerated fashion that was tinged with tolerant good humor, as if to say, "Silly grown-ups, who make mountains out of molehills."

"These are the reasons the grown-ups have given me, when I asked, 'Why is Cassandra Ventura on the unit?' "

Cassandra rolled her eyes again, then looked up to the right, then up to the left, then back to the right.

"What do you think?" I asked. "Do these things seem like problems to you?"

"I don't know."

"I'm interested in your thoughts. There isn't a wrong or right answer to my questions. We're just exploring."

"I don't know," she repeated.

"You don't know?"

"I don't remember."

"You don't remember what? If you do those things? If people think those are problems? Or you don't remember what I just said?"

Again she shrugged and rolled her eyes.

*　　　*　　　*

I pushed one of the plain pieces of paper in front of Cassandra, then I opened the small box. Inside was an assortment of marking pens, pencils, and crayons. "I want you to draw me a picture of your family."

She hesitated. "I'm not a very good draw-er."

"That's okay. They can just be stick figures, if you want. You can make them any way that's easy for you."

"Like bubbles? Instead of sticks, can I draw them round, like bubbles?"

"If that's what you want."

"Fish!" she said with sudden animation. "I draw really good fish. I figured out this way. Let me show you." She picked up an orange crayon. "See? You make a circle. Then you draw a little triangle on one end with the point sticking against the circle and that's the tail. See?" She made several more fish along the side of the paper. "Can I make them fish?"

"You decide," I replied.

But she didn't make fish. And she didn't make stick figures. Instead, Cassandra dropped the crayon and took a pencil. She began to draw very small, very carefully proportioned people. First a man, then a girl, then a smaller girl, then a woman. A pause. Cassandra considered the picture. Then she added another figure next to the mother. This was a second man. Then she added a third man. Another pause.

Everything thus far had been done in pencil. Indeed, she'd chosen a very sharp, hard-lead pencil and so the drawings were quite faint. She then put the pencil down and reached over for the box, pulling it closer. Looking through, she picked out different crayons and set about placing her family in a pleasant scene of grass, blue sky, and bright sunshine. She worked carefully, coloring in the grass after drawing the lines and then the sky. She assiduously avoided coloring over the orange fish so that it looked almost as if they were balloons in the air. She pressed hard when making the sun, turning it waxy yellow, many of the rays extending out over the crayoned blue of the sky.

While Cassandra had been careful not to color over her fish at the edge of the paper, she had had no such compunctions about coloring over the family. They were hardly visible through the blue she'd used for the sky.

"There," she said, then paused to regard the picture. "No, wait." She reached out and took up a black magic marker. Carefully she penned in a smiling face on the sun. "That's better. That's a happy picture now, isn't it?" Then she continued with the black marker and drew a strange little blobby shape in the sky not far from the sun. It had three protrusions, making it look rather like a clover leaf without the stem.

"You've worked hard on that. Can you tell me about it? Who are these people in the family?"

"Welllll," she said in a slow, drawn-out voice, "that's my dad." She pointed to the first faint figure. "That's my sister Magdalena. And that's my sister Mona. And that's my mom. And that's Daddy David. And that's Uncle Beck."

"And where are you in this picture?" I asked.

"I'm not in this picture. Am I supposed to be in this picture? I thought you said you wanted a picture of my family."

I nodded.

"You wanted me in the family?" she asked.

"Well, if you wanted to draw everyone in your family, it might include you, mightn't it? . . . but then again . . . however you see it, that's good. There isn't a right or wrong way of doing it."

"Everyone? You wanted everyone? I didn't know you said everyone. I didn't know you meant everyone."

Cassandra reached over and picked out an assortment of crayons—red, yellow, blue, green. Down in the right-hand corner of the picture she began to draw several small snakes, all with smiley faces. She made about ten of them of different sizes.

"This is becoming quite an intricate picture," I said. "Can you tell me about these?"

"This is Mother Snake and this is Father Snake and these are the kid snakes. And this is Minister Snake. And this is Cowboy Snake. And this is Fairy Snake. They're my brothers and sisters, these ones. He's my brother and he's my brother and this one's my sister."

"Ah," I said. "Your mom only told me about your sisters Mona and Magdalena."

"These are my other brothers. In my other family. From when I was abducted. I lived in a whole other family then, and these are my brothers and sisters from there. I called them 'Minister' and 'Cowboy' and 'Fairy' because that's how they liked to dress up. Well, not him. He really was a minister. He was a grown-up. Like seventeen, I think. But Cowboy and Fairy were my age. Well, Fairy was younger. She was three. I took care of her."

"I see. Your mother didn't mention your other family."

Cassandra grinned then. It was an openly saucy expression. "Maybe she doesn't know."

Or maybe I don't know, I was thinking. There was something too playful about her behavior, making it feel manipulative to me. I was getting a sense of smoke and mirrors about Cassandra, that she was astute at giving what she surmised I wanted so that I never noticed what wasn't being offered.

"And that's me, there," she said and pointed to the clover-shaped blob in the sky.

"Ah," I said, "so you are in the picture now?"

"Yup." She looked up at me and smiled. "But I'm up there 'cause I'm an alien."

I'd been working on the unit almost two years. Feeling frustration with the attitude of the administration in Washington toward special education and foreseeing the inevitable cutbacks and job losses that would result from administration policy changes, I had decided to take a break from teaching. Some years earlier, I'd completed my psychology credentials, so this seemed the right time to move in that direction. My intention had been to join a small clinic where a friend of mine worked. It was located in a city I had lived in previously, a city I knew and loved well and where I already had a good social network. What had attracted me most, however, was a chance to work with the clinic's director. He not only had a formidable reputation in child psychiatry, which was reason enough to want to learn from him, but he was also a skilled administrator, known for his creative thinking. Breaking free from the often restrictive attitudes of psychiatry, he had sought to set up the clinic with a more holistic approach, drawing together professionals from several allied fields—child psychology, psychiatry, pediatrics, social work—to work together in a broad, cross-disciplinary manner. This ability to "think outside the box" appealed to me greatly.

How I'd left the small town where I had been teaching with the intention of taking up a position in that wealthy, well-funded, broad-minded private clinic and ended up instead working in the claustrophobic world of a closed psychiatric crisis and assessment unit for children in a metropolitan general hospital was somewhat of a mystery even to me. It had involved one of those encounters one can only write off later as "fate," when a colleague of a colleague contacted me late one Sunday afternoon, saying something about being familiar with my former project in elective mutism and would I be willing to give an in-service to staff at the hospital. While on the unit to do the in-service, I found out they were desperately looking for a specialist in psychologically based language problems. I was not such a specialist, but I was free for a few months, since times had not quite coordinated between the end of the school year and the opening of the position at the clinic. I said if they were interested, I'd be willing to give it my best shot. They were and I did. And months zoomed by. The position at the clinic came and went and I remained at the hospital.

It was a good choice. No doubt the clinic would also have suited me well, and I still had occasional idle dreams of switching over at some later date, but I loved the gritty, front-line feel of working in a hospital. We were a short-term facility, designed primarily for diagnosis and assessment, as well as acute crisis intervention, and as a county-funded institution, many of the cases referred to us came from the poor under-belly of society. The continual struggles for enough time, enough money, enough choices never went away, lending a certain frisson to the work and provoking among the staff an attitude akin to that of comrades-in-arms in a MASH unit. Like a good political debate, this kind of edgy atmosphere stimulated me. I enjoyed, too, the flexibility of my position, which allowed me to continue liaising with many of my patients long after they had left the hospital unit and returned to their homes and schools, and I enjoyed being a "language specialist," of seeing the many variations of one presenting problem.

Which is how Cassandra came my way.

In the beginning Cassandra Ventura's life had looked promising. Her father was a security guard. Her mother had been a secretary but gave up work when Cassandra's elder sister, Magdalena, came along. During those years, the family exuded the American dream. They worked hard, were committed members of their church, helped out in community activities. Dad was a regular on the company bowling team. Mom baked cakes that won prizes and sewed enviably well, providing the two girls with elaborate costumes at Halloween, new dresses at Easter, matching outfits for the school pictures.

Behind closed doors, however, it was a very different scene, one of drug problems and domestic violence. Mr. Ventura claimed never to have abused the children until that final incident. Before that point, it had been only his wife who had suffered the cruel put-downs, the beatings, the dishes smashed over her head. But then on that night, six-year-old Magdalena had tried to intervene, getting physically between her arguing parents. Mr. Ventura swung out at her, meaning only to push her aside. She fell and was knocked unconscious. That proved the breaking point for Mrs. Ventura. She could no longer keep up the pretense of being a happy family. Taking the girls, she fled to a women's refuge. The next day she went to the police.

It unraveled swiftly from there. As well as the domestic abuse, Mrs. Ventura also revealed her husband had long-term drug problems and had been using his position as a security guard to procure a regular supply of cocaine. The criminal trial that followed was ugly and rancorous and made worse because it required testimony not only from his wife but also Magdalena. Mr. Ventura was jailed for eighteen months.

Mrs. Ventura rebuilt her life with rather disconcerting speed. All within the space of time her husband was in jail, she managed to file for divorce; meet and move in with another man, whose name was David Navarro; relocate to a new community about an hour's drive from the city; and give birth to a third daughter, Mona.

Cassandra had been three at the time of her father's imprisonment. Two years later, when she was in kindergarten, she came out of school to find a car waiting for her. When the man in the driver's seat said he was Daddy, she hesitated. She didn't actually remember her natural father well, so she didn't know if this was him or not. When he tried to call her over, she replied that she needed to wait until Magdalena came out. He said, "I have some of your old toys here. I thought you might want them." So she went to see.

When Magdalena came out from her third-grade

class, there was no sign of her younger sister. Her mother was called. The police were called. Nothing. No trace. Cassandra had disappeared.

The Navarros' efforts to find Cassandra were unrelenting. Police bulletins, news reports, searches over several states, posters in the local grocery store, on the side of milk cartons, efforts through Mr. Ventura's parole officer—everything anyone could think of was tried in an effort to find out what happened that afternoon—but nothing turned up. It was as if Cassandra and her father had, as the old cliché goes, simply vanished into thin air.

Twenty-six months passed without any word of Cassandra's whereabouts. Then three states away, a young man working in a 7-Eleven convenience store discovered a small girl in the alley behind the store going through their garbage. Suspicious that she was there to steal something, he gave chase when she tried to run away, and caught her. When she wouldn't speak to him, wouldn't answer his questions about her name or where she lived, he called the manager. The manager realized immediately that the girl was too young to be alone in such a place at that time of day, and he was concerned about her unkempt appearance; so he called the police. It was Cassandra.

No one ever knew precisely what had happened to her during those twenty-six months. Cassandra was totally mute for the first weeks after her return. Her father, when found, was in a drug-addled stupor, and he seemed incapable of giving much information beyond indicating the motive behind the abduction had been revenge against his ex-wife. "I wanted to make her suffer for what she'd done" was his only real explanation.

Cassandra had been not quite six when she was abducted and was now approaching eight. She was very dirty and suffering from malnutrition, giving the impression she had spent at least part of the time living rough or in very poor conditions. No one knew whether this was in the company of her father or others, because her father gave a muddled, inconsistent picture and Cassandra said nothing. Even when she did begin to speak again, she usually refused to talk about the abduction. The few things she did say turned out to be mostly lies.

The longed-for homecoming proved to be nothing like Cassandra's mother had dreamt about for so long. In place of the cheerful, loving daughter who had been abducted that autumn afternoon, she welcomed home a wary, mute stranger.

Cassandra found it impossible to settle back into her former life, which, in fact, was not her "old life" at all, but rather a completely different one from what she'd been living before the abduction. She hated her stepfather and wouldn't tolerate him in the room. She refused to talk to him or even look at him. She fought constantly with Magdalena and did many small, nasty vengeful things to her. With her new sister, Mona, she was so spiteful and short-tempered that her mother didn't dare leave the two of them alone together.

Cassandra startled easily, was prone to unexpected tantrums, suffered horrific nightmares, and alternated between shouting at everyone and not speaking at all. She lied constantly, stole from everyone in the family, and had chaotic eating problems, tending to hoard and hide food, or else taking too much, consuming it too fast, and vomiting it back up, occasionally while still at the table. She also had digestive problems and was plagued by many other minor illnesses associated with a compromised immune system.

In addition, it appeared Cassandra had not attended school at all during the time she was gone. Indications when she was in kindergarten were that Cassandra, like her elder sister, would be an able student. Old enough to be in second grade when she returned, she was now behind in everything and could neither read nor do basic adding and subtracting.

Cassandra's mother and stepfather attempted to deal with the situation as appropriately as they could. Her parents decided to restart Cassandra's education from the beginning, so she was placed in first grade, a year below where she should have been for her age. This still left plenty of catching up, as the academic year was well under way when she returned, so she was also given extensive resource help. To deal with the psychological trauma of the abduction, Cassandra had individual therapy with a child psychologist for twelve weeks, which was the length of time covered by the Navarros' insurance.

And Cassandra did start to recover. She began to speak reliably again. First it was at home and then, more slowly, at school, although she could still be oddly unpredictable and sometimes went silent for hours and occasionally even days. She was making reasonable academic progress and generally keeping up with her class. At home she was still difficult and prone to tantrums, but the family felt this was improving, too.

Yet . . .

It was Cassandra's third-grade teacher, Earlene Baker, who kept pressure on the Navarro family to seek further help for their daughter. Mrs. Baker found Cassandra's behavior disconcerting and difficult to cope with in the classroom. She was most concerned about the amount of very manipulative behavior Cassandra engaged in, which mostly took the form of lying and "storytelling." A number of the lies, she said, seemed completely pointless, such as coming to school in a pair of running shoes she wore almost every day and insisting they were new. Many others were malicious, such as on one occasion when Cassandra had purposely hidden her schoolwork and then told the school staff that another child had stolen it from her. The only thing that had saved the other child from serious trouble was a playground aide who had happened to notice Cassandra placing something carefully into a trash bin outside the school and had later gone to investigate. Most of the lies, however, were about hideous but outlandish things, like her little sister falling in the canal and being swept under the culvert but then being rescued by an unidentified boy who just happened to be passing.

Mrs. Baker said she was aware that in all likelihood Cassandra had suffered terribly during her abduction and she tried to take this into account, but even so, why would a nine-year-old spend recess cheerfully helping the school janitor sweep leaves and then come in and say he had tried to push her down the stairs?

Mrs. Baker also wondered if Cassandra could be suffering petit mal seizures. It was a bit of joke with everyone at school, even Cassandra, that she "should have been born blond" because she could be very "ditzy"— not paying attention to what was going on around her, not remembering obvious details about ordinary things. Mrs. Baker didn't always find the behavior funny. She felt the forgetfulness, which could be very abrupt and out of the blue, was often manipulative in nature and just a further extension of the lying. Occasionally, however, she said Cassandra did genuinely seem not to remember things that had just happened, and this occurred often enough for it to interfere with learning and social interactions. This led Mrs. Baker to wonder if there could be a neurological underpinning for such behavior.

Cassandra's erratic speech also bothered her. Most of the time, Mrs. Baker said, Cassandra was chatty to a point of being verbose; however, every once in a while she'd suddenly refuse to speak to anyone, and this could last anywhere up to a few days. Mrs. Baker saw no particular pattern to these silences, but they did occur at home as well. Cassandra's mother was resigned to them, feeling they were another outshoot of the traumatic abduction and the best response was to give Cassandra peace and support and not call attention to them. Mrs. Baker couldn't be this lackadaisical because not talking interfered with the learning process. Given the randomness of the behavior, Mrs. Baker's mind again went back to the question of a neurological basis. When she spoke to me, she mentioned Cassandra's father's drug problems and wondered if Cassandra had been the victim of any drug-taking while she was with her father, or if there had been some kind of horrible abuse that might have caused brain damage, which was now throwing up these odd neurological signs.

The final concern was what Mrs. Baker called Cassandra's "creepy" behaviors—actions that, while there was nothing inherently wrong with Cassandra's doing them, made Mrs. Baker uneasy. Among these was a tendency for Cassandra to turn otherwise ordinary conversations into nonsense. She would be chatting normally and then unexpectedly get what Mrs. Baker described as her "Bad Seed" look. Suddenly her replies would become off-topic, occasionally provocative, and often make little sense. This was a very disconcerting behavior, Mrs. Baker said, because it "felt crazy." And very off-putting. Other children quickly became disconcerted or irritated and avoided her.

Another creepy behavior was Cassandra's tendency to pretend she was some kind of animal, like a vulture or a bear, and then only relate to people using shrieks or growls. Often she picked a violent animal and then used the animal's normal aggression as an excuse for hitting, biting, spitting, or doing other hurtful things. Mrs. Baker said Cassandra often did this playfully, as if she were in control of the behavior and it was only a game; however, she could persist with the animal-like behavior for several hours, despite repeated requests to stop or even punishment.

Neurological investigations turned up no evidence of seizures. The doctors concluded Cassandra's problems were psychological, most likely part of post-traumatic stress disorder resulting from the abduction, a diagnosis she already carried. She was given a prescription for antidepressant medication and sent home.

Mrs. Baker didn't see a significant change in Cassandra on the antidepressant, so she persisted in her efforts to pressure the parents into getting more treatment for Cassandra. She claimed the various difficult behaviors were soon going to make it impossible to keep Cassandra in regular education. She kept insisting the parents continue searching for help. Consequently, Cassandra was eventually referred to one of the senior child psychiatrists affiliated with our unit at the hospital. He spent time in Cassandra's school, observing her, then met with both Cassandra and her parents. In the end he decided it would be beneficial to bring Cassandra to the unit as an inpatient for observation and assessment.

The child psychiatrist, Dave Menotti, was to oversee the case, but I was given the individual daily therapy sessions with Cassandra. Dave's thinking was that my experience with psychogenic language problems might prove useful here, even though her occasional mutism was not the presenting problem. He described her to me as a child "where something doesn't add up," which I knew meant we were still very much in the diagnostic stage. While we assumed we had the source of her problems—the twenty-six-month abduction—we had no understanding of how that pieced together with her difficulties now.

Cassandra and I sat together at the table, examining the drawing she had done of her family.

"That's really quite an elaborate picture. Can you tell me more about it?"

"There I am. Up in the sky," she said. "I look down on everyone. I can see everyone. I can see everything from the sky."

"That sounds interesting, being able to see everything."

She nodded. "I like being an alien."

"If *I* were an alien, I think I would feel lonely," I said, "because I'd feel I was different from everyone else. I'd feel like an outsider."

"No, not me. I like it," she replied. "Because I can travel in a rocket ship."

Cassandra was a rather wriggly little girl, squirming around in her seat, bending her head down and around in a way that allowed her to look up at me while I regarded the picture. There was something coy about her behavior. This made me wonder if she had chosen to draw herself as an alien because she genuinely felt like an alien or if she had chosen to do it as a way of engaging me, as a sort of savvy assessment of what she'd thought a therapist would be interested in.

"And here we have your family," I said. "Yes? Your mother, your stepfather, your two sisters—"

"And the fish. The fish, too," she interrupted and pointed to them.

"Ah, I thought they were leftover from when you were experimenting with shapes . . ."

"No, they're living in the sky like it was an aquarium. Goldfish. Really, they're a family, too. That big one's the dad. And that's the mom goldfish. And those are the babies. They belong to my other family."

"I see."

"Those are my other family there. Remember, because I told you already. They're outside the aquarium, looking in. That's why they're small." She pointed to the snakes. "Really they're not snakes. They got snake costumes on."

"They're not snakes?"

Cassandra laughed at this. "Silly! They're people!" She laughed again. "That's Daddy Snake and Mama Snake and the kid Snakes. And there's the Minister Snake. And that's Cowboy Snake. And that's Fairy Snake."

"I thought you just said they were people," I replied, a little confused.

"They are," she said cheerfully. " 'Snake' is their last name. That's because they dress up in snake costumes all the time, so that's why people started calling them that. And really I'm Cassandra Snake when I live with them."

"Why do they dress up in snake costumes?"

"Ding-dong, willy-nilly, Peter Pan!" she replied in an unexpectedly loud, singsong voice.

I sat back.

She laughed shrilly.

I sat quietly without speaking.

"Ding-dong, willy-nilly, Peter Pan!"

She laughed again, writhed in her seat, and fluttered her hands. Then taking up a black marking pen, she drew strong black lines across the picture in a random, rather frenzied manner. The lines didn't color over anything or appear to be there to cover up anything. The way she did them, they appeared to be just marks, slashes across the page, as if her inner environment had become too much to control and these marks simply exploded forth like lightning strikes.

Saying nothing, I just sat, waiting.

This outburst lasted about three minutes. Then slowly Cassandra came back into herself and grew quieter. She was still laughing in a rather peculiar way. It was almost what I'd describe as a lascivious, sleazy kind of laugh. Certainly it implied sexuality to me, which, I suppose, given the "snakes" and the outburst regarding "ding-dong," "willy," and "Peter," was perfectly possible.

Still I said absolutely nothing. I kept my expression as bland as possible so that she would not interpret my silence as disapproving, but I continued to sit motionless.

At last Cassandra fell completely quiet. The interesting thing about this episode, to my mind, was that not once did she take her eyes off me during the whole course of it. Her eye contact was quite extraordinary, but it also implied to me that my reaction was very important to this whole little drama. I sensed she was doing it for me, that she was expecting me to behave in a certain manner as well and she had to keep a close watch in order to see what I was going to do or, possibly, to adjust her own behavior as necessary.

When she was finally reduced to sitting quietly again in the chair beside me, her great dark eyes still fixed on my face, I said, "You know, I think you did that as a way of getting away from what we were talking about. Sometimes magicians do that trick. They say, 'Look over here,' because they want your attention over here so that you aren't paying attention to over there and they can hide something away without your noticing."

There was a long, long silence. She pressed her hands together prayer fashion and pushed them down between her legs on the chair. Straightening her elbows, this pushed her shoulders up, like a frozen shrug. Her eyes were still locked on mine.

There was a flicker. She looked away for just a very brief moment, then back at me. "Can I go now?" she asked. "I'm tired. I'm done with this. I want to go back to the dayroom."

The children's psychiatric unit was on the seventh floor of the hospital. When one first came off the elevator and turned left, there was a long corridor that contained administrative offices, many of which were not affiliated with our unit. At the far end were the two sets of double locked doors through which one entered the unit itself. Immediately beyond the doors to the left was the nurses' station, and to the right, the dayroom where the children gathered to relax and play when they weren't in the unit classroom, attending therapy sessions, or participating in activities. The sleeping rooms were down two short corridors that branched off the opposite side of the dayroom from the nurses' station. Most accommodated two children each, although there were four single rooms. All locked. In all, the unit could accommodate twenty-eight children between the ages of three and eleven.

Beyond the dayroom, to the left of the nurses' station, was a third short corridor, and it was here where the two therapy rooms were, plus a miscellany of utilitarian rooms—an examination room, a med room, a walk-in linen room, and an odd little room that was about twenty feet long but only about six feet wide. Various kinds of technical equipment, like video cameras, recorders, and monitors, were stored just inside the door, whereas at the far end, there was a teeny, tiny kitchen, narrow as a boat's galley.

It was down among these rooms that I had my office, which I shared with Helen, a clinical social worker, whose main task was liaising with children after they had left. Consequently, she spent only a small amount of time each week actually on the unit, and I normally had the office to myself.

The room was a curious mixture of the industrial and the macabre. A set of cast-iron pipes went through the room. This would have been ordinary enough, had they been in the corner of the room or ordinary-sized pipes, associated with something like the central heating. These, however, sprung up about three feet in from the near-side wall and varied in size between three and six inches in diameter, so it was like having a stand of trees in the office. Iron trees. Or rather, just their trunks, passing through the room.

Moreover, in the old days, the room had been used for electric shock therapy. This had long since been discontinued, but the evidence was still there in the form of odd knobs and disconnected wires and the indentations of long-since-removed equipment on the walls. These things had since been painted over, indeed, many times, giving them a blobby, indistinct form.

Midst this, Helen and I had managed to squeeze in our two desks, a large table, and two sizable bookshelves. As always, Helen's side of the room was a triumph of order and organization. My side looked, as Helen succinctly put it, as if the condemned-building notice was overdue.

I had just returned to my desk from the session with Cassandra when there was a quick rap at the door, and it opened. Nancy Anderson stuck her head in. She was the charge nurse on the unit during the weekdays. In her fifties, a tall, strongly built woman of African American origins, Nancy had made a career of psychiatric nursing. She loved the job; she loved the kids, and decades of experience had given her a clear understanding of life's absurdities, which meant her reaction to most things was a good laugh.

"This one's for you," she said, waving a piece of paper.

"What is it?" I asked and reached over for it.

"He's asked specially for you. Read your research on elective mutism. Saw that article in the paper. Wants *you*."

"Oh, good," I muttered sarcastically.

I hated these—cases where the parents wanted a specific therapist or therapy—because they often came with wildly unrealistic expectations. Many were looking for miracle workers, nothing less, and it seldom worked out that miracles were in the cards.

"Harry's looked it over," Nancy said. "He says why don't you arrange an opportunity to see the child sometime this week. There's a space in his schedule to interview the parents next Friday, if that works for you. If they want to go ahead with something, if it looks right, there's a space coming open on the unit a week next Wednesday."

I took the paper from Nancy. "Geez. This is out in Quentin. Did Harry notice that?"

Nancy lifted her eyebrows in a "no idea" expression.

"That's almost two hundred miles. It's going to take over three hours of driving just one way. It'll use up my entire day just to observe the kid for forty-five minutes."

"I think that's why they're thinking of inpatient."

"Surely they've got services in Quentin."

"Well, they want *you*."

I started reading. It was a personal letter from a man named Mason Sloane. He was the grandfather of the boy in question and the letter was written on the letterhead of a well-known regional bank.

Oddly, to my mind, the first thing Mr. Sloane established was his family business pedigree. They were majority shareholders in the bank, which had been founded in the late 1800s by his grandfather. Ownership and operation of the bank had passed from father to son through the generations and was now managed by Mr. Sloane's son, who was a prominent businessman in Quentin, a small city of about thirty thousand.

What drew Mr. Sloane to me was an article he had

read in the city's Sunday newspaper about my research into elective mutism. He had a four-year-old grandson named Drake, his only child's only child. The boy did not speak outside the home. Mr. Sloane said he was an exceptionally intelligent and lively boy; however, he had always refused to speak to almost everyone. The family had taken him to various specialists locally with no success. When Mr. Sloane read about my work, he knew *here* was Drake's problem. And *I* was the solution. Drake had elective mutism and if he came to see me, he would be cured.

The rest of the letter outlined how money was no object nor was distance or effort. They'd do anything to see Drake had the help he needed and I was it. All I had to do was name my price and make the arrangements.

Sitting back in my desk chair, I sighed. The article he was referring to in the newspaper had been one of those things that had seemed like a good idea at the time I did it. This was before I'd gained any insight into how important it was to journalists to write dramatic stories, even if there wasn't actually any drama in your work to write about, and how, if you *did* get suckered into talking about your favorite bit of research, a reporter desperate to prove to his boss he can write something more exciting than this week's round of society weddings was not the best guy to open up to. What I had hoped would be an article providing general information on this surprisingly common childhood problem metamorphosed into pop psychology sound bites that not only had never come out of my mouth but also diminished my treatment methods, making them sound effortlessly, almost arrogantly effective, as if there were no margins for error at all.

There was more to worry about in Mr. Sloane's letter, however. It was clear from the tone that he had already made several sweeping assumptions: that Drake was a perfectly ordinary boy just waiting to be cured, that "cure" was just a matter of finding someone with the magic to do it, and that enough money could fix anything.

The way the hierarchy was set up at the hospital meant each child who entered the unit was assigned his or her own team of specialists, which would include nursing and care staff, psychologists, occupational or physical therapists and educators from the unit, plus liaison people, who would continue to work with the child when he or she returned to the community. Each such team was always headed by a child psychiatrist. Even if one of us in an allied position had been responsible for referring a child to the unit with the intention of working more intensively on a problem ourselves, nonetheless, the case leader was still one of the psychiatrists. This was because the unit was, first and foremost, a medical facility. The child psychiatrists, by virtue of also being medical doctors, were thus always at the top of the pecking order. Moreover, it was they alone who were able to prescribe drug treatment in addition to the other forms of therapy.

I wasn't known for being a natural team player, certainly not back in my teaching days, when I'd rather relished the "outsider" status provided by being in special education, and I had always been inclined to rebellion. However, I found this hierarchical approach worked well in the tightly structured hospital setting. I was grateful not to be in a position to make the ultimate decisions, which were often very gray and, thus, very difficult, and frequently had grave consequences. Even more, however, I enjoyed the intellectual stimulation provided by regular interaction with professionals whose background and training were very different from my own.

We had five child psychiatrists, four men and a woman, and they were, all of them, sharp, erudite individuals. My favorite among them was Dave Menotti, who was affable and witty and most likely to come down from "Heaven"—our term for the corridor on the floor above where the psychiatrists' offices were—to fraternize with us. Harry Patel, however, was the psychiatrist I most looked forward to leading my team. He was a quiet man who seldom socialized, so it was hard to get to know him personally. A native of New Delhi—indeed, a fairly recent immigrant—he often gave the impression of not quite having a command of English, and this contributed to his slightly aloof nature. But this wasn't true. Harry just didn't waste words if none were needed. And Harry was stunningly good at what he did. I would have expected the difference of cultures to work against him, but this hadn't happened. Indeed, perhaps it was this that gave him such astute powers of observation, because I found he could see depth even in the most ordinary of situations. Faint nuances of behavior, fleeting expressions, sighs, silences. He took them all in. He worked with incredible delicacy, never pushing the children, never leading, only following. I loved watching him in action, and I loved even more the chance at his guidance.

So, even though I had qualms about Mr. Sloane's letter regarding his grandson, if Harry suggested we observe the child, I was happy to do so. Thus, I cleared my schedule, packed up my "box of tricks," and set out for the long journey to Quentin.

$\mathcal{I}$ enjoyed the drive out to Quentin, appreciating a chance to get away from the city for the day. It was late winter going into spring and the weather was gorgeous in that heartbreaking way of a dying season. The snow was gone, the landscape gray and brown, and yet there was an expectancy to it, a nascent joie de vivre. Moreover, I loved driving itself and the freedom and solitude of being on the open road.

I reached the preschool just after eleven, which gave me about forty-five minutes to observe Drake in his class. Martina, Drake's teacher, greeted me in the school office.

"We've been expecting you," she said cheerfully. "We've had at least five phone calls this morning."

I raised my eyebrows in surprise. "Really? From whom?"

"Mr. Sloane. To see if you had come."

"Drake's father?"

"No, Mason Sloane, Drake's grandfather. We all call Drake's father 'Walter.' Mr. Sloane is his father." She laughed. "It can be even more confusing than that, because Mr. Sloane always refers to his son as 'Watty,' while Walter's wife calls him 'Skip.'" Then a friendly grin. "But 'Mr.' always refers to the old man."

"And he's been calling? Here?"

Good-naturedly, Martina rolled her eyes. "Welcome to Sloaneville."

Drake was not at all what I'd anticipated. His macho soap-opera name had put me in mind of aristocrats or oversexed mallards. When I first saw him in the classroom, however, I didn't even realize Drake was a boy. Not only were his features soft and feminine, but his hairstyle was a girl's. At least in my book. He was blond with thick, shiny, straight hair, and it was cut in what I could only describe as a bob. And not even a "Dutch boy" bob. This was a long, shoulder-length bob with well-trimmed bangs of the sort you might see in pictures of boys in medieval times. I had not seen any boys look like this lately, however. Even back in the 1960s and 1970s when there was a certain vogue for long-haired boys' styles, they were not the court-of-King-Arthur fashion this boy wore.

Drake also defied the stereotypic personality of an elective mute. In my experience, the majority of children with this disorder were shy and withdrawn. Drake, however, was participating joyfully in a rollicking singing and dancing game with the other children. He wasn't singing, of course, but he was having a high old time joining in with the movements, his actions open and uninhibited.

At least pretty much they were "open and uninhibited," because that was the other unusual thing about him. He was not dancing alone. Accompanying him was an enormous stuffed tiger, which he clutched tightly around the neck with one arm. It had brilliantly hued orange-and-black stripes, a merry, almost cartoonish face, a big fluffy white belly, and was formed into a permanent sitting position. And quite honestly it was almost as tall as Drake was.

Taken aback by this Prince-Valiant-meets-Calvin-and-Hobbes combination, I just stared.

He was fun to watch. This kid had megawatt charisma. The other children in the class were unfazed by his silence, his odd name, his crazy hairstyle, or his having a life-sized tiger for a sidekick. They actively sought his company and included him in everything happening. Drake responded to each overture with enthusiastic charm. Indeed, he responded just as eagerly to the teachers. I observed him focusing well, listening attentively to instructions, following directions easily and cheerfully. From everything I observed that morning, Drake was a happy, well-adjusted little character.

After the children left, I joined Martina for lunch in the teachers' lounge. "He's certainly not what I expected," I said. "I'm going to admit right here that seeing him in the classroom, I wouldn't have identified him as having the level of problems he apparently has. What's your take on all this?"

"Have you met the family yet?"

"No."

She raised her eyebrows meaningfully. "Well, I won't say anything more, then. I'll let you form your own opinion."

Comprehending, I nodded.

A pause.

"So tell me about the mutism," I said.

"It's absolute. In all the time he's been here, I've never heard a single word out of him. In fact, he almost makes no noise of any kind. He does speak at home. He just won't speak here in front of anyone else."

"So what have you tried?" I asked.

Martina shrugged. "To be honest, not much. He's only four. I've had other kids with these kinds of problems. Usually, like him, they're only children. Or first-born. They come in really shy and frightened and feel a bit besieged by all this new activity. Normally, I just give them time and eventually they do settle in and start talking."

"So you've had experience before with elective mutism?"

She nodded. "I've been teaching preschool almost twenty-five years now. You see all kinds. I can remember this one little girl. Her name was Stormy, of all things. Which was quite a misnomer. Tiny, pale, mousy little thing, and she wouldn't say a word. Would hardly breathe. She sat all folded up on her chair, and you could just tell she was overwhelmed. Her mother was really shy as well, so I think it was a family trait. And yeah, she was totally mute, just like Drake. Wouldn't say a thing. It must have taken six months or more with her. But we just stayed patient and finally she started.

"So this is what I told Drake's family," Martina continued. "Just give him time. He'll settle in. But Christ, that grandfather. Nothing is good enough for that man. Nothing happens fast enough. He runs his life like it's a business. In fact, I think he'd like to run everybody's life like a business, and I'm quite sure he does at home. He's absolutely fixated on 'meeting targets,' on everything 'being within normal guidelines.' That's the whole reason they brought Drake into this program. To 'get him to meet normal guidelines.' I mean, hell, what's that when it's at home? There's huge latitude when you're talking 'normal' at age four. But obviously, whatever we're doing, we're not doing it well enough, because now you're here. He didn't even have the courtesy to inform us, to give us a chance to review the situation. Just bang. 'Time's up. You're finished.' "

"So you don't really think Drake's mutism is a problem?" I asked.

Martina shrugged. "I dunno. I wouldn't want to say at this point, really. I don't see the point of giving him that kind of label. If it were my kid, I would have just left well enough alone, because he's doing really well in all other respects. So I would have just given him time to grow. He's a young one. An August birthday. I personally wouldn't start him in kindergarten this year, which, of course, is what they want to do when fall comes. Yes, he is definitely bright enough. No question of that. But what's the hurry? The rat race will still be there. So I'd say, 'Here, sonny, play another year.' I think that's all he needs."

"What's with the stuffed toy?" I asked.

"Ahh. That's 'Friend.' That's what we've named it; I think just because you always tend to say, 'Where's his friend?' Drake doesn't call it anything, of course. Or if he does, we don't know about it. But if you want to see him get distressed, try taking Friend off him."

"It's a little . . . big, isn't it?"

"Tell me about it. And it goes absolutely everywhere.

To lunch. On the playground. To the toilets. Now, that's fun! I say, 'Let's leave Friend out here so he doesn't get dirty while you go potty,' and I might as well be saying, 'I'm going to cut Friend up into little pieces and stuff him down this toilet while you're in there.' "

I grinned. "Wishful thinking?"

Martina grinned back. "If I tell you we actually got stuck in one of the toilet cubicles one day because of Friend, you'll get the picture. Just some places that you, a kid, and a three-foot tiger can't go."

"So what's your take on Friend?" I asked. "Security blanket?"

"Oh, no, Friend's much more than that. He's a proper friend. You know. The kind you have to set a place for at the table. Drake is an imaginative little boy. We're handicapped, of course, not having him say anything, but you can tell when watching him that he's 'talking' to Friend. And he's quite insistent that Friend be given his own paintbrush or crayons or cracker at snacktime. My guess is that Friend is more than just a security blanket. I suspect we've got a very intelligent, creative child here, and Friend's the only one with access to his world."

After lunch I was to spend half an hour of individual assessment time with Drake. I was shown into the room where the youngest children in the program—the two-year-olds—met, because they only came in the mornings, so the room was empty in the afternoons. It was a lovely room, bright and spacious, painted pale green and white, with a generous number of attractive toys. I was concerned that these would distract Drake, making him uninterested in one-to-one work with me, especially as he himself would be tired by that point. However, I needn't have worried. He entered willingly with Martina and when she introduced me, he happily sat down in one of the small chairs beside me at the table. Well, he and Friend.

He was a very attractive child. Indeed, he was more than attractive. There was about him a cherubic beauty. Porcelain skin, delicate little Cupid's-bow mouth, sparkly brown eyes with lashes so long they fell in the "to die for" category. He was like one of those dolls-for-adults, those "collectors' pieces" that are never meant to be played with. His girlish haircut contributed to this rarified aura.

And he was a *very* charming child. Looking up with wonderfully smiley eyes, as he sat beside me, his expression was of eager, almost squirmy anticipation, like a happy puppy. It made me feel just as eager.

"Hi, my name's Torey, and know what? I've come here today just to see you! You and I are going to do some interesting things together."

More excited squirming, more gleeful smiling.

"And look. I've got a box all full of fun things for us to do. Shall we open it and see?"

Drake didn't try to open the box himself, but he looked at it with anticipation. I reached over and pulled the box toward us. This was the "bag of tricks" I traveled with when I went to assess children or work with them in schools. The container had originally been a presentation box for a gift of fruit, and as the fruit had had to travel by carrier, it was sturdily made. It was low and flat with a lid that lifted off. Inside I kept a whole assortment of things I thought might be helpful in encouraging children to talk—puppets, paper dolls, plain and colored paper, a whole collection of different pens, pencils, and crayons in a smaller box, some stickers, a couple of picture books, a Richard Scarry's word book, a joke book, a coloring book, a paperback full of puzzles, two Matchbox cars, a family of dollhouse dolls, an old, broken Instamatic camera, some plastic animals, some plastic soldiers, and whatever "clever" things currently had my fancy. At the moment it was a "fortune-telling" fish, which was really no more than a piece of plastic that flipped around when warmed by the heat of the hand.

I took out the Richard Scarry book. This was a favorite of mine, simply because there were so many pictures in such variety that I could do an infinite number of things with them.

Paging through, I came to two pages illustrating numbers. One whale. Two walruses. Three piggy banks. And so forth, with delightful pictures accompanying. "Look. Here's counting. Can you count?"

Drake nodded enthusiastically.

"How far?"

He held up both hands. Then one by one, he put his fingers down, as if counting them. But, of course, he made no sound.

I nodded. "Okay, let's do these. Look. One whale. He's big, isn't he? See how much of the page he takes up? Have you ever seen a whale?"

He shook his head but then stretched his hands way up over his head. The meaning of what he was trying to communicate was perfectly clear.

"And look, two walruses. Aren't they funny-looking?"

Drake gave a breathy, noiseless little chuckle.

"Three piggy banks."

Drake was hooked in the activity now. He was leaning forward. He had pulled Friend in close to join us, perhaps to show the tiger the book, too, and he pointed to the next row of pictures, which showed four bells. They were the sort that had handles, like old school bells. Drake tapped the page enthusiastically and then tapped my shoulder to get my attention. I looked up. Cheerfully, he moved his hand up and down to indicate he was ringing such a bell.

I hesitated, not speaking.

He tried again, imitating the movement of shaking one of these handled bells up and down. He smiled in eager anticipation of my recognition of his action.

I still hesitated. Truth was, I didn't want to reinforce his gesturing. In my research I'd found children had a much harder time speaking to people with whom they had already formed a nonverbal relationship, so it wouldn't be helpful for us to go that way. But it was hard not to respond to such a charming little boy.

And this, I was thinking, was perhaps a good deal of the problem. He was so engaging, so keen, and, indeed, so sociable that he didn't really need words to get people to interact with him.

Then I thought: why? Speech is natural and innate. Why not do it? What was the payoff for Drake to stay silent when he so clearly wanted to communicate with people?

*F*ollowing my assessment with Drake came a meeting with his parents. Only it turned out not to be his parents. It was his mother and Mason Sloane, his paternal grandfather. There was no explanation offered as to where Drake's father, Walter, was.

Mason Sloane shook hands with me in a firm, businesslike manner. He was a short man, shorter than I was, mostly bald, and with a very red complexion. Despite being well over sixty, he was fit and muscular with the sort of physique one usually associates more with manual labor. Not in this case, however. His hands and nails were so well cared for that they looked professionally manicured. His clothes were precise and elegant, and he wore an expensive watch and two rings.

Drake's mother, in contrast, was tall and very thin. She was quite a beautiful woman in the delicate, rather nervous way you find in thoroughbred horses. Her coloring was Mediterranean. She had long dark hair and the same liquid, deerlike eyes as Drake had, only deeper and darker. Her name was Lucia, and when she spoke, I realized she was Italian. Not an American of Italian descent but actually from Italy. Her English was heavily accented and, indeed, not very good.

No one had mentioned this fact to me. When I heard Lucia speak, my mind instantly leaped to Drake's mutism. Did Lucia talk to Drake in Italian at home? Was this perhaps his problem? Could the mutism be due to language confusion? Was it possible he simply didn't have a good enough command of English? Which would explain a whole lot.

All three of us sat down in the small child-sized chairs at the equally small table.

"You've seen Drake now," Mason Sloane said. "I am sure you can tell what a very intelligent little boy he is."

I smiled and nodded. "Yes, I'm very impressed. He's lovely."

"So what is your diagnosis?" he asked.

"I'm not really in a position to give a diagnosis at this point," I replied.

"You've seen him?"

"Yes. But more is involved than just giving a label, because it's important that the label be correct. Moreover, a diagnosis in isolation isn't very helpful."

"This is your specialty, isn't it? You have a lot of experience with elective mutism. That's what I was led to believe in that article," he replied.

"Yes, I've had experience and I've worked with many elective mutes, but I've also come out here as part of a team. It would be inappropriate for me to give the impression I'm solely responsible for diagnosis or treatment. The hospital unit I work for doesn't function that way."

"Why? It's straightforward, isn't it? He doesn't talk. Nothing else is wrong with him. He talks at home; he doesn't talk at school. That's elective mutism, isn't it? Your article said that the vast majority of children you worked with spoke to you in the first session. So I was assuming it was just a matter of your coming out here and getting him started. So didn't you get him to talk?"

"This was an assessment, Mr. Sloane. It would be inappropriate for me to come in and work with Drake without assessing what the problem is first."

"All this talk of 'inappropriate' sounds like a smoke screen, if you ask me. Or a way to get money out of us. We've already told you what the problem is. We engaged you to come out, diagnose him with elective mutism, and fix that."

"Yes, I know. But that isn't quite the way things work," I replied. "First there is an assessment."

"So you didn't get him to talk?" he said.

"No."

"So was the article not right?"

"The article was right. But the article was about my research. This is an assessment. I came out to assess Drake. Because I'm employed by the hospital unit, I work as part of their team. So before I can work with a child, I have to go back and talk to the psychiatrist who will head the case. Assuming we want to proceed."

Mr. Sloane frowned. "We *wanted* just you. We don't need a psychiatrist. Drake isn't mentally ill, for God's sake. We were employing *you*. I thought we made that very clear."

Drawing in a deep, rather frustrated breath, I sat back in the chair. Or at least as much back as one can sit in a chair designed for a three-year-old.

"We wanted *just* you," he said again. "To come out here. To see him, get him to talk at school. I said money is no object. We'll pay you whatever you charge. Whatever the costs of your coming out here. Just do what you said you could do in the newspaper."

I sighed. "I'm sorry. It doesn't work that way."

"Great!" he said and banged the table with his hand. "So it was all lies! You call yourself a professional! If people ran banks the way you damned doctors work, the whole country would be bankrupt."

Before I realized what was happening, he leaped up from his chair. He stormed out of the room, slamming the door hard behind him.

Astonished, I stared at the door through which he'd just disappeared. Then I looked back. Lucia remained sitting, motionless. She had her head down, but then raised it and very briefly exchanged a glance with me before lowering it again. It wasn't a revealing glance, however, so I couldn't discern what she was thinking.

I had instant pity for her. It had to be hell living in the shadow of a man with such strong views, imperious demands, and an astoundingly short fuse.

Silence followed. It wasn't very long. A moment or two, perhaps less than a minute, but it was acutely uncomfortable. I didn't know whether to sympathize aloud with her and risk humiliating her or whether to express amazement at his behavior and risk putting her on the defensive. In the end I opted for no comment at all and decided to plow ahead as if this were all perfectly normal and I were used to it.

"Drake's teacher says he talks normally at home," I said.

Lucia nodded. She still had her head down. Her

hands twisted nervously in her lap. I thought she was
going to cry.

"Can you describe how he speaks to you?"

She shrugged slightly without looking up. "How do I
describe that? I don't know. He speaks normally. Like
any boy. He says normal things."

"How old was he when he started to speak?"

She hesitated. "When he was . . . nine months old?" It
came out more a question than an answer. "Yes, nine
months old. I think this is right. This is what I remember."

"That's quite young, isn't it? Especially for a boy.
What were his first words?"

Again, she seemed rather flustered. I was trying to
puzzle out if it was due to shyness or perhaps difficulty
coping in English. I couldn't tell.

" 'Kitty,' " she said at last. "Because he much likes
our cat."

This seemed odd to me. The way muscle coordination
works in the mouth, most babies' first words begin with
D or *B*. Combined with normal babbling, this produces
"da-da" or "ba-ba." The hard *c* sound that would be
necessary to produce "kitty" comes quite a bit later.

"Does Drake speak in Italian with you?" I asked.

She reddened and looked away. I got the immediate
sense that she'd been told not to speak in her native
tongue to her son and was now embarrassed to admit to
me she did. It wasn't hard to imagine the grandfather
making such a demand. Or perhaps others had already
implied that bilingualism was at the root of Drake's
problems, and she was now reluctant to admit that, in
spite of this, he and she still spoke Italian to each other.
Whatever, she didn't answer immediately.

I sat quietly and let the silence grow.

Finally she nodded. "Yes, I sometimes speak Italian to him." However, she then backed off and corrected herself, saying, "No. No, I mean, he does not speak it."

"You're saying you speak to Drake in Italian, but he does not speak Italian back to you?"

"Sometimes. Only sometimes. I mean, only sometimes that I speak Italian. I too speak English. Much of the time. Most of the time."

"But about Drake. Does he speak in Italian when he is talking to you? Or does he speak in English?"

"In English. Only in English." Then a hesitation. "Although he can understand Italian."

I nodded and smiled. "It's all right if he speaks Italian at home. I don't want to make you feel you shouldn't be speaking to your son in your native tongue. I've worked with many bilingual children and I think the advantages of growing up with a second language far outweigh any problems it might cause in the preschool years. In my experience, while there may be a little confusion when they're starting to speak, virtually all children outgrow that quickly and have no problems in the long run. Nonetheless, it's important to know if this could be happening in Drake's case. If bilingualism is causing Drake's mutism, we need to know in order to help him. Because I would work with this differently than if the mutism were due to psychological reasons."

A slight nod of her head, but she still didn't look at me.

"So . . . ?" I asked, waiting for her to admit to the Italian.

Head down and turned a little away from me, Lucia didn't respond.

"Okay," I said and knew to move on. "Does Drake

speak to anyone outside the immediate family? Aunts or uncles, perhaps? Or cousins? Neighborhood children?"

"No. No one."

"So, just you and your husband? Just at home to the two of you?"

"No." Her voice became very meek.

"How do you mean, 'no'?"

"He speaks just to me."

"Just to you?" I said, surprised. "You mean he doesn't speak to his father either?"

She shook her head.

"What age was Drake when this happened? When did he stop?"

"He's never spoken to his father."

"*Never?*" This degree of selectivity caught me by surprise. It wasn't unique in my experience, but it was very, very unusual and tended to point to a markedly more severe problem than Drake appeared to have.

"My husband does the work, so he is not in the house much," she said. "He is in his father's bank. And on the weekends he does the golf. And he does the boat on the lake with his father in the summer. These are all important for his work. So he does not spend much time in the house when Drake is awake."

Our conversation continued. I asked a few more questions, explored a few more avenues; then finally I said, "If you want me to work with Drake, I'd be happy to. Unfortunately, we have to consider the distance. Normally I see children with elective mutism in their school setting, since that's usually where the mutism occurs, and I work with them two or three times a week until we get the problem sorted out. But there really isn't any way I could do that here, so far from the city. I'm afraid the only way I could work with Drake would be if he came into the unit at the hospital as an inpatient. It doesn't sound like Mr. Sloane would be very agreeable to that. And to be truthful, Mrs. Sloane, I'm not so sure I'd be agreeable either. That's a very drastic measure. Drake is young. Elective mutism with preschoolers seldom needs such a major intervention as hospitalization, so I wouldn't be very comfortable taking him away from home unless it were really, really necessary. You might prefer to find someone here locally to work with Drake and, if you wish, my unit could offer to liaise with them and support whoever took it on."

She nodded. "It was good of you to come so far and I am sorry it was for nothing, but I think you are right. We will leave it. I think Drake will be just fine."

I felt disgruntled after the meeting. It hadn't been a satisfactory visit for a variety of reasons. Mason Sloane's actions, while they did not particularly upset me, had certainly impeded my opportunity to accomplish anything useful. His expectations were unrealistic and his attitude untenable. At the end of the day, the fact remained that there was a child who did need support.

I felt Drake's mutism was worth further investigation simply because it did seem unusually extensive; nonetheless, experience told me that in all likelihood the problem was minor. I suspected Lucia was not admitting the degree to which she spoke Italian to Drake and that his mutism was influenced by his not being wholly comfortable in English. My hunch was that everything would come right quite easily with a bit of very gentle intervention in a supportive environment, but that was the key: "supportive environment." Sympathetic adults, a relaxed atmosphere, and time for Drake to master two languages were crucial, if there were to be no long-lasting problems. Unfortunately, I went away from the meeting dissatisfied that Drake would receive that. Instead, I was left with the concern that Lucia and the grandfather were locked in some kind of battle of wills or in a series of accusations and denials over the use of Italian in the home and this was causing a poisonous environment, which Drake was reflecting with his mutism.

Anyway, that's what I considered. However, having lots of time to think as I made the long drive back to the city, a couple of spare not-fitting-in thoughts refused to fall silent. One was Drake himself. He was an extroverted, charismatic little boy who gave such a clear impression of wanting to communicate. This was not at all the typical profile of an elective mute. Nor was it typical of children who had bilingual problems. In my experience with young bilingual children, the extroverted, confident ones would happily bull ahead with whatever mixture of the two languages they had available and not worry whether they were right or not. I had encountered more than a few who were electively mute due to bilingualism, but in all the cases these were very shy, private children by nature who feared humiliation when making mistakes. Moreover, of what I could remember, they had all come from homes where no English was spoken at all, so their problems came from having no chance to practice English outside the public arena of the classroom.

The other odd thing was Lucia's comment that Drake had never spoken to his father. This did not fit at all with bilingualism, and I had never encountered a bilingual child who did not speak to everyone at home. Moreover, not speaking to immediate family members in the privacy of the home is an unusual pattern, even when elective mutism stems purely from emotional issues. In my own research it had been closely associated with serious child abuse and severe family dysfunction. Again, Drake's open, gregarious manner did not give the impression of such a traumatized child. However, I knew not to presume.

Chapter

6

*I*nto my next session with Cassandra I took with me one of my favorite therapeutic props, a box of dolls. These were called Sasha dolls. They were about sixteen inches high with beige nonethnic-colored skin; smooth, stylized limbs; and wistful, enigmatic expressions that were neither clearly happy nor sad. That alone set them apart in an era when virtually all other dolls had vacantly delirious grins that would better suit a stoned hippie.

I now had eight of these dolls, three of which were baby dolls, and the other five—two boys and three girls—had the proportions of a child in middle childhood. Through the years I had made or acquired a large wardrobe of clothes, plus many other small accoutrements, so I now used an apple box to accommodate it all. Wanting to give the apple box a little more longevity, to say nothing of a little more style, I had covered it in bright green wrapping paper with tiny cartoon rabbits all over it that I'd found in a store one Easter.

Cassandra noticed the box straightaway when she came into the therapy room. She looked at it, looked back at me with an interested, curious expression on her face, and then approached the box.

"It looks like a present, doesn't it, with all that wrapping paper," I said. "It's not really, though. So it doesn't need to be unwrapped. If you put your hands on the bottom, you can lift the top off because the paper is wrapped separately around the top of the box and the bottom."

Carefully, Cassandra eased the lid off the apple box. "Look!" she cried. "Look at all these dollies! And look at all the clothes!"

"Yes. And we're going to use those things in our work together." I sat down at the table.

"This is the kind of work I like!" she replied and reached in to take out a red-haired doll wearing a long blue patterned dress.

"There are a couple of things, however, I want to talk about first," I said, "before we get down to work. When you were in here yesterday, I asked you if you knew why you had come to the unit and you didn't seem quite sure. So I want to make certain that's clear to you."

Cassandra appeared to be paying little attention to me. She was enthusiastically rooting through the box, looking at various clothes, trying them up against the red-haired doll.

"Sometimes when kids come to the unit, they think they must have done something wrong and leaving their families to come to the hospital is a punishment for that.

It's important to understand that isn't true. You didn't come here because you've done anything wrong—"

"Yes, I have," she interjected in a casual, almost cheeky voice. She didn't look up at me.

"You think you've come here because you *have* done something wrong?"

"I put a frog in the blender! Whirr!" She reached out with one finger to press an imaginary switch. "Just like I'm going to do with this dolly right now. Here's a blender," she said, pointing to a bare space on the table. She held the doll upside down by its feet and lowered it into the imaginary blender. "Whirr! It's chopping it all up. Look at the blood. It's gone all bloody. Whirr!"

She looked up cheerfully. "And now I'm going to take the lid off. The blender's running and I take the lid off. WHIRRRRR! The blood spatters all over you! You're all bloody now. Ha-ha-ha-ha-ha!"

O-kaaaay. I sat back. I was definitely getting a better sense of what Earlene Baker had meant by Cassandra's "creepy" behaviors.

"I'm taking the lid off again. It's still running. Whirr! Blood and guts going all over. All over you. Splash! Splash!" Cassandra threw the doll into the air and made wild gestures with her hands to indicate splashing.

I remained silent. I didn't want to get drawn into questioning Cassandra on her imaginary blender. I suspected it was simply a replay of the old joke: "What is red and green and goes two hundred miles per hour? A frog in a blender." As with our conversation the day before, there was a vaguely manipulative feel to what she was saying, a sense that she was trying to shock me or engage me in a way she could control. Even if it were a true event and she had really put a frog in a blender, I wanted time to suss why she had chosen to insert this topic into the conversation here. So, instead of responding to her comments, I reached into the box and took out a doll, too. It was a blond boy doll dressed in hiking shorts and a T-shirt. I walked him along the side of the table.

"I haven't got a doll," Cassandra announced, even though she was still holding on to the red-haired doll. "Mine's all chopped up. Here, put yours in the blender."

"You know what this boy's wondering?" I asked and walked the doll closer to her.

"Unh-uh. And I don't care."

"He's wondering, why does that girl want to play that game?"

"What game?"

"This boy says, 'Why do you want to pretend something that's not true?'"

"Because I want to."

"He says, 'Why do you do that?'"

"Because it's fun," she said rather defiantly.

"This boy says, 'Sometimes when I do that, it is because I don't want to talk about something else. When I play a silly game, people get distracted and stop asking me.'"

"Not me. I do it because it's fun," she replied. "Funnest thing in the whole world and so that's what I do. Squish up frogs. And other stuff. I step on anything I see and watch its guts squirt out."

I held my doll in a standing position on the table. "This boy says, 'I have yucky feelings sometimes. I don't know what they are. I don't know how to explain them. Sometimes they make me do things I don't mean to and

I get into trouble. But if I play a silly game, people won't ask me about these feelings.' "

"You're stupid," Cassandra replied. "That never happens to me. It happens to you because you're stupid. You should go in the blender." She reached over to pull the doll out of my hand.

"I'm not stupid. I'm just scared," I said for the doll. "Being scared doesn't mean I'm stupid. It just means it's hard for me to think because I'm too frightened sometimes. And when I'm that frightened, I don't want someone to get angry at me and put me in the blender."

"You belong in the blender. You're very bad. Very, very, very, very bad. Come here. Get ground up." She reached for the doll again.

Holding on to it with some effort, I kept the boy doll standing upright on the table. "I'm not bad," I said for the doll. "Being scared doesn't mean I'm bad."

"Yes, it does. You're bad and stupid. Everybody's bad and stupid. The whole world is bad and stupid. Everything should be ground up in the blender!"

This outburst seemed to explode out of her physically, and she leaped up, throwing her doll high into the air. It fell to the floor and she picked it up. Holding it by the legs, she pounded its head against the linoleum in a frantic way.

"Cassandra?" I said.

She paid no attention to me.

"Cassandra, I can't allow you to do that. The doll will break if you treat it that way."

She continued to hammer the doll's head against the floor with vicious, uncontrolled swings.

Rising from the chair, I came around behind her,

leaned over her, and stopped the movement of her arms. "It's all right to have angry feelings, but I can't let you turn your anger into actions if it will hurt things. It's time to stop now."

As I spoke, it was as if a wizard cast a spell over the room. Cassandra froze the moment I touched her. When I removed the doll from her hands, her fingers retained their positioning, even though they were no longer holding anything.

Setting the doll back on the table, I returned to my seat. "You had some very strong feelings just then, didn't you?"

Cassandra lowered her hand. Still sitting on the floor, she stared straight ahead.

"That's all right. In here it's okay to have such feelings. And if they get too strong, I'll always be able to stop them."

Still looking into the space in front of her, she remained motionless.

"However, it's easier to cope with strong feelings when we have words for them. So one of the things you and I will do together is try and find ways to express your feelings with words. Then they won't be so scary."

Cassandra still didn't move.

The strength of her emotions seemed to have literally paralyzed her, so I thought rather than pursue them at this point, it would be better to help Cassandra reestablish equilibrium. I reached into the box and took out a girl doll with long dark hair.

"I'm going to change her clothes," I said. "Right now she is wearing pajamas, but I think it's time for some day clothes, don't you?"

Cassandra looked over at my doll. It was a slow, almost turgid movement, as if she were having to turn through a thick fluid. She said nothing.

"What about this long dress? If we look through the box, we'll find a sunbonnet that matches it. Would you look for it for me?"

Cassandra regarded me. She didn't answer.

"The lady who made this outfit wanted it to seem old-fashioned. Like perhaps one of the dolls was traveling west on a wagon train in the old days. So she made this long dress with lace on it like they wore in those days and a sunbonnet, because often the women and girls would walk alongside the wagon as they traveled and they didn't want to get a sunburn."

Cassandra stared at the doll in my hands.

"Cassandra?"

Again, the slow, solemn turning of her head.

"When we work together in here, I'll always keep you safe."

She glanced only briefly at my face and then away, staring into the space beside my chair.

"Sometimes we're going to work on hard things together, but you will decide how fast we go. We're not going to do anything that is too scary or too difficult. And I'm strong. If your feelings get too big, I'll help you with them. They won't be too big for me to handle. And I won't be scared by them."

She continued to stare, unfocused.

"Cassandra?"

She didn't respond.

I reached out and turned her face toward me. "How does that sound to you?"

She didn't meet my eyes. Even though I had re-oriented her head, she kept her eyes averted.

A pause.

I lowered my hand. Leaning forward, I sorted through the apple box until I found the sunbonnet.

"Look. Here it is. See, it matches the dress."

She regarded the sunbonnet.

"Would you like to try it on her?" I held the dark-haired doll out to her.

She took it. Laying the doll on the table, she carefully pulled on the sunbonnet and tied it under the doll's chin. Then she held the doll up.

I smiled. "What do you think?"

She didn't say. Indeed, she didn't speak again for the remainder of the session.

The next morning when Cassandra arrived for her session, she was once more her usual outgoing self. I had the box of dolls sitting on the table again, but this time she went right past them and over to the shelves behind me.

"I want to draw today," she said. "I can do what I want in here, can't I? Isn't that the way it's supposed to work?"

"You'd like to draw today?"

"That's the way it worked at the psychologist's I went to before. 'Cause I've been places like this before. If you thought you were special, you're not. My other psychologist's name was Dr. Brown. Adele Brown. But she wasn't brown. She was pink. Whitey-pink. Ugly whitey-pink. She was ugly. You're ugly. I think you're ugly, too."

"I see."

"And at ugly whitey-pink Adele Brown's, I could do

whatever I wanted. That's what she said. That I could do whatever I wanted. So that's what I can do in here, too."

"You're telling me you want to do whatever you please," I said.

"Yup. And I'm going to. And you can't stop me."

"You can do as you please in here as long as it doesn't involve destroying things or hurting yourself or me. I would stop you then. That isn't allowed here."

Cassandra looked at me, a rather evil glint in her eye. "You can't stop me doing anything, if I really want."

"If it's necessary, I can," I said quietly, "because those are the rules here and they're here to protect us. So I won't allow you to break them. But I am quite certain that isn't how we want to spend our time."

"You couldn't stop my daddy. He's bigger and stronger than you."

"You feel your daddy is very powerful and he can do what he wants. But if he were here, he'd have to follow the rules, too. In here I don't allow anyone to destroy things or hurt people."

"My daddy's the Hulk! Boom!" she cried and threw her hands out expansively. "Nobody can stop him when he turns into the Hulk. He'd beat you up in a minute! Boom! When he gets angry, he goes from being ordinary to being huge. A huge green monster. All his clothes rip apart." She leaped from the chair and demonstrated by pretending to tear off her clothes. "Even his underpants rip apart. Then you see his big green weenie. His weenie would hit you on the head and you'd fall down dead."

"That's what you picture happening," I said.

"Yeah!" she cried enthusiastically, leaping around. "That's what I want to happen. I want to see you dead."

I smiled slightly and didn't speak.

"That's what *would* happen!" she said, as if I'd rebuffed her. "My daddy would kill you with his dick."

"You seem excited by that idea."

"Yeah! You'd be dead! My daddy's so much stronger than you! Then I'd stomp up and down on your guts!"

"Cassandra, sit down, please."

She didn't. She continued jumping up and down.

"Cassandra, sit down, please."

She continued to jump. However, the quality of the jumping changed almost immediately from frenzied to defiant.

I watched her. Part of the reason I'd asked her to sit down was to help her keep from being swamped by what I sensed were very strong, scary emotions, but partly it was also to see how in control of her behavior she actually was, how much of it she was directing.

Quite a lot, it seemed. She jumped boldly a few more times, staring me right in the eye, challenging me to stop her. When I simply sat but insisted again she also sit down, she gave two or three more jumps to save face, then stopped and sat down.

Silence followed. Cassandra looked at me. Again I noticed what extraordinary eye contact she had. When caught in her gaze, I had almost a sense of violation. I found it hard not to want to escape it.

A dominance technique? Had she discovered this was a good way to gain power over others? Or was it more self-protective than that? Was she watching me so carefully because she felt the need to anticipate what I was going to do next? I didn't know.

More silence. Cassandra kept watching me.

"Know what? I don't like you," she said finally.

"Yes, so you've said. Why is that?" I asked.

"I don't like the way you look. I think you're ugly. I'm not going to work for you. I'm not going to do anything but sit here."

"Well, I'm sorry to hear that because it will certainly be very boring sitting here every day, doing nothing," I replied.

"I'm going to do it because it'll make you mad," Cassandra said. "Whatever you want me to do, I'm not going to do it. So you might as well know that now."

"You sound very concerned about who's in control here."

"I'm not going to listen to you either."

"Once I had a boy in here whose name was Liam. One of the first things he told me was that I couldn't make him do anything he didn't want. He wasn't going to do any work for me. He wasn't going to listen to a single thing I said."

Which was a story. I'd never had a Liam. But I'd found one of the best techniques for approaching problem areas was to ascribe the difficult behaviors or incidents to someone else.

"Liam thought that if he was—" I continued.

"I'm not listening to you," Cassandra said. She put her hands over her ears.

"Liam thought that if he knew everything that was going to happen, then—"

"I'm not listening," she said, hands still clamped over her ears. "La-la-la-la-la!" she started to sing in an effort to drown out my words.

"Yes, you're right. If you don't want to listen, I can't

make you listen. Just like I can't make you talk, if you decide you don't want to talk. You decide things like that. And as I said yesterday, we will not do anything that feels too scary or too difficult. If it feels too scary to listen, then we'll start with not listening."

Cassandra exploded up gleefully, throwing her hands in the air. "So I can do anything I want in here! You just said so yourself! I can do anything and you can't stop me."

I sat back and smiled with what I hoped was a very patient smile.

"I'm going to draw," Cassandra announced. "That's what I want to do." She flounced around the table to where the paper was kept on the shelves behind me and took a handful of sheets. She returned to the table, opened my box of tricks, and took out the smaller box containing the crayons and marking pens.

Then a pause.

She pushed the first sheet of paper over in front of me. "I want you to draw first. Draw a squiggle."

"How do you mean?"

"Draw a squiggle, so that I can draw. That's what my other psychologist did. She always drew a squiggle and then I would make a picture from it."

"I see," I said. "So you want me to do the same?"

"That's what Dr. Brown did."

"You like things to go exactly the same, don't you? You don't want any surprises."

"Just do it," Cassandra said. "I'm telling you, and you got to do anything I say."

"You want these sessions to be just like Dr. Brown's sessions. You want to tell me what to do."

"Would you quit repeating what I say? Draw." She shoved the pen right under my nose.

This demand to draw felt to me less like an effort to connect and communicate and more like a plain old-fashioned power struggle of the sort I'd had much experience with while teaching. Consequently, I said, "No, thank you."

"Yes. I say."

"No. In here each person is responsible for her own behavior. You have the right to decide what you are going to do, but you don't have the right to decide for me."

"Dr. Brown let me. It's what you let kids do at the psychologist's. You're so stupid. You don't know anything. I'm supposed to be able to do what I want in here, and I want you to draw a squiggle."

"You know what I hear you saying?" I said. "I hear you saying you want to control everything in here. You want to be able to say what you will do and you want to be able to say what I will do, too."

"That's how it's supposed to be. How long have you been a psychologist? You sure don't know anything about it."

"I see."

"You don't see or you'd do it. You don't see anything. You're stupid. You don't know anything about doing your job."

A moment's silent standoff. She glared at me, fixing me very firmly with her gaze.

"I don't like you," she said sulkily. "You're a big pain. I don't like being in here. I'm not going to come anymore." Frustrated, she sat down in the chair opposite me at the table.

Yet more silence.

She sighed heavily and flopped forward on the table. "You want Cooperative Girl," she muttered.

A pause.

"You said I could come in here." Her voice was low and still petulant. "But you don't want me. You want Cooperative Girl."

"I hear you saying you can't be yourself because you aren't able to tell me what to do."

"Shut up."

"I'm thinking that you feel worried about coming here unless you can control everything that might happen."

She clamped her hands over her ears and lowered her forehead down until it was against the tabletop.

Several moments passed.

Then gradually she lifted her head and lowered her hands. She remained hunched well forward over the tabletop and she sat very still, staring down at the wood pattern of the Formica. There was almost a meditative quality to it, a quieting, and it lasted two or three minutes, which is a sizable amount of time, if one is simply sitting without speaking. I watched her carefully.

"I can tell you something," she said very softly, her head still down.

"All right."

"It's a secret, so you've got to not tell anyone. But I can explain why I got so many problems and got to be in here."

Cassandra tilted her head to the side slightly, enough to look at me sidelong. For a moment or two she held my gaze. "You know my teacher?"

"Mrs. Baker? Yes."

"Well, one day . . . this was last term. Before Christmas. I was at my desk doing my workbook and she leaned over me . . . and she put her hand between my legs and felt me."

I watched her.

"She said if I could come in after school, she'd show me something. I didn't want to and I was sort of shaking my head. Like this. Real slow, like, because I didn't want the other kids to see. I didn't want them to know what she was doing to me. I didn't want to come in after school, but she said if I didn't, she'd tell my parents that I had stole some money, even though I hadn't done it. But she said she'd say that to them and they'd believe her."

"I see," I said.

"So I went in after school. She was there with her girlfriend. She's a lesbian and they were making love with each other. She asked if I wanted to do it, too. I didn't want to. I know that's wrong and I wanted to run away, but she said she'd tell my mom and get me in big trouble if I didn't do what she wanted. She said nobody was going to believe me over a teacher. So I had to let her and her girlfriend tongue me."

"So you're telling me that you think the reason you have problems and are here is because Mrs. Baker did sexual things with you?"

Solemnly, Cassandra nodded.

I hesitated.

She quickly read my uncertainty. "It's true!" she said with sudden vehemence. "It is the truth and no one will believe me. It's just like she said. Everyone will believe her and not me. And I got to pay for it."

"I think the reason people have a hard time believing

you, Cassandra, is because in the past you have sometimes had trouble telling the truth. This makes it hard
for people to know if what you are saying has really
happened or not."

"It has. And it's your fault. No one believes me. No
one takes my side. Nobody understands anything." And
with this Cassandra broke into inconsolable sobs.

State law required all allegations of child abuse be reported, so I had no choice but to go immediately to Dave Menotti with Cassandra's accusations regarding Mrs. Baker. I was quite certain she was not telling the truth. Not only did her allegations sound outlandish in terms of their content, the logistics just didn't fit. Mrs. Baker not only had a husband, but he usually stopped by the school at the end of the day to give her a ride home, as they had only one car. A friendly bear of a man, he was in the room, helping his wife rearrange classroom furniture the day I had visited. So the odds did not seem high that she also had a secret lesbian lover who joined her after school in molesting the children. Nonetheless, these were serious allegations. Without evidence that they were untrue, it would be negligent—and unforgivable—to simply ignore them.

In the early afternoon Dave and I sat together watching the videotape of the session. What came through in a way that hadn't been so obvious to me during the sessions was what a strange girl Cassandra was. There was no other way to put it. You watched her and you just got this eerie, uncomfortable sense of how odd she was.

The other thing I noticed was the lack of any discernible pattern to her behavior. Other than a desire to control the session, which had been present in all our meetings, Cassandra's behavior was diffuse and erratic. Watching the session, I was struck by how much of my floundering was simply because I still had no idea what I was dealing with. She switched from being aggressive to being coquettish to being domineering to being babyish and dependent without giving any indication of how these related to one another. Moreover, she made these switches so quickly I saw myself struggling to keep up. As soon as I tried to address one problem, she was off doing something else.

Dave said this indicated a "poorly organized personality" and added that this was, in his experience, the precursor to borderline personality disorder. In adults, this emotional disturbance shows itself as a pattern of behaviors that includes poor interpersonal relationships; intense and inappropriate emotions; unstable, often unpredictable moods; and impulsive and manipulative behaviors. So he speculated aloud that this might be what was forming.

We both agreed that Cassandra showed many indicators of having been sexually abused, including her comments about her father's penis and the graphic description of what she alleged her teacher had done to her. However, there was no way at this point to discern when or where or how the abuse had taken place or what it had involved. Like me, Dave felt there was not much credibility in her allegations against Mrs. Baker, but he was intrigued that Cassandra should pick Mrs. Baker to accuse. Why? he asked. Did Cassandra perceive Mrs. Baker as a threat and was thus attempting to get rid of her? Or was it just the opposite? Did she actually *like* Mrs. Baker and was using these allegations to make herself appear special to Mrs. Baker in our eyes? Or was she doing it to ensure some kind of connection to Mrs. Baker, feeling that even the negative uproar lies would cause was preferable to having no attention at all? I replied, what about the possibility that she'd simply lost contact with reality? Perhaps in her imagination these things *had* happened and she wasn't able to discern that they were thoughts and not actions.

Dave's and my conversation digressed then, wandering back to the issue of how hard it was to know how to treat someone when the individual's observable behaviors could be interpreted so many ways. I remarked that the tape reflected well the lack of focus in the sessions and my feeling that I was spending all my time reacting rather than acting. There wasn't really much more direction in what I was doing than in what she was doing.

Dave replied that we weren't lacking focus. Her abduction was the source of Cassandra's difficulties and the focus of our work was understanding how that trauma had affected her and finding a way of helping her deal with that experience.

I hadn't really needed reminding of this. Indeed, I said, that was half my problem. I'd spent a lot of time investigating the current research into treatment of traumatized children and had made detailed plans for dealing with the issues surrounding the abduction. The problem was that so far I hadn't managed to squeeze in even one of my planned exercises. Focusing on the trauma of the abduction was what I *wanted* to do, but that was just never where we ended up going.

Dave smiled gently. *"Au contraire, mam'selle,"* he said. "I think that's just where you're going." And he rose from his seat, clapping me on the shoulder as he did so. "The trick," he added, "is fitting what you know to the events, not fitting the events to what you know."

The day after I'd returned from Quentin, I reported back to Harry Patel regarding my visit to see Drake Sloane. I told Harry that, yes, indeed, Drake was electively mute and the preschool had tried interventions, which had thus far been unsuccessful. I mentioned the possibility of bilingualism as a contributing factor and did say there were a few peculiarities to the case, such as the restrictive nature of Drake's mutism. My overall impression, however, was of a reasonably well-adjusted child who, given an environment sensitive and appropriate to his needs, would most likely outgrow the difficulty without further treatment.

Which sadly couldn't be said about Drake's grandfather, I added. I told Harry how I'd found the old man to be difficult, demanding, and meddlesome and how I suspected that if there were any serious problems, they lay in the family dynamics and not in the boy. Then I mentioned how I'd unintentionally antagonized the old man and he'd stomped out on me. So, regardless of my findings, that was the end of the story.

Or so I'd thought.

Sitting in my office with Dave Menotti, going over

the videotape of Cassandra's session, I heard a quick rap at the door.

It opened and Harry popped his head in. "Oops, sorry to interrupt," he said, "but I'm just leaving to go over to the medical center, and I wanted to say before I missed you, Torey, that Drake Sloane is coming into the unit on Sunday."

My eyes widened with surprise.

"Had a call from Mason Sloane, who said they'd had a family meeting and Drake's parents decided they wanted this problem sorted out."

Mason Sloane decided, more likely.

As I didn't work weekends, I wasn't on the unit when Drake was admitted, but, of course, I was slated for his individual therapy sessions. When I arrived on Monday, I found Drake curled up on the couch in the dayroom watching cartoons, his huge stuffed tiger, Friend, sitting beside him.

"Hi, Drake!" I called as I walked through the dayroom to the nurses' station. "Remember me?"

He nodded enthusiastically, smiled broadly, and waved, then started to get down to come over.

"You wait there just a second while I talk to Nurse Nancy and then I'll come get you. Then we'll go do something fun. Okay?"

Grabbing Friend around the neck in such an vigorous hug that they both toppled over, he laughed and nodded.

Before starting the session, I wanted to find out how Drake had adjusted to his first day on the ward and what Nancy's general impressions were, so I stepped into the small room behind the nurses' station and closed the door.

"*What* a sweetie!" Nancy said. "He's been just good as gold since he's come. There were some tears last night. I mean, poor little tadpole. And his mama must have had a very wet pillow last night, too. She lingered so long yesterday. You could just see it in her face."

This I could imagine. My impression during my visit to Quentin was not only that Lucia loved her son very dearly, but that Drake may have served as a buffer between her and the rest of the world. Indeed, my general sense was that both Mason Sloane and Lucia had more problems than Drake.

Truth was, I was not happy with the Sloanes' decision to bring Drake for inpatient treatment. Without evidence of devastating levels of dysfunction, the boy was, in my opinion, way too young to be separated from his mother and left for days in an institutional setting. Elective mutism on its own is not indicative of serious pathology. To hospitalize a four-year-old for not speaking at school falls into the category of "burning the house down to roast the pig," in my opinion. This left me far more concerned about the psychological damage *we* could do by separating a preschooler from his family and familiar surroundings for days, if not weeks, than what would occur from leaving the elective mutism untreated. Unfortunately, he was not my child and it was not my choice. If parents made this kind of decision and had the insurance or finances to see it through, our hospital unit was designed for diagnostic purposes. So my best course of action was to swallow my own opinions and simply to get on with the job as quickly and straightforwardly as possible, so that he could go home.

I didn't foresee any problems in this. My treatment essentially involved very little more than arriving as an outsider with whom the child had not already established a silent relationship, setting up the expectations he/she could and would talk with me, and then presenting the child with opportunities to do so. Among children for whom there was no other significant pathology, this "method" had worked very well and my success rate was almost a 100 percent within the first session. So I set myself the personal goal of having Drake ready to go home by the next weekend.

The therapy room wasn't large, and it suffered from being painted a really nasty institutional gray, but otherwise it was an acceptable room. Long and narrow in shape, it had a sunny south-facing window on the far end that overlooked the trees in the hospital courtyard below. On the right-hand side of the room was the one-way mirror with an observation room on the other side. Usually there weren't any observers, but located in there was also a video camera that recorded all sessions. On the left-hand side of the room was a low set of shelves running the entire length of the wall. These contained a small selection of playroom items commonly used in therapy—puppets, toy cars, plastic people and animals, paper, crayons, pens, plus a Playmobil dollhouse, a Fisher-Price garage, and part of a Playmobil hospital set. A Dick Bruna alphabet frieze had been put up on the wall above the shelves along with four large posters of Dick Bruna's popular rabbit character, Miffy, displayed at rakish•angles. Their bright primary colors and imaginative arrangement against the gray walls in the long, narrow room gave me the feel of being amid the cheap and cheerful decor of a student dormitory.

I always carried my own box of materials with me, the same box I'd taken out to Quentin, and I set it on the tabletop. Drake immediately settled into the chair opposite, putting Friend on the chair beside him. Friend was so enormous that he actually sat taller in the chair than Drake.

Drake proved an enthusiastic companion. If he was lonely or frightened at being separated from his family, he didn't show it. His expression was bright-eyed and animated; his whole body wriggled with anticipation.

"So what do you think about all this?" I said. "Do you like being here?"

He nodded eagerly.

"What's been your favorite part?"

He gestured with his hands. I had no idea what he was trying to communicate but he did so fervently, then looked up at me with expectancy.

"You know what I think, Drake? I think it would be so much easier if you used words. I really do want to understand what you are saying. I want to know all about what you like to do and the things that happen when we aren't together. I'm really, really interested. But we need words for that, don't you think?"

Drake nodded.

"Your mom has told me you use words with her. I'm thinking it would be helpful if you used words to talk to me, too. So that's what you and I are going to do in here together. I'm going to help you to start using words. You see, my special job is working with boys and girls who find it hard to talk. Just like you. Just exactly like you. So I'm very good at helping people start to talk again."

This seemed to please Drake enormously. He nodded enthusiastically, as if I were suggesting just the best idea in the world.

I was struck yet again by his physical presence. He was such a gorgeous kid. His features were so symmetrical and well formed, his eyes so vibrant. I was even growing accustomed to his unusual hairstyle. It was part of him, part of what made him seem so ethereal, like a lost angel.

"Because I've worked with lots of other boys and girls who've had trouble talking, just like you, I know how hard it is to get started. I know it can be scary when you've been used to not talking. But usually it's just the first time that's hard. We'll work together. I'll be right here, helping you. And I know you can do it."

Again, the wholehearted nod.

I reached into my box and pulled out a set of cards I'd made. They were about five by seven inches in size and made from magazine pictures I'd cut out and pasted. Each showed a clear, appealing picture of common items: a car, a cat, a dog, a man, a child, and so on. I chose one that was very popular. It was a close-up of a little red-haired boy and a black cat. The boy was holding an ice cream cone and as he licked it on one side, the cat, long pink tongue extended, was reaching out to lick it on the opposite side of the cone. Children never failed to respond both to the inherent humor in the picture and to the almost universal desire to share experiences with animals.

Drake laughed noiselessly and pointed to the boy and

the cat and then looked up to assure himself that I too was seeing how funny it was.

"Yes, that's a good picture, isn't it? What's happening? What's this?" I asked, pointing to the cat.

He gestured, tapping his finger against the picture.

"Yes, what is that? What's it a picture of? What animal is this?"

He was exhaling, pushing air out quite audibly but it was nowhere near a word. Just breath.

"What is this? What animal is this?" I continued pointing to the cat. My experience in getting elective mutes over this first hump of speech was that I had to provide an opportunity to speak early on in the session and then pleasantly but persistently keep at the request, ignoring the silence that was thrown up; indeed, never allowing the silence to develop any kind of potency. So I continued to ask, rephrasing the question repeatedly, tapping the picture, pointing to it, staying forever on task.

Right from the onset, Drake appeared to make a genuine effort. He exhaled. He made noisy breathy sounds that didn't approximate words, but nonetheless appeared to be authentic attempts.

Because he was so young and because he did seem to be working hard, I didn't want to stress Drake too much by becoming more insistent, as I often did with older children. So I changed tactics. "Is this a dog? Is this boy sharing his ice cream cone with his dog?"

Drake grinned and shook his head.

"Is it a dinosaur? Is the horse eating his ice cream cone?"

Again, the cheerful shake of the head.

"Is it Friend?"

Drake laughed noiselessly and shook his head hard.

I went on through half a dozen other absurd possibilities until Drake seemed almost unable to control his hilarity at this funny game. Then I said, "What animal *is* it?"

He opened his mouth wide and leaned down close to the picture.

"What animal is this? Come on. Let's use the word."

He kept his mouth wide open.

I made my voice suddenly intense. "What animal is this?" Not anger, just focused no-nonsense intensity.

Drake got the message immediately. His laughter dropped away abruptly and he stared at the picture. Reaching over, he clutched Friend around the neck. His body began to rock slightly back and forth in the chair. His eyes remained fixed on the picture.

"What animal is this? Here. Now, Drake. What animal is this?"

Deep, noisy respirations.

"What animal is this?" I tapped the card more insistently. "Tell me what we have here. What's this?"

He started to cry. This too was almost noiseless. He didn't even whimper, but huge tears formed and rolled over his cheeks.

"I know it's hard," I said. "It's hard and it's scary when you haven't been used to talking, but only the first time is so bad. Once this is over, it won't be this hard again. What animal is this?"

A long moment of intensely expectant hesitation. Then he put his head down on the table and sobbed.

Chapter

9

$\mathcal{I}$ had to give up.

Giving up, however, wasn't the obvious decision it appeared to be. An extraordinary degree of manipulation underlies many cases of elective mutism. In almost all instances, it is unconscious behavior, but it is manipulation nonetheless. So a child bursting into tears isn't usually enough to deter me. Even with a child who doesn't appear manipulative, to stop at the first sign of tears tends to reinforce the mutism as a successful defense. So stopping wasn't a decision I took lightly. However, given Drake's age, I was very concerned about putting him under too much pressure. Moreover, all along he genuinely had appeared to be trying. Thus, it seemed wise to go with my instinct to stop.

So I said, "You've been working very hard. This isn't easy. I know." He had pulled Friend across and sat, face buried in the fake fur of the tiger's head.

Taking a tissue, I leaned over to mop him up. "You did try hard, didn't you?"

He nodded.

"Here, come here." I opened my arms. He and Friend came willingly onto my lap for a hug. "Don't worry about it," I said. "Don't feel bad. When it's time, it'll happen."

After taking Drake back to the ward, I returned to the observation room and started to rewind the videotape. It was a puzzling session. Drake *had* given me the impression of trying so hard. Right from the visit out in Quentin, he had not seemed fearful, obstinate, withdrawn, or in any other way unwilling to comply. He had always appeared focused and genuinely enthusiastic for what we were doing. So why hadn't my methods worked straightaway?

Popping the tape out of the machine, I took it back to my office to play it on the VCR there. Helen was in the room when I came in. A tall, slim, quite elegant woman in her early fifties, Helen had a tenderhearted, maternal approach to working with the children, which was quite different from my more pragmatic methods. When I put the tape in, I said, "If you have a sec, would you watch this with me?"

"What a cutie!" she cried, seeing Drake on the screen. "How absolutely adorable. And look that big toy tiger!"

We then watched the tape in silence.

The advantage of videotaping sessions was that it allowed the opportunity to go back and see all that was missed. For me, occasionally this could be quite a lot, because I have quite an extraordinary ability to focus on what I am doing. The plus side is that I seldom miss even the subtlest cues from whatever I am centered on. The minus side is that I can miss everything else. Indeed, I had become the subject of much good-natured teasing after one video showed me so absorbed in how quickly and accurately a child was doing an eye-hand coordination task that I failed to notice he had climbed entirely out of his chair and up onto the table on all fours while he was doing it. The tape showed me effortlessly adjusting my positioning to follow the child as he moved across the table and eventually back down into his chair again and during this whole time I'd never realized the boy had left his seat. My colleagues found this hysterical. And, needless to say, I now greatly appreciated the opportunity to see what I'd missed by viewing the session videos!

Consequently, on this occasion I was expecting to see clues in Drake's behavior that I had overlooked during the session. With Helen's added perspective, I hoped it would become clear to me why I'd failed to get him to talk and how I needed to adjust my approach for our next time together.

What I saw, however, was . . . nothing. Nothing at all different from what I'd perceived during the session itself. Drake came in eagerly. He engaged well with me, seemed attentive and interested in what we were doing, appeared motivated to try what I asked of him. And he did try. Again and again. What the videotape made clear was how hard he'd applied himself right from the beginning and then the heartbreaking decline of his mood when he did not achieve what I wanted. Watching it, I was relieved I'd stopped when I did.

I looked at Helen when the screen turned to snow.

"He *can* talk?" she asked.

"Yes."

"Because that's my first impression. The boy can't speak. You're *sure* he speaks? He's not deaf or anything?"

"No, he's definitely not deaf. And yes, I'm sure he speaks. He talks at home to the mother. The big question mark in my mind remains bilingualism. He may be speaking only Italian to her," I said.

"Have you tried speaking Italian to him?"

I grinned sheepishly. "If I knew Italian . . ."

"Yeah, well," Helen conceded. Then she added, "But if it were bilingualism, wouldn't he at least be able to repeat the words for you, even if he couldn't use them himself? Or wouldn't he try to use the Italian word or something?"

"Not if he's electively mute."

Helen sat back in her desk chair and slowly shook her head. "Then I'm no help. I didn't see anything there you didn't see."

Turning off the video recorder and monitor, I returned to my desk and started to go through the telephone messages that had piled up. While most were the usual communiqués with other professionals over the various children I was involved with, one came from the hospital's geriatrics department. Geriatrics? Curious, I lifted it out of the pile and dialed the number.

The phone was answered by a geriatric social worker named Joy Hansen. Ah, she said in a bright-sounding voice, what she wanted to talk to me about might be "a bit of a stretch" but she wondered if I'd give an opinion. My name had come to her via Dave Menotti, she said.

She and Dave had been having coffee in the hospital cafeteria and she'd been discussing a case with him. He suggested perhaps I'd have some insight.

Intrigued, I asked for more information.

Joy had a patient named Gerhardine Sharple, who was currently in the stroke rehabilitation unit, housed in a nearby medical complex. Gerhardine, known as Gerda, was eighty-two. She had been in good health and living independently up until five weeks earlier, when she had had a massive stroke. After the initial stay in the hospital, she was then released to the rehabilitation unit and seemed to be making a reasonable recovery. However, there was an ongoing problem with her speech. Strokes often interfere with the language center in the brain, causing loss of communicative speech, which is known as stroke-induced aphasia. In Gerda's case, she had recovered certain elements of speech almost immediately. In particular, she was capable of responding appropriately if she was asked simple, concrete questions. However, in spite of intensive speech therapy work, two problems remained. One, while she had demonstrated the ability to respond appropriately to questions, this did not mean she always complied with the request. And two, she produced no spontaneous speech whatsoever.

Joy said Gerda had been widowed many, many years before. She had been living alone in a small isolated farm. The house, a two-story clapboard of the sort commonly built at the turn of the twentieth century, stood amid ancient, half-dead cottonwoods and was surrounded by miles of sagebrush and little else. Although the emergency services had found things clean and tidy, the property was dilapidated in the way of the rural poor, and a haven for small animals. More than a dozen chickens ran happily in the yard, a goat was in the half-collapsed barn, and sixteen cats shared the house. Indeed, Joy said, Gerda seemed a stereotypically reclusive "cat lady" and, as a consequence, she had had little contact with neighboring farms.

She did have a family, but they were widely dispersed. Her daughter, married to a Spaniard, had been living in Spain for decades, and her son lived half a continent away in Detroit. Joy had contacted the son, whose name was Edward, and said he seemed distant and largely unconcerned. He had taken the news of his mother's stroke with a disgruntled moan and characterized Gerda as "difficult." He said he'd tried on two or three occasions to get her to see that the only real way he could take care of her in her old age was if she moved to Detroit where he and his family lived. Gerda had flatly refused. She was even unwilling to consider selling the house, he said, even though she could get a good price for that property, because it was a desirable location for rural development. He'd pointed that fact out to her several times. Why did she want to keep it? It was far more space than one person needed and starting to get very run-down because she couldn't afford the up-keep and was simply past being able to do any of it herself. But his mother was difficult. She would never compromise to make it easier for anyone. He was a self-made man, he explained. He'd come up from nothing. Got a good education, married into a good family, started a successful business. He had made something of himself, but it was still hard work. He couldn't be at his mother's beck and

The daughter was even less involved. When social workers had entered Gerda's house after the stroke, they found photographs of the daughter, her Spanish husband, and their two children, but there was no way to tell when the photos had been taken. They couldn't even find reference to the daughter's name in the house. This was possibly not due to any purposeful removal but simply because Gerda did not seem to be a "keeper." Her house was immaculately clean, in spite of all the cats, but also spartan. Joy had obtained the daughter's name—Anna—from Edward, but this was clearly not a close family. He and his sister, who had returned to the States only twice since her marriage twenty-three years earlier, had no more contact than Christmas cards.

So that was the situation, Joy said. Social Services were now dealing with Gerda's immediate future. She could only remain in the rehabilitation unit as long as it was apparent she was actually in the active stages of rehabilitation. For most stroke patients this lasted three to six weeks. In the doctors' opinion, Gerda seemed to have made this initial recovery. Now decisions on her future placement had to be made, such as how much longer would she need full nursing care and would she be able to resume an independent life eventually? Could she care for herself in an isolated location such as her own home? At the moment, assisted care seemed more appropriate, or, indeed, full-time nursing home placement. Of course, all of this required money. A decision ▓ded to be made, which would most likely entail sell-▓ ▓ouse to finance assisted-living arrangements.

▓ ▓ As the social worker, she had spent time ▓ these various scenarios with Gerda, and Joy's overall impression of the old woman was not one of a stroke victim so much as a very depressed individual. Depression, Joy said, is common among elderly patients who lose their independence and suddenly find themselves sleeping in strange beds, eating strange food, and having to live according to strangers' rules. Joy was accustomed to dealing with that, but in this instance, it was grossly complicated by Gerda's lack of speech. Joy had consulted the gerontologist supervising Gerda's case and told him that she felt Gerda's mutism might be largely psychological, due most likely to depression. The gerontologist put Gerda on Zoloft, which, if anything, had made Gerda even more subdued.

This lack of speech spelled bad news for Gerda, Joy said. Whatever the reason, it gave the professionals grave concern regarding her ability to resume any level of independent living. Joy had tried to explain this to Gerda, tried to stress how important it was to work hard on talking with people in the rehabilitation unit because otherwise Joy wouldn't be able to stop a nursing home placement.

I asked, "Have there been any psychiatric problems in her past?"

"No. But then, she's of that generation. Her son said that Gerda's parents were homesteaders. Part of the German immigration about the turn of the century. If people suffered psychiatric problems in that era, they just toughed it out. No one sought help."

"And what have they done with Gerda's animals?" I asked.

"I don't know what's happened to the chickens and things," Joy replied. "The cats they put to sleep, I think."

"All sixteen?"

"Social Services went in after the ambulance took her. There really wasn't much choice."

"Were the cats poorly cared for?"

"No. Not really. It was spotlessly clean there. And in fact, they found more cat food in the cupboard than people food. But there were just too many of them. No one could be expected to house sixteen cats during such a long period of hospitalization. Especially as she well might not come back at all. It just seemed the better thing to do. Kinder in the long run, you know? Sixteen cats are too many to re-home."

I didn't say anything in response to that. Joy sounded depressed herself about Gerda's case. It was a sad story in so many ways—the lack of connection, the familial disinterest, the isolation, the loss of independence—one of those small heartbreaking stories of small, heartbreaking lives, of people who don't really matter to anyone. What struck me as the final cruelty, however, was the decision to put her cats to sleep without giving her any say, without any warning, without any opportunity to change things. To Gerda when she found out, I'm sure it was as if they'd simply said, "We're sorry but your loved ones were too much work for us while you were ill, so we've gassed them all." And now she genuinely did have no connection with this world. No wonder she was depressed.

Joy went on to say that this was the point they were at when she ran into Dave Menotti. During their conversation together, he had mentioned my interest in language disorders and said perhaps I could offer an opinion on the extent to which Gerda's poor speech was physiological or psychological. Would I be willing? she asked.

Ah, I said. This was all very interesting. And very sad, too, and I genuinely wished I could help. Unfortunately, I had absolutely no experience working with the elderly in any capacity beyond funding my college years as a nurse's aide. I had never worked with language problems in anyone who was over sixteen. Indeed, my recollection of the academic literature was that there was very little information available regarding adult elective mutism. When such behavior occurred in adulthood, it tended to be associated with much more serious psychiatric problems, such as schizophrenia or other psychoses, and was not usually treated as a disorder in its own right.

Down the phone line I could hear Joy make that soft click of the tongue, that faint noise denoting hopelessness. A small silence followed. Then she said, "You wouldn't want to just have a look at her, would you? She's in the Oakfield Rehabilitation Center. It's only about three blocks from the hospital. If we could just get through to her, just get her to understand how critical it is she cooperates, if she wants any chance of an independent life. Dave thought maybe you'd at least have ideas."

That evening I spent a couple of hours at the library on a nearby university campus searching for information on adult mutism. I found nothing except the references I already knew about regarding psychotic mutism and a few others regarding advanced Alzheimer's disease or obscure brain tumors or anomalies. Joy's plea, however, stayed with me. Consequently, I finally decided I would stop by on my way into work and see Gerda. Not because I had any qualifications. I didn't and I knew I didn't. And certainly not because I had any magic. Truth is, I had no real good reason. I did hear way back in my mind, however, what a mentor had said to me at eighteen when I had protested at being too ill-equipped to work with a seriously disturbed child: "When things are hopeless, nothing you do will make it worse. So it's always worth taking the risk to see if just, just possibly something you do will make it better."

Chapter

10

$\mathcal{I}$ walked down the long corridor of the rehabilitation center, dank with disinfectant and the steam-and-musk mix of institutional food and bodily fluids. It was early. Breakfast trays were only just being cleared away. In some rooms, nurses' aides were still spoon-feeding patients.

Gerda's room was second to last on the right. As I approached, I was aware of feeling nervous. What on earth would I do with her? I could hardly pop open my box and pull out the puppets or crayons.

She was sitting up in bed. Her breakfast tray had been removed, but the little adjustable bed table was still pushed across in front of her.

I don't know what I'd expected but it was something different than I saw. She looked unexpectedly young. Or, I suppose said better, she looked unexpectedly "not old." Her hair, which was completely white, had a yellowish cast that could almost have been mistaken for a pale blond, and it was loose around her shoulders. And long. Longer than mine. No doubt she normally wore it pulled up in a bun, and such a style would have given her a more predictable little-old-lady look, but the way it was here now, parted on the side—long, loose, and straight—she seemed ageless as an ancient sculpture. This sense was enhanced by her skin. Though it had the fragile crepeyness of age, she had few wrinkles, especially across her forehead, which was smooth to a point of being almost waxy looking. She was of obvious northern Germanic heritage, with pale eyes and prominent features. Although she was not overweight, her bones were big and blunt, giving the impression of a tall, sturdy woman.

"Hello," I said. "My name is Torey. Joy Hansen has asked me to come see you. I work with people who have problems speaking. I'm not a speech therapist, so I won't be doing those sorts of things with you. My work is more with people who are able to talk but find it hard to do so."

Pulling over a plastic chair that was next to the wall, I sat down. Gerda regarded me. Her gaze was straightforward but not at all readable. I couldn't tell if she was pleased at a new face, if she was appraising me, or, indeed, if she was simply watching me because I moved.

"How long have you been at Oakfield?" I asked.

She continued to gaze at me. Seconds passed, feeling like minutes. She didn't respond.

Thinking perhaps this was the wrong kind of question, that age and the stroke as well as simply the loss of normal routine might make it difficult to recall how long she had been in, I changed to: "How was your breakfast?"

She gave me the same unflinching, unreadable stare.

And it was the unreadable aspect that was making things difficult for me. I was accustomed to being able to discern more information nonverbally than I was getting here. I genuinely could not tell if she was refusing to speak or if she was unable to speak or even possibly that she was not hearing me properly. Her expression was not so blank as to give the impression of nobody home, but there was a definite possibility that whoever was in there was not turning the lights on.

"What did you have for breakfast?" I asked.

She looked away then. It was done slowly, giving the action ever so faintly a feeling of misery.

Had the food been awful? Or something she loathed? Or was she simply fed up at having one more stranger in her room demanding stupid information from her?

"You must be tired of all this," I said. "All of us coming and going. All of us keeping you to our schedules and our activities. When I was in the hospital, that's what I remember as being the worst part. I especially hated the mornings. It's so hard to sleep at night because they leave so many lights on and make so much noise, but then just when exhaustion finally takes over and you go to sleep, in they come at 6:30 and wake you up again. And for what? They'd always get you up, just so you could wait. I always thought, 'Why don't they leave us sleeping in peace?' "

She looked back as I said that, and her look was not guarded this time. I could easily read the quiet despair.

"All this change must be very upsetting for you. Has anyone talked to you about it?" I asked.

Gerda looked at me a long moment. It was a deep, searching look, and then slowly she shook her head. A sigh followed. Then she lay back in her bed and turned away from me.

"That's what I'm here for," I said. "Because what you've gone through is difficult and frightening. And if we can talk about it, perhaps we can put some things right."

Silence.

More silence.

It wasn't "working" silence, which was the kind of silence I could manipulate to bring words from reluctant speakers, nor was it the kind of silence that was my trick in trade because I'd learned how not to be uncomfortable with it. This was just silence. Total and immovable.

"How would you like me to address you?" I asked. "Shall I call you Mrs. Sharple? Or is it all right to call you Gerda?"

No response.

"My great-aunt was named Gerda," I said. "I never met her because she lived in Germany, but I liked her very much. When I was small, she always sent me a papier-mâché egg at Easter with little gifts in it. Among the things inside the egg was always a tiny little wooden rabbit wearing lederhosen and playing a musical instrument. Each Easter it was a different rabbit with a different instrument. I have a whole orchestra of them now, each only about two inches high. So when I heard your name, it reminded me of my aunt. I cared for her very much. So, if you don't mind, I'd like to call you Gerda."

She had turned back to look at me while I was talking.

"Gerda's a German name. Which part did your family come from?"

She didn't answer.

."My family is originally from Emden. It's on the coast, near the Dutch border. My grandfather grew up there. Gerda was his sister and she lived in Emden all her life."

No response.

"Is your family from the north of Germany?"

She nodded.

"Which part?"

No response.

This conversation was hard work. Should I persist? Continue chattering one-sidedly? Ask more questions? Use the same direct, expectant techniques that had worked so well with the children? I was having a small crisis of confidence. What if she couldn't talk? What if she felt under horrible pressure to do something she was physically unable to do? Who was I to be sitting here, trying to elicit speech from a stroke victim? I was overstretching myself and I knew it.

Unobtrusively, I tried to glance at my watch. My time was already up. I was supposed to be on the children's unit in only five minutes' time.

"I need to go now, because I work over at the hospital and I see I'm running late for my next appointment," I said.

She had looked away already.

I felt bad saying that because it sounded as if I were trying to get away, so I added, "I'll stop back, okay?"

She didn't respond.

"Okay," I said for her.

My next appointment was, in fact, Drake, and I wasn't feeling a whole lot more confident about him.

Ever since I'd left our unsuccessful session, he had been on my mind. I didn't want to establish a nonverbal relationship with him, as this would make it more difficult to break the cycle of mutism; on the other hand, I also didn't want to spiral into the kind of negativity that would make him fearful and unhappy in our sessions. If that happened, then anxiety would become the barrier.

Indeed, I'd been thinking quite a bit about anxiety in the interim, as anxiety lies at the root of elective mutism for many children. With some the mutism is a manifestation of social phobia. In these instances, the child tends to have an excessively shy personality and often comes from a family where one or both parents have also had a history of acute shyness in childhood, indicating that there well may be a genetic component at work. For other children, the anxiety seems to be more closely related to stage fright, to fears of performance and failure. With these children, the parents may be confident and outgoing themselves. Baffled by the shyness, they often put heavy pressure on the child to be more social, which exacerbates the problem.

Anxiety isn't such an issue for the third major group of children displaying elective mutism. For these children, speaking is a control issue, and withholding speech is an expression of complex psychological problems similar to those found in anorexia or encopresis. These children tend to have strong-willed, perfectionistic personalities and often form tempestuous but symbiotically close relationships with a primary caretaker to whom they speak normally.

Drake, however, didn't seem to fit any of these profiles. This left only one other group in my experience:

those children who are mute in reaction to trauma. This group includes children who have had a sudden appalling injury to the mouth, often coinciding with the age when the child is starting to speak. One such little boy I'd worked with had caught and badly ripped his mouth on a playground swing. The fright of the accident stopped him speaking altogether for several months. Then latterly he would speak only when in the safety of his house. This group also includes children who have witnessed deeply traumatizing events and are literally shocked speechless, as in the case of another young boy who had witnessed his sister's murder. Mostly, however, it takes in children who have been severely abused and are affected either by the trauma of the abuse or by the threat "not to tell."

Severe abuse was already in my mind in regard to Drake, because in my research, his kind of mutism, which was very complete and excluded even close family members, had been a marker of serious dysfunction in the family; and, of course, serious dysfunction often goes hand in hand with serious abuse. I found this so sad even to think about. He was such a joyous little boy—lively, intelligent, eager to please—the kind of little boy I'd imagine anyone would be absolutely delighted to have. It was heartbreaking to consider he might be experiencing a whole other world behind closed doors. It was daunting to consider how to go about uncovering it.

If Drake had any residual misgivings about his unhappy time with me the previous day, he didn't show it. When I appeared in the dayroom where he and Friend were watching cartoons, he grinned broadly and jumped up.

"I've got something fun for us to do today," I said, as we walked together down to the therapy room.

Drake smiled beguilingly. Honestly, the kid could have charmed ducks off water, as my grandmother always used to say.

Since he had become so upset the day before, I decided to choose a very different kind of activity. In the therapy room, I shoved the table back and seated us on the floor in front of the two-way mirror because I wanted to be able to scrutinize Drake's behavior on the videotape afterward. Then I held up a bottle.

"Know what this is?" I asked, as I unscrewed the top. "Bubbles!" Lifting the little wand out, I blew through it, and a cascade of bubbles flowed between us.

Drake clapped his hands with delight.

I made bubbles several more times. Then I held the wand and bubble liquid out to him. "Here, you try," I said.

He smiled joyfully at me.

"Here, like this." I blew on the wand gently and a few bubbles came out. "You try."

He smiled more.

I dipped the wand into the liquid and coaxed him again.

More grinning, but he wouldn't try.

Getting up, I brought over a flat dish with a huge wand. I poured some of the solution into the dish. "What do you think is going to happen when I dip this big wand into the bubble liquid?" I lifted it up, pulling an enormous iridescent bubble from the water.

Amazed at the size of it, Drake jumped up and down with excitement. I whirled the wand and a basketball-sized bubble escaped and floated toward him, which he gleefully popped.

"It's easy to do. Here, you try it," I said and set the wand back in the dish.

Drake came over and took the wand from the liquid. His first bubble didn't work, but on his second try, he managed to produce a series of bubbles each about the size of a baseball. One popped on Friend's head, and this sent Drake into spasms of delight.

For several minutes, he was absorbed in making bubbles with the large wand. He played very uninhibitedly with them once they started to float, chasing after them, trying to loop them with the wand, kicking them, poking them. He repeatedly wafted bubbles over Friend and gleefully let them pop on the stuffed toy.

I watched him as he played. There was a rather jerky quality to his movements, which I hadn't noticed in his usual activities. It caught my attention, but it was still very subtle. Not something I would actually identify as unusual.

It was intriguing to observe the attention he gave Friend. He was definitely more engaged in playing with Friend than with me. Throughout, he made absolutely no noise, which was eerie to observe. It felt almost as if real life had had the sound turned off, because the only noise in the room was the hushed slap of his sneakers against the floor. What gave it an almost surreal aura was that this was a scene of such gaiety. Capering after the bubbles, Drake gave the impression that he was laughing, giggling, whooping for joy as he played. However, he wasn't even breathing audibly.

"Look here," I said and reached in my bag of tricks. "I have a different kind of bubble maker. It's a pipe. See? You dip it in the dish and then blow." I demonstrated. Dozens and dozens of small bubbles tumbled around us.

Drake danced after them, batting at them with his hands.

"Here, you try."

He grinned at me.

I loaded the pipe with bubble liquid. "Here."

He continued to smile cheerfully, but he didn't take it.

I gave a little puff of the pipe to create a small flow of bubbles, then held it out again. "You do it."

Gleefully grinning, he slapped at the bubbles but still didn't respond to my request to take the pipe.

At that point the penny did finally drop for me. If you behave very beguilingly, people don't tend to force their will on you. Particularly if you are small and cute, to boot. Drake's charismatic cheerfulness was an avoidance technique. Now, the question was, avoiding what?

*W*hile I was blowing bubbles with Drake, I could hear a terrible commotion going on out on the ward. Yelling and crying was followed by the heavy sound of feet, which signaled extra staff arriving in an effort to control whatever was going on. My first thoughts were that the uproar would alarm Drake, because certainly it sounded frightening. He paused for only the very briefest moment in his exuberant enjoyment of the bubbles to listen; however, beyond that, he gave it no attention. My second thoughts, of course, were to wonder myself what was going on out there. It was pretty unignorable, so I was naturally curious.

No need to wonder long, however, because once the session with Drake was over and we came out into the dayroom, Nancy Anderson beckoned me over. "If you're looking for your next one, she's in lockdown."

Cassandra.

"Lockdown" was the unit term for the isolation or

seclusion room where children were placed when they completely lost control. It was a kind of ultralevel of time-out, used mainly when children became very violent and presented a serious danger to themselves or others. The seclusion room was a small cubicle—about six by six feet—with no furniture. The walls and floors were covered with a heavy-duty canvaslike material over a thin layer of foam rubber, so that a child could safely calm down and regain control without injuring her- or himself. In the old days, we called such rooms padded cells.

According to Nancy, Cassandra had been hyper all morning, bouncing around loudly and boisterously, constantly testing the patience of the staff and provoking the other children. Then she started "playing pterodactyl," which involved standing on the arms of the dayroom chairs while shrieking loudly, her own arms outspread, and then leaping on anyone who walked past and pretending to tear at their clothes and skin.

Cassandra frequently pretended to be a vicious bird or animal. Needless to say, this was the kind of game that got old fast, because it was noisy and physical and often quite aggressive, but on most occasions she would stop when asked insistently enough. However, on this particular morning she "woke up really wound up," as Nancy put it, and had been in trouble several different times already.

We'd noticed Cassandra had a tendency to zero in on children with weak or dependent personalities and would pester them ceaselessly, if not stopped. One girl named Heather had caught Cassandra's attention in the morning. Heather was a dumpy, obese ten-year-old whose problems included much very infantile behavior.

Cassandra had somehow discovered Heather was afraid of birds, and this may have influenced her choice in becoming a pterodactyl. Whatever the reason, she had been harassing Heather with her screeching and flapping since before breakfast.

Early on, Cassandra's behavior had simply been annoying, and she was told to stop several times and, indeed, put into ordinary time-out. Although paying lip service to the staff in regard to understanding why she couldn't keep playing and professing to be in better control of herself, Cassandra persistently returned to playing pterodactyl, and it became more aggressive as the morning wore on. Latterly, she had been dashing about, climbing up on the backs of the dayroom chairs and launching herself in quite a dangerous fashion at whoever passed. When she managed to knock Heather heavily to the ground doing this, the staff snapped. Cassandra was told to go into time-out to calm down. She ignored them. Staff came over to take hold of her and make her comply when she lost complete control and started raging furiously. She simply "went off the radar," as Nancy described it. Small and wiry as Cassandra was, she required five adults to hold her and get her into the seclusion room.

I was disconcerted by this news. The truth was, in the time she had been on the unit, Cassandra's behavior seemed to be deteriorating. She was becoming more difficult and bizarre, not less so. The other sad truth was that Cassandra was proving an extremely difficult child for any of us to like. She was an emotional mercenary, bonding only so long as it served her and then moving on to the next person. She seemed largely unconcerned by what others felt, thought, or wanted. We were coming to realize she was a startlingly bright, perceptive girl. Unfortunately, she applied these abilities to seeking out people's weak spots. She was particularly good at recognizing innocent attachments to things or sensitive feelings about weight, appearance, intellect, or skill levels, and she would exploit these heartlessly, saying deliberately hurtful or offensive things in an effort to get what she wanted. In day-to-day life she was unpredictably moody, swinging quickly between being loud and excitable one moment to being silent and withdrawn, or going from being friendly and caring to being calloused and spiteful. Moreover, Cassandra seemed to have little sense of accountability for her actions. If you confronted her about doing any of these things, her response was always "I didn't do that." Or "It wasn't my fault." Or, if really pushed, "I don't remember." As much as I wanted to remain open-minded about Cassandra, I had to admit the words *antisocial personality* and *sociopath* had passed through my mind more than once.

I stowed my stuff behind the counter in the nurses' station and went over to the seclusion room door. There was a small observation window made of glass with embedded chicken wire, or at least what looked like chicken wire to me. I gazed through. Cassandra was huddled on the floor in the far corner. She raised her head when I appeared at the window.

Unlocking the door, I went in and closed it behind me. I stayed against it until I had a chance to suss out Cassandra's state because I didn't want to be locked in myself unless necessary.

"You're having a bad morning?" I asked quietly.

Cassandra didn't answer. She simply shrieked. It was a loud, wordless cry of the sort you'd give if someone startled you from behind. Except, of course, she'd known all along I was there.

I sat down on the padded floor.

She shrieked again in the same piercing manner.

"Are you still a pterodactyl?" I ventured.

She nodded.

Dealing with pterodactyls not being part of my normal repertoire, I paused a long moment trying to decide the best tack to take. This hesitation seemed to annoy Cassandra. She screeched fiercely right at me.

"Pterodactyls seem like very angry creatures to me," I said finally. "Powerful. Dangerous. They want to kill things. From what the staff told me, you sound like you've felt very angry this morning."

Another pterodactyl scream. Indeed, this brought Cassandra to her feet, and she spread her arms like wings.

"What sorts of things would make a pterodactyl angry?" I asked rhetorically and didn't look at her. "It would be helpful for me to know that."

Again, more pterodactyl shrieks and flying motions. Up until this point Cassandra had not moved from where she'd been when I came in; however, now she started to circle the small seclusion room, screeching and flapping, her neck going in and out rather like an excited chicken's.

Her circles were tight at first, avoiding the place where I was sitting against the door, but she became more and more expansive.

At first I thought this was okay, that she was working off some of the anger that had so overwhelmed her, that she needed this physical activity to release it before she would be able to regain enough control of herself to come out of lockdown. However, after a few moments of watching her, I changed my mind. Becoming more physical in enacting her pterodactyl fantasy seemed to agitate her, not calm her down. She ceased responding directly to my questions and just flew around the room, screaming and flapping.

The circles kept getting larger and coming closer to me. I realized I would shortly be in pterodactyl attack range, and this didn't seem a healthy way to go, so abruptly, I said, "No!"

This sudden sharp voice startled Cassandra. She halted, her arms still extended.

"No," I said more quietly. "It's all right to play pterodactyls, but it isn't all right to hurt people. If you come rushing at me, you may hurt me."

I seemed to lose her again. After that momentary pause, she started to scream and threw herself wildly off the padded walls.

"No!" I said. She thumped into me.

I didn't want to get into a really physical confrontation with Cassandra in that small space, but I'd be forced into it if she rushed at me; so I pulled out the necklace I always wore. It was a St. Christopher medal, a gift from a boyfriend, and normally wasn't visible because it was on a long chain, and I wore it inside my shirt. "Do you see this?"

She wasn't looking.

"Cassandra? See this? This medal? It's a St. Christopher medal. I wear it to protect me."

She shrieked defiantly.

"This is my pterodactyl protection medal," I said.

"Everywhere else in the room pterodactyls can fly, but when I pull my medal out, it protects me. This area is safe here. This area right around me."

Of course, the first thing Cassandra did was fly directly at me.

I rose to my feet and caught hold of her arms, forcing them down. "No, where I am is a pterodactyl-free zone. I have my medal out." Then I let her go and gently pushed her toward the rest of the room. "It's all right for pterodactyls to be in the room. But they fly out there. Not here. This space is safe."

Cassandra circled the room and came back to attack me again. Again I grabbed hold of her arms, forced them down, held a moment, and then turned her free again, pushing her away from me.

Whatever was happening in this process—Cassandra's flying at me, my catching her arms, pushing them down, telling her it was all right to be in the rest of the room but not here—seemed to mesmerize Cassandra. She was not really fighting with me. Her arms were easy to push down and hold and she did not struggle; however, she did it over and over again, and there was a hypnotic, almost mechanical sense to her actions. I couldn't manage to get a peek at my watch, but this "game" went on for what felt like forever. Again and again and again she repeated it, showing no sign of wearing down. Or out.

Finally, on the next round when I caught her, I didn't let her go after I'd lowered her arms. Instead, I said, "Aren't you getting tired? Why don't you sit down here very close to me? If you do that, the medal will protect you, too. We'll both be safe from pterodactyls."

She was having none of it. She struggled free and circled the room again.

And again the pterodactyl attacked me. And again I suggested she come inside the protective range of my St. Christopher medal. And again she broke free.

And again.

And again.

And again.

And several more agains after that. And every time I would say the same thing and she would have the same response.

This must have lasted at least ten more minutes. Finally, when she was panting and hoarse from screaming, she stopped and didn't struggle to free herself from my grasp.

"Here, sit down," I said.

Cassandra hesitated.

"Sit here beside me. It's safe here." Letting go of her, I sat down on the floor and patted the area beside me.

She sat. And once she was beside me, she reached out her hand. "I want to see that medal," she said. These were the first words she'd used since I'd arrived.

Cautiously, I lifted the medal away from my neck and showed it to her, keeping a hand on the chain so that she couldn't jerk it. She fingered the slightly raised features of the image.

"I don't think this really works," she said.

"Yes, it does," I replied. "It was blessed by the pope."

Her eyebrows shot up in surprise and she looked at me. "Are you Catholic?" she asked.

"No," I said.

"It won't work for you, then."

"Yes, it will. Blessings will work for anybody who tries to do good because of them."

Still fingering the medal, she fell silent a long moment.

"See, it's already working," I said. "All the ptero-dactyls are gone from here now, aren't they?"

Very faintly, she nodded.

There was silence then, a quiet, tired silence.

"I want to sit in your lap," she said at last.

"Okay."

She clambered onto my crossed legs. Gripping my wrists, she wrapped my arms around her. "I want you to hold me."

So I did.

"I'm your baby. Hold me like I'm your baby."

"You want to feel safe and close like a baby," I said. She nodded.

"This feels safe, doesn't it?" I said.

Cassandra nodded again. "You're my mom. You keep me safe."

"You want your mom to keep you safe."

"Moms should keep their babies safe, shouldn't they?" she replied. "So nothing bad can happen to them."

There was a long moment's silence then.

"Sometimes it makes us very angry when unfair things happen to us," I said. "Things that shouldn't have happened. Things we should have been safe from."

She didn't respond.

"Sometimes we feel so angry, it's like we have ptero-dactyls inside us. We're that mad about things being un-fair. And yet often what we still really, really mean by all that anger is that we just want to feel safe, to have peo-ple keep us safe when we can't manage it for ourselves."

"I'm your baby. I came out of your wee-wee place."

"And sometimes if conversations get too scary, we need to think of something else quick, so that we won't think about things we don't want to."

"I want to sucky on your breasts."

"You want to be a very small baby, don't you?" I said. "A little tiny baby whose mother will take very good care of her."

Cassandra nodded and tucked her head in under my chin.

A very long spell of silence followed then, lasting perhaps as much as six or seven minutes. I just held her. She remained absolutely motionless. Slowly, slowly her muscles relaxed.

"Well," I said finally, "I think our time is almost up."

Cassandra nodded faintly.

"Shall we go back out on the ward?"

"Okay."

$\mathscr{P}$terodactyls suddenly became our theme. The moment we came into the therapy room, Cassandra would say, "I want to play the pterodactyl game again."

On the first occasion, I said, "How do you mean?"

"I'm going to be a pterodactyl. I'm going to get up here on this ledge and be looking for prey." She leaped up onto the table. "And you come by. You don't see me and I'm going to swoop down and attack you."

"I see. Can you tell me more how this game goes?" I asked.

She had jumped down but she leaped back up onto the table again and stretched her arms wide with excitement. "Yeah! I'm big. Huge! I got a wingspan of a hundred feet! I'm the biggest pterodactyl in the whole valley. On the whole continent, even, and I fight with everyone and I win. And you're walking by. You don't see me. But you're really scared, because, like, you're a rabbit. And I dive down and kill you!"

As unappealing as the idea of being savaged by a pterodactyl was, this was the first time Cassandra appeared to engage with me in any meaningful manner, and it seemed as good a place as any to start in allowing her to express what were clearly intensely angry feelings; so I said, "Okay, I'll be the rabbit." I went back to the door of the therapy room.

Eagerly Cassandra flapped her arms up and down, then folded them in against her body like wings. She made a loud screeching noise.

I minced across the floor, looking one way and another. "I wonder where I can find some nice grass to eat. I'm feeling very hungry."

Cassandra launched herself off the table with a force I hadn't really anticipated, and my falling to the ground under the talons of the pterodactyl was not so pretend.

"I'm going to kill you! I'm tearing you to shreds. I'm ripping out your eyes now." She dived at my head, plucking at my eyes with her hands. Her fingertips brushed my skin but kept just within the standards of pretend play. "I'm tearing you to shreds. Everything's bloody now! Blood and guts everywhere! Look at all this blood! I've killed you. You're dead now."

She pulled back. I lay "dead" and didn't move. Clambering back on the table, Cassandra spread her imaginary wings again and shrieked wildly. Then she dived again. Despite having already killed and dismembered me and my still lying there dead, she once again tore out my eyes and shredded my body and got blood everywhere. Blood seemed to feature big in this scenario.

And then again. And again. Repeatedly she dived down from the table to "kill you some more" and make "the biggest mess with blood and guts." At last Cassandra said, "Okay, get up now."

I sat up.

"Now, do it again. Come from the door."

"What am I this time?" I asked.

"You're a rabbit. You don't know anything. Rabbits are really stupid. So you think it's okay to go out and eat grass. You don't even stop to think there might be something really dangerous out there waiting to get you. Hop, to show you're a rabbit."

So I enacted the drama again and we had an almost identical scenario. The pterodactyl flew down from its perch on the cliffside, attacked the rabbit, pulled its eyes out, tore it to shreds so that it bled everywhere, and then flew away, leaving it for dead. As before, the pterodactyl continued to kill the rabbit several more times after it had already died.

"Okay," Cassandra said, "let's do it again."

"What am I this time?" I asked.

"You're still a rabbit."

"Why am I a rabbit?" I asked.

"Because, like I said, rabbits are really stupid," Cassandra replied.

"What makes you think they're stupid?" I asked.

"Because they're really weak."

"How do you know that?"

"Because they let anyone do anything to them and they don't fight back. They don't even make a noise," she said. And we reenacted the scenario yet again in almost exactly the same way.

After killing and shredding me several more times, Cassandra said yet again, "Okay, get up now and go back to the door."

"No," I said, "I've had enough. I'm going to remain a person. I'm going to sit down here."

"I can still kill you. Pterodactyls can kill people. They can kill anyone. Anyone, anything living today, a pterodactyl can kill. They've got a twenty-foot wingspan."

She flew at me.

"But I've got my medal. See?" I pulled out the St. Christopher medal from my shirt. "This means this is now a pterodactyl-free zone, this here, around me. It means I'm safe and can't be attacked."

"No sir. Pterodactyls can kill anyone." Arms outstretched, she rammed into me full force. It wasn't a pretend hit.

I grabbed hold of her, wrapping my arms tightly around her in a way that pinned her own arms to her sides. "The rules are, I won't allow you to hurt anyone. I won't allow you to hurt me. I won't allow you to hurt yourself. Do you understand?"

Cassandra immediately burst into tears.

I continued to restrain her for a moment or two longer, as much to communicate my strength as to prevent any further movement on her part. Then slowly I loosened my grip. Cassandra turned and put her arms around my waist, burying her face in my clothes. I held her close for several minutes until she stopped crying.

"That was scary, wasn't it? It was a good game, but I think it was a very scary game, too," I said. "It's all right to play scary games in here, because I'll always set limits on them. For example, with this game, when I take the St. Christopher medal out, it's over. This room becomes a pterodactyl-free zone. If the pterodactyl is still attacking, I will stop it."

Cassandra needed a few more moments to compose

herself. I then went over to the table. Things were generally in disarray there—the chairs had all been knocked over, some papers had been scattered—so I bent and righted a chair and told her to sit down. Then I set the other chairs upright, shuffled the papers together and set them up on the table, and afterward went to my box. Opening it, I took out a small cloth bag. I returned to the table and sat down opposite Cassandra.

"We're going to do something different now." I opened the bag and poured the contents out onto the table. "Do you know what these are?"

Cassandra nodded faintly. "Poker chips."

"That's right. Do you know what poker is?"

"It's a card game. People gamble with it."

"That's right. Chips represent money. That's why there are four colors here. White ones, red ones, green ones, and blue ones. Each color is worth a different amount of money."

Cassandra nodded.

"We're going to play a game of our own. Not poker, but we're going to use poker chips."

I watched Cassandra closely as I spoke. Gone was the hyperactive mania that had marked the pterodactyl game; gone, too, was the wriggling, taunting manipulator. She sat quietly and attentively.

"But before we start playing, we're going to do something else we need for the game," I said. Pulling over one of the pieces of paper on the end of the table, I turned it horizontally, uncapped a pen, and drew five equally spaced lines down the paper, dividing it into six columns. "I'm going to put the names of different kinds of feelings here. Top of this column: happy. Top of this column: sad. Top of this column: angry. Top of this column . . ." I paused and looked up. "Can you think of another feeling I can write here?"

"Disgusted?" Cassandra ventured.

"Good, yeah. I hadn't thought of that one." I wrote "disgusted."

"Being afraid," Cassandra volunteered.

"Good. Let's think of all the feelings we can."

"There's no more space," Cassandra pointed out.

"That's all right. I'll make another page. We can make as many pages as we can think up feelings to write." I divided another sheet into columns.

"Lonely."

"Good. More?"

"Excited."

"Okay. More?"

"Unhappy."

"Well, I have 'sad.' Do you think that's the same or different as 'unhappy'?"

Cassandra considered a moment. "Different. 'Cause you might be sad if your cat got run over or something, and then you'd be unhappy, too, because you didn't have no more cat. But sometimes when you're sad there isn't a reason. You just feel sad. But if you're unhappy, you're not happy anymore."

While I didn't fully understand this reasoning, I could tell she thought of them as two separate emotions, so I included them separately.

"Can you think of others?" I asked, after I'd written down "unhappy."

"Ummmm." She pressed her fingers to her lips and thought. "I know! Confusion."

"Good."

"Joy. Because that's different from 'happy.' 'Happy' is a quiet feeling but 'joy' is a big feeling."

I smiled. "That's a very clever distinction. Any more?"

"Bored. And tired."

"You think 'tired' is a feeling?" I asked.

She nodded.

I wrote it down.

"And what about when someone feels really, really, really angry?" I suggested. "So angry they can't stand it. Sort of like they have a pterodactyl in them? Is that different from just plain angry?"

"Probably it's 'hate.'" She paused. "No. I can hate, like, school, but I'm not really super angry about it. They're different. Put 'super angry.'" She paused again and then her face lit up. "No, I know! Put 'pterodactyl' there. In that column. Call that 'pterodactyl feeling.' And put a flower in the 'joy' one. We'll call that 'flower feeling.'" A brief thinking pause followed. "Love's a feeling. We haven't put that there. Put 'love.' And then draw a baby under it. Call that 'baby feeling.'"

She was suddenly into this. Leaning across the table she grabbed the paper to pull it over. "I want to draw the pictures, okay? And we're going to call each one by the kind of feeling they are. 'Baby feeling,' 'flower feeling,' 'pterodactyl feeling.'" She opened the small box containing the colored markers and took out a fine-tipped black one. "And for 'lonely,' we're going to draw an alien and write 'alien feeling.'" She wrote that below and drew a clubby little shape like she'd drawn on her first day with me. "And for 'bored,' it's going to be a squiggly line, like this. 'Squiggly line feeling.' And 'tired' is going to be 'in bed feeling.' " Cassandra drew a little stick figure in a bed under it. "And 'hate' is going to be 'snake feeling.' "

This hadn't actually been part of the plan, this giving identities to the various feelings, but I didn't interfere. Wearing as this session had been, it was the first one where I felt Cassandra and I had been working together and not against each other. So I sat back. The rest of the time she spent hard at work, naming and illustrating her feelings.

$\mathcal{I}$n the afternoon I sat down to view again the video-tape of my session with Drake. Playing parts of it over and over, I scrutinized his responses to the bubble blowing.

What struck me most—and not for the first time—was that he made virtually no noise at all. Even his grunts and puffs of air were largely silent. And as before when I had noted this, he did not appear to be purposefully controlling this. I observed nothing that indicated he was actively holding himself in, keeping control of himself enough not to speak. Indeed, he did not appear to be monitoring himself any more than any other four-year-old would. He behaved in as open and carefree a manner as any little boy at play. The only difference was silence. As carefully as I looked at the videotape, I was unable to see anything I hadn't seen before.

Perhaps most notable in what I did see was Drake's

gentle but persistent refusal to blow on the bubble wand or bubble pipe himself. He had happily joined in the bubble-making when it involved only lifting the wand from the solution; however, he would not even try to blow. Why?

My gut instinct was that there was something physically wrong. Drake wasn't refusing to make bubbles, and indeed, he wasn't refusing to make speech. For whatever reason, he simply wasn't able to do it. That sense came through strongly at that moment.

Of course, this was exactly what Helen had said when she had first seen him on tape, too. And the truth was, this had actually been my original instinct clear back during that first observation in Quentin, even though I had come into the classroom knowing ahead of time that he was speaking at home. Too many of us were coming to the same conclusion for there not to be some substance in it.

But . . . then what about his speaking at home? What was the quality of that? Was it possible there was some physical impediment that made it hard for him to speak and this, in turn, made him reluctant to speak outside the family? Had he possibly been laughed at or harassed for speaking slowly or poorly and now refused to do it at all? But if so, why had the family or the school not mentioned an impediment?

Hmmmmm.

I rewound the videotape. Taking it back to the place where Drake was playing with Friend, I watched again as he engaged the stuffed tiger. At that point he appeared very uninhibited and generally unaware of me. All his focus was on the bubbles and Friend. And not a noise. Not a single noise.

I studied the faint jerkiness in his movements that I'd noted during the session. It wasn't much, wasn't anything I'd consider out of the norm for a four-year-old just mastering large muscle control. Were there any syndromes involving muscles that might inhibit speech? Could it be cerebral palsy? Aphasia of some kind? Or *could* it be something so straightforward as a hearing loss? Had a minor loss, such as could be caused by infant ear infections, made him self-conscious of speaking outside the home because he couldn't hear his own voice well?

Here was one advantage of his family's insistence on having Drake as an inpatient, I thought. All the resources to pursue these questions were right here and I didn't need further consents to make use of them. So I picked up the phone and rang the hospital audiology department to make an appointment for a full workup on Drake's hearing.

When I was finished, I phoned Drake's home number. Lucia answered. We chatted a few moments. I told her Drake had settled in well and was working very hard, and what a pleasant little boy I found him to be. And then I asked about his speech.

Both Harry Patel and I had asked Lucia previously about Drake's speech, and so had the staff during the intake interview when Drake had arrived on the unit. Now, however, I wanted specific details. I didn't say anything about my increasing suspicions that Drake had physical problems. I simply wanted to hear her version of it, and I was hoping she might be more relaxed over the phone, because she did not have to make eye contact with me or worry about her father-in-law's presence.

Indeed, Lucia did seem friendlier and more forthcoming than she had in person. She talked willingly about her conversations with Drake. When I asked if he spoke freely to her whenever they were alone—for instance, did he speak to her when they were alone at the park or alone in the car, as well as alone at home—she admitted no. Even then he was silent because "he doesn't want to be overheard." In fact, she said he could be quite shy talking with her, too. Mostly it was at bedtime or if they had a little "cuddle time" together during the day that he would speak.

I asked what sorts of things they talked about. Lucia said it was just ordinary stuff. He would tell her about what he had done at preschool or about something fun they were planning. Just the usual conversations like you have with young children, she said. Sometimes they sang songs together, she added. Or other times when she read him a story, he would talk about the pictures with her.

I asked if she had ever overheard him talking to Friend. She said no. She said again how little he actually spoke. Even with her. So I asked why she thought that was. Is he able to form words all right? I queried. Is it hard for him to speak?

He's normal, she replied immediately, but there wasn't any defensiveness in her words. Just hesitant, she said. Just shy about talking.

But is his speech good? I persisted. Can he speak clearly? Can he make the usual speech sounds all right?

Yes, she said more emphatically. He's normal. His speech is normal. He just doesn't do it much. And then she added, "I can let you hear him, if you want."

"What?" I said, surprised.

"I can send you a tape recording of him speaking. The school wanted us to make it. They thought they could play it for Drake at school and say, 'Here you are. Here is Drake's voice.' And this was their hope that he would start to speak then and wouldn't be afraid to do it in front of the other children."

I was pleased at this unexpected news, because both audiology and I could make fair assessments of what was going on if we could hear him speaking. "That's great," I said. "I'd be very interested if you could send a copy of this tape to me, please."

The next morning on the way to work, I stopped again at the rehabilitation center to see Gerda. As with the first morning, Gerda was sitting up in her bed, her long white hair loose around her shoulders. Over her nightgown she was wearing a pink bed jacket, a very old-fashioned article of clothing that I'd only ever seen in pictures of women in maternity hospitals in the 1940s.

"Hello. Me again," I said. "How are you doing this morning?"

She had very blue eyes. They were that deep, pure color that is often described as "China blue," referenced, I think, from Blue Willow dishes. For a brief moment she turned them on me. There was something I couldn't quite catch in her expression, but it felt like an odd mixture of curiosity and gloom, as if she were inquisitive as to why I was there but simultaneously feeling "What's the use?" It made me think perhaps the specialist was right and depression was her main enemy.

When I made eye contact, she looked away. Indeed, she looked right at the wall and didn't turn back.

I pulled the plastic chair over and sat down. Setting my box of tricks down on the floor, I opened it and took out an old *Reader's Digest* magazine. I always carried a few of these because most of the stories had a low reading level and teenagers with reading problems usually didn't feel so self-conscious when asked to read aloud from an adult magazine. Moreover, there were jokes and funny stories, and these often proved valuable when trying to charm a recalcitrant older child or adolescent into being cooperative.

Moving aside the breakfast tray, which still hadn't been collected, I laid the magazine in front of Gerda and positioned myself so I could see it, too.

"I'm going to have you do this for me," I said. I opened to the "It Pays to Enrich Your Word Power" section. "Have you ever read this magazine before?"

Contrary as any child I'd worked with, Gerda simply refused to look at the magazine. She continued to keep her head averted, staring at the wall beside the bed.

"I always enjoy this section. See? Here's the word. And then you choose which of the definitions fit."

No luck.

"Gerda, here." I reached over and touched her chin with my fingers, gently trying to reposition her face.

Clearly she hadn't expected me to do this, and she startled. I was able to move her head quite easily. For the briefest moment, our eyes locked.

"I'm hard to get rid of," I said and smiled. "You might as well know that now. Once I start coming, you're stuck with me."

She didn't jerk away, but she shifted her eyes.

I tapped the magazine. "Let's do this, okay? Humor me. I know you respond to the other staff when they ask you things; so please respond to me. I'll go away sooner if we get through this."

She looked down at the magazine.

"The first word is *chortle*," I said. "Now, does *chortle* mean 'A: to shout,' 'B: moan softly,' 'C: laugh throatily,' or 'D: grunt'?"

In a very quiet voice, Gerda said, "C."

"Yup. Good. That's right. In fact," I said, "did you know that word was invented by Lewis Carroll? The guy who wrote *Alice in Wonderland*? He made it up from the words *chuckle* and *snort*."

She was watching me as I spoke.

"Next one: 'Radar, a system for locating objects using: A: radioactivity, B: sound waves, C: gravity, D: radio waves.' "

Again very quietly, "B." She had a vague German accent.

"Here. Would you read the next one?" I pushed the magazine over into a better position for her to see it.

She looked at it. No response.

"Here. Right here. We're looking at the third one."

Still she did not read it. Or even try.

"Please?" I said.

Silence.

I was formulating my next move in face of this opposition when Gerda said very softly. "I need my glasses."

Ah. Oh.

I looked up, embarrassed. "I'm sorry. I didn't think about that. Are your glasses in the bedside stand?"

There was a moment's silence where the noises of the rehabilitation center swirled in fluidly around us like surf around rocks. At last she shook her head.

"No?" I said. "Where are your glasses?"

She shook her head.

"You don't know?"

She shook her head.

And I was thinking, here she was, almost six weeks after the stroke, and in all this time no one among the staff had wondered if she wore glasses and, if so, where they might be.

"All right," I said. I closed the magazine and put it in my lap.

A pause while I considered what to do next. I was floundering. Probably it showed.

I regarded the magazine.

Silence.

"You know what?" I said at last. "I'm going to read to you. Sit back. Here." I got up and shifted the table with the breakfast tray on it down past the foot of the bed so that the staff couldn't miss it. "Get comfortable. Do you want this pillow?" Then I sat down again and opened the *Reader's Digest*. "What shall we go for?" I asked. "A story about orchids, someone who grows orchids? Or this one, called 'The Lake That Went Down the Plughole'? Or 'Sing a Song of Blackbirds,' which looks like it is about bird-watching and backyard birds?"

Gerda looked at me with the most uncomprehending look. Her forehead was creased, her brows drawn down in a questioning expression, as if I were speaking in a totally foreign language.

I waited for her to respond in some manner, spoken

or not, but she didn't. Finally, I said, "Well, today I'll choose. Let's find out about the lake that went down the plughole, because that sounds pretty unusual." And I settled back into the orange plastic chair and began to read.

$\mathcal{T}$he tape of Drake's voice hadn't arrived before my next session with him, so I thought I would try yet another tactic.

"We're going to play a game today," I said to him, once we were in the therapy room. "Look. I've got candy." I opened a bag of M&M's. "Do you like candy?"

He nodded enthusiastically.

"I thought you might. You'd be a very strange little boy if you didn't like candy, wouldn't you?"

Drake immediately saw the humor in this and laughed noiselessly.

"I'm going to put the candy here on the table. And I'm going to set this doll here." I poured a small pile of M&M's out in one area, then took one of the Sasha baby dolls out and set it upright on the tabletop. "And let's set Friend here, all right? I'm not going to take him away. Just set him in this other chair on this side of the table. Because guess what? Friend is going to help us today, too!"

This tickled Drake. He clapped his hands gleefully.

"Okay, here we go," I said. I pointed to the candy. "What's this?"

Drake smiled beguilingly.

"Some people use words to tell what things are, don't they? If someone asked me what that is, I'd tell them 'candy.' But you know what? There's another way of saying it. Do you know what it is?"

He shook his head.

"Like this." And I made the American Sign Language sign for "candy." "These movements are a special language. You do all the talking with your hands and not words at all. And in this language, this motion here is used to say 'candy.'"

An odd expression crossed Drake's face, which seemed to be a kind of hesitance, almost a physical falling back from me. Then abruptly he smiled.

"For a moment, you seemed a little worried there," I said.

The tentative expression had vanished. He grinned cheerfully.

"This kind of language is called 'sign language' and this—" and I demonstrated, "—we call a sign. It's the sign for 'candy.' Can you make this sign with your hands?"

He didn't even try. He just sat. When I continued sitting patiently, he looked away, looked at Friend, then down at the floor.

"Come on. Have a try," I said encouragingly. "Here." I reached over and lifted his right hand. "And when you make the sign for 'candy' to me, I'll know you want some and I'll give you a piece. How's that?"

Instead of doing it, he let his hands drop back to the table when I let them go.

I stood up and walked around the table to Friend. Leaning over the toy tiger, I lifted his front paws and endeavored best I could to make him sign "candy."

"Look," I said. "Friend wants some candy. So he is making the sign." I reached over and put an M&M in front of Friend, and then I made Friend sign again.

The absurdity of a giant stuffed tiger signing anything—and he *really* wasn't very good at it—suddenly struck me. I got a fit of the giggles and started to laugh. Indeed, I couldn't stop.

This delighted Drake. He started to laugh, too.

"Yes, this is very funny, isn't it? Friend really can't sign very well, can he, because he doesn't have any fingers!" I said amid my chuckles.

Grinning, Drake shook his head.

"Here, you try. Come here and see if you can make Friend do a better job than I have."

Drake got up from his chair and came around. He made even more of a hash of it than I had, but it was uproariously funny to both of us.

"No, no, like this," I said and made the sign myself. And Drake imitated it back.

"That's right. Like that." And I gave an M&M to him.

It was only at that moment he realized what he had done, that he had made the sign himself. The laughter fell away immediately. There was a heartbeat's hesitation and then came a curious, almost expectant expression.

"Can you do it again?" I asked.

A long pause. Then he did it very quickly, almost as if not to be caught doing it.

"Good! Good job. Here." I gave him a second M&M.

I returned to my chair and sat down. As I did so, Drake reached out and tapped my arm. I looked at him and immediately he signed "candy" again. I laughed and gave another piece.

"Now, here is a new sign. What do you think this is?" I drew my index and middle fingers of each hand back from my eyes.

For a moment Drake wrinkled his brow in concentration, then shook his head.

"It's an animal. What animal has stripes like this going back from his eyes?"

Still Drake couldn't guess.

"It's an animal right in this room. Right now!" I said.

Drake exploded with joy. Leaping from his chair, he shot around the table and grabbed Friend tightly around the neck.

"That's right! This is the sign for 'tiger.' And we have a tiger right here, don't we? Can you make this 'tiger' sign, too?"

Drake promptly complied.

"But we don't just want to call him 'Tiger,' do we? That would be like my calling you 'Boy.' We want to call him by his name. 'Friend.' Here is the sign for 'Friend.' See. Fingers coming together like this, because friends like to be together."

Drake imitated my gesture.

"That's right! How good you are at this! You can learn these signs very quickly, can't you? And isn't it nice to be able to say his name? Now if I ask 'What is your tiger's name?' you can tell me, can't you? All by yourself!"

Clearly delighted, Drake leaped up and down, turning in a circle as he did so such that his long hair lifted up off his shoulders in a jerky twirl. He signed Tiger-"Friend" as he did so.

It was an immensely pleasurable session. I taught him the sign for "doll" but he learned so fast that I also taught him "up," "down," and "under." We made up games with these signs and spent the rest of the session communicating eagerly with each other.

When the time came to leave, Drake grabbed Friend tightly around the neck and tore out the door, dragging the tiger behind him. Then he stopped halfway down the corridor. He turned and ran back to me, embracing my legs.

I knelt down to his height. Drake lifted his fingers to his lips and signed "kiss."

As I stood in the corridor outside the therapy room and watched Drake and Friend heading back to the day-room, I was both encouraged and bewildered. The ease with which he had acquired and used the signs was fascinating, because if he were withholding communication for psychological reasons, I would have expected considerable hesitance in signing also. While Drake had held back initially, once he overcame that, he had signed enthusiastically. This indicated either he wasn't withholding speech for psychological reasons or that the reasons he withheld were very specifically to do with speech itself and not with communication. There was a much bigger surprise in all this, however, and that was Drake's signing "kiss." I had not taught him that sign.

So? What was going on? Logic told me someone else must have already been teaching Drake to sign. If so, who? And why had no one mentioned it? And if he knew them, why had Drake never used any to try and communicate with us? It did occur to me that I might be reading more into all of this than was there. American Sign Language is very intuitive, relying on movements that are easily connected to the meaning of the word. The sign for "kiss" involves touching the tips of the fingers to the lips, which could be a gesture he and his mother might have developed spontaneously between them. The second part of the sign involves then touching the cheek, which I wouldn't have expected him to come up with on his own; however, it was conceivable I'd overinterpreted the gesture. Perhaps it was just accidental movement.

I met with Harry Patel later in the afternoon that day to bring him up to date on my sessions with Drake. I took along two of the videotapes, having marked out particular parts for him to watch and give me his assessment. We spent about forty-five minutes going over the case together.

I asked Harry if he thought Drake's lack of speech could be a purely physical problem. I was thinking primarily of aphasia, which is a type of brain damage that disrupts speech at the neurological level before it ever reaches the parts of the body involved in speech production. I hadn't seen any particular indicators of neurological problems in Drake, except perhaps the slight jerkiness in some of his movements. On the other hand, I had had several children previously who were presented to me as electively mute but turned out to be aphasic. I did acknowledge that in all the instances it had been fairly easy to identify indicators of brain damage, either via the child's history or via observable behaviors. On the other hand, during my time teaching I had come across some much more subtle examples of aphasia. None of these had been mistaken for elective mutism, but some had gone undetected for many years and they had caused a quirky dysfluency in expression. In an extreme form, perhaps it could mimic elective mutism.

Harry said, "We have other problems. Mason Sloane phoned this morning. He was anxious to know how things are coming. I told him we had made arrangements for Drake to be seen by the audiology department. Well! *That* didn't please him." Harry widened his eyes in a telling expression. "He got very angry and accused us of just being in it for the money. He said, did we think they were stupid? Did we think his own family would not notice if Drake was deaf? Of course they have had all that investigated long ago. He said, in fact, two years ago, Drake was seen at the Mayo Clinic in Minnesota. He had a very thorough investigation to ascertain why he was not speaking normally and there was absolutely no evidence of physical involvement whatsoever."

"Gosh," I said in surprise. Stuff kept turning up on this kid that none of us had had any idea existed. I didn't need to mention how incredibly helpful it would have been for the family to share everything with us at the onset, because contrary to popular opinion, we weren't in it for the money. We were genuinely trying to help this boy and if we didn't know something existed, then it was hardly our fault if we duplicated it.

"Well, anyway, I've asked him if we can see this report," Harry said. Then he gave an impish grin. "Know what the son-of-a-canine said back when I said why had they not sent this at first? He said, 'You don't need that. What you need is to deliver the goods.' That's exactly what he said. Like it was a product he had ordered. He said, 'Your therapist needs to get on and do what she said she could in that newspaper article'!"

I rolled my eyes.

The next day, the audiocassette from Lucia arrived. I was very curious to listen to it. Not only did I want to hear Drake's voice, but I also wanted to hear the quality of his speech: how fluently he spoke, how well he formed the words themselves, how he used vocabulary and grammar, how he pitched his speech. This would tell me a great deal about where we actually were with this problem, including whether it was likely to be a physical disability, a neurological problem, or a psychological one.

I popped the tape into the cassette recorder immediately and sat down at my desk. The tape was scratchy, as if it had been played often, but it was clear enough. First there was Lucia's voice, soft and maternal-sounding, chatting in the way one does with small children. She was speaking in English, but she didn't sound very confident. There was also a very faint nervousness to her tone that made me more convinced than ever that she did not normally speak in English to Drake. Two or three minutes of tape spent listening to her talk about animals and noises animals make. Lucia imitated several herself. I could hear the presence of another person in the room, but no one else spoke. Then came a hesitation. It grew long, leaving me with nothing but the static of the tape.

Then Lucia started to recite a nursery rhyme.

> *Hickety, pickety, my black hen,*
> *She lays eggs for gentlemen;*
> *Sometimes nine*
> *And sometimes ten,*
> *Hickety, pickety, my black hen.*

Immediately a little voice joined in.

At first Drake spoke in unison with her, and it was hard for me to hear what he was saying. They continued repeating nursery rhymes together, reciting three or four common ones.

"Now," Lucia said, " 'Dance to Your Daddy.' Can you do that one?"

And a little voice alone started saying,

> *Dance to your daddy,*
> *My little babby;*
> *Dance to your daddy,*
> *My little lamb.*
> *You shall have a fishy*
> *In your little dishy;*
> *You shall have a fishy*
> *When the boat comes in.*

Lucia responded animatedly, "You know that very well! Good boy! Can you sing that now? You know the tune. Here, I will sing it with you."

This wasn't a nursery rhyme I was very familiar with, and I had never before heard the rather haunting little tune that went with it. Lucia and Drake sang it together, and then she said, "Can you sing it now yourself for me?"

He sang alone. He had a soulful little voice, almost as if pleading for the fish in the rhyme. It was unexpectedly skillful singing for such a young child; he held the tune well and made the words plain.

And the tape ended.

That was all there was. Only one nursery rhyme said and then sung alone. No conversation. No interaction beyond saying the rhymes together and getting him to recite the final one on his own.

Hmmmmm.

All I could determine with any certainty from the tape was that he could, indeed, speak. His voice was clear and strong. He spoke with an American accent. The words were well enunciated and said in a manner that gave them correct meaning. In fact, even during the song Drake gave meaning to the words. This indicated that, unlike children with autistic spectrum disorders, he not only understood the communicative value of words but that he was also capable of using them appropriately. The tape didn't tell me much else, however.

I played it again.

And again.

And again.

Trying to garner every little bit of information from it I could, I played the tape so many times over that the little tune lodged in my brain and dogged me the rest of the day.

He *did* speak. That was a vital confirmation. Moreover, he spoke clearly, with no trace of a speech impediment or bilingual accent. He gave appropriate meaning to the words as he said them. He did not sound shy. Although he didn't speak until asked to do so, he did not hesitate once he was asked. He complied immediately. Nor were there any untoward pauses or silences.

Nonetheless, I found the tape unfulfilling. Perhaps this was because I'd assumed it would be conversation, which would allow me to get so much more from it, or perhaps it was simply because it left me with more questions than it answered. If Drake could speak this well, why wasn't he doing it spontaneously? Even on the tape with Lucia, there did not appear to be any spontaneous speech. Why? How had such a young child come to be so silent, especially when he did not seem to have the anxious or withdrawn personality normally associated with such silence? Drake was in all other respects such a charismatic little guy. He always made joyful efforts to socialize with the children on the unit, the other staff, and me on every occasion. So what was going on here? If he spoke without hesitation when asked by his mother, why was he refusing to make even the faintest vocal sounds with me, with his schoolteachers, with even the other members of his family? How could he, on one hand, be a warm outgoing child who interacted so enthusiastically, and on the other, so determinedly silent that not even an audible laugh escaped him? Something didn't add up here.

$\mathcal{I}$n preparation for our next session together I had set out on the table the papers with the columns of feelings that Cassandra had so carefully done. However, when Cassandra came in, she immediately said, "I don't want to do that." She dismissively flapped her hand at the table.

I pulled out a chair to sit down.

"I want to play pterodactyls," she said. "Like we did last time." Before I could say anything, she had leaped up on top of the table, stamping her feet meaningfully near to my fingers.

"All right," I said and shuffled the papers back together to put them safely out of the way. "But remember there are rules. I won't let you hurt me or yourself. And when I take out my medal here, the area around me becomes a pterodactyl-free zone."

"Yeah, yeah," Cassandra said glibly.

"No, I want you to hear me, Cassandra. I don't want you to say later, 'I don't remember that.'"

"I *do* hear you," she replied. "Can't you tell? I'm looking right at you. So are my ears. I can't hear you more than that." She grimaced. "You're so uptight, you know. You got to have everything your way."

"So how will we play? I asked. "What shall I do?"

Cassandra had turned sideways when I was talking about the rules. For a moment she was staring downward at the table, but now she looked at me out of the corner of her eye without turning her head.

"You've wrecked it," she said. "I don't want to play anything now. I don't like you, you know that? I don't want to do stuff with you. You're stupid!"

"You feel angry because I interrupted your plans by reminding you of the rules?"

"Why do you think I want to play some stupid pretend game anyway? Only babies do stuff like that. You can't make me play that."

My first instinct was to refute what she was saying. I certainly hadn't been trying to make her play the pterodactyl game. I held back, however. This was less due to some august psychological technique than simple confusion. We seemed to have switched sides very quickly, and I wasn't sure how this had occurred.

A moment's silence passed between us.

"Well," I said at last, "if you don't want to do that, let's work with these." I picked up the feelings papers again.

"I'm not going to do anything in here. You can't make me. You can't make me stay in here if I don't want. I can call the police on you."

"Cassandra, you seem upset today. Can you tell me why?"

"I'm not going to stay in here."

"You don't want to stay in here. I hear you saying that. You have very strong feelings about having to stay with me today. You wish you could leave. You want that so much you wish you could call the police on me, so that I would be forced to let you leave. I do hear you saying those things. But can you help me understand why you feel like this? Because our problem at the moment is, this is your time with me. Even though you have very strong feelings about staying, you still need to stay in here."

"You're trying to lock me up!"

"Can you tell me what is so upsetting right now?"

She cried out. It was a furious, frustrated cry accompanied by clenched fists and a truly enraged expression, but she didn't move from where she stood beside the table. Indeed, she seemed to have rooted treelike, all her muscles gone so taut as to gnarl around her bones.

Bewildered, I watched her.

A moment passed. Two, three. I'm not sure how long this was in minutes. Only a few, I'm sure, but it felt longer.

Then, still standing, she began to wet herself.

This caught me completely unawares and I didn't react for a moment.

Cassandra looked down at herself. She didn't show any particular embarrassment or even surprise at what was happening, nor did she appear to make any effort to stop. Instead, she spread her legs and continued to urinate through her clothes.

My first coherent thought was that she was unwell. Perhaps she had developed a urinary infection or was coming down with the rather nasty flu making its way around the children's ward. This would account not only for wetting herself but also for her difficult mood.

I came over and put my arm around her shoulders. "Are you feeling okay?" I asked.

She looked up at me with an oddly uncomprehending expression on her face. "Seizure" flashed through my mind. While teaching, I had had children with epilepsy who lost bowel and bladder control during the process of grand mal seizures. Cassandra was obviously not having a grand mal seizure, but the fleeting vacancy in her expression was reminiscent of that odd, out-of-sync look that accompanies some seizures.

"Are you okay?" I asked again.

Cassandra recovered herself quickly. She said in a very little-girl voice, "Babies come out of your wee-wee place."

Not anticipating this comment at all, I was caught unawares yet again by this kid. I had my own blank moment just then.

So Cassandra spoke again. "Babies come out in your wee."

"Babies come out of their own special place," I said. "While this special place is down between a woman's legs, it's not the same place as urine comes out."

"Urine. You-rine. I say 'wee.' Wee-wee. We, we have babies come out." She pointed saucily to me and to herself.

"I'm thinking we need to go get some cloths and clean this up," I replied. "Urine doesn't belong on the floor. Someone might slip."

"You might slip. You might fall on my you-rine and die. You're thinking we need to get some cloths. I'm thinking you might have a baby and it will come out in your wee."

To be honest, at just that moment, what I was *really*

thinking was that a psychiatric unit was a pretty appropriate placement for Cassandra.

I had misgivings about taking Cassandra out onto the unit to help me to find cloths and a bucket, because she was being so unpredictable. I wasn't too sure about having her help me clean the mess up, either, because I was concerned it might overstimulate her, as there seemed to be a sexual association with wetting herself. Nonetheless, there was still enough practical, real-world teacher in me to want her to connect her actions with their natural consequences. So out we went.

Being a hospital, we didn't have the kind of mop-and-bucket ordinariness that had always been part of the schools where I'd taught. Here any mess was responded to by full-time cleaning staff ever ready with their antiseptic scrubs and special equipment. It took some dedicated searching to locate something we ordinary mortals could take back to the therapy room.

Cassandra was unexpectedly compliant. She didn't speak at all while we were out on the unit, but followed meekly and did as she was told. I took her first to her room so that she could change her clothes. Afterward she came with me to the dayroom, where she accepted and carried cloths and disinfectant while I ferreted out latex gloves and a bucket. We returned then to the therapy room.

"Here are the things you need to clean the floor," I said.

I expected her to rebel or, at the very least, respond with her brash, negative comments. She didn't. Cassandra pulled on the gloves, then knelt with the cloths and straightforwardly cleaned the urine up from the floor.

When she had finished, she rose to her feet and let the cloths drop into the bucket with a heavy plop. Continuing to stare into the water, she said without looking up, "Do you like me?"

"Yes, I like you," I said.

"Do you really like me?" She raised her head then and met my eyes.

"Yes, I really like you," I replied.

"Then why do you make me do this?"

"Because urine doesn't belong on the floor. Someone could slip and hurt themselves. So if you have been unable to get to the toilet in time and, as a consequence, wet your pants, it is necessary for you to clean it up."

She frowned. "I didn't wet my pants." Her voice wasn't defiant but rather simple and clear-cut.

I regarded her.

"And if that was pee on the floor," she said, "I'm going to tell my mom you made me touch it. She'll call the police on you, because that's dirty. You shouldn't make kids touch stuff like that."

"Cassandra, yes, you did wet your pants. I don't know what's going on here that makes you say you didn't, but I was here, too. And yes, you did wet your pants."

Cassandra looked down at herself, but of course, because she had changed clothes, her pants were dry. She looked back up at me with an incredulous expression, as if I had made it all up. And, indeed, for just that moment, everything felt hideously surreal to me, as if her version might be a possibility, as if we'd stepped into some kind of mirror world without my noticing.

"Cassandra, I'm not very happy right now, because I can't understand what's going on. You just wet your pants. About twenty minutes ago. And we went out onto the unit. We went to your bedroom and you changed your clothes and that's why you're dry now. We got the cleaning equipment and came back here to wipe it up. I'm not sure if you are confused about what happened or if you have forgotten what happened or if you are simply still angry with me and feel in the mood to argue. But it is hard for us to understand each other when we have these kinds of conversations."

She started to cry then. They were not angry tears so much as despairing. "You don't like me," she sobbed. "No one likes me. It's horrible here. You treat me terrible and I want to go home."

To say I was confused at the end of that session was certainly an understatement. On one hand, Cassandra had a history of being very manipulative, sometimes pathologically so. It was fairly easy to interpret what had just happened as a deliberate effort to avoid responsibility, a calculated lie that threw the blame for her behavior onto me. Nor was it much of a stretch to interpret it as sociopathic behavior, that she was construing the events in an attempt to dominate me, that having assessed it was important to me to be understanding and accepting, she now sought to twist me into the dangerous and humiliating position of abuser.

But . . .

At that moment I couldn't put my finger on "but." Something felt seriously weird. Things just didn't fit together in a way that made sense. Often when finishing sessions with children I would come away filled with unanswered questions, with the feeling that there was much more I had to understand before I'd know what to do. This, however, was a normal kind of not understanding, the kind where I knew it was me; I knew I simply needed more information, more time, or more insight. These instances were like doing a jigsaw puzzle where I didn't know the picture that was being formed. I knew from the onset I didn't know. And I knew likewise that it was unrealistic to expect to know until I'd found a sufficient number of pieces and fitted them into place. So that kind of not knowing was a normal state.

This was different. There was a bizarre, Alice-in-Wonderland quality to working with Cassandra. It felt as if every time I went to add another piece to her particular jigsaw puzzle, it changed into a completely different puzzle from the one I'd been adding pieces to before.

I didn't have the time immediately after the session to think further on it, because I had a staff meeting and then needed to go out in the early afternoon to do two assessments.

It was after five when I returned to the unit, so Dave Menotti had already gone home. Not that I'd really had plans to consult with him over Cassandra so late in the day. Not that I'd even intended to do anything more with it myself at that point. However, as I came into the office, I unexpectedly saw the videotape of our session that morning sitting on my desk. In all the brouhaha over cleaning up after Cassandra had wet herself, I hadn't gotten around to taking the videotape out of the machine in the observation room. Most likely someone else had wanted to record in the therapy room, and seeing my tape still in the machine, that person had brought it in and left it on my desk.

Impulsively, I popped it into the video recorder in the office and turned on the monitor, thinking I'd watch a few highlights to give me something to mull over during my commute home. I quickly got caught up in the tape, however; and instead of just whizzing through for highlights, I ended up watching it all.

Something odd caught my attention.

Just after Cassandra had wet herself, she said to me, "Babies come out in your wee." And then, when I had used the word *urine,* she had replied, "I say 'wee.' Wee-wee. We, we have babies come out."

At the end of the session, however, when Cassandra had denied responsibility for wetting herself, she said, "If that was pee on the floor, I'm going to tell my mom you made me touch it."

Why would she use *wee* in one reference and *pee* in another? Linguistically, it is unusual for children to alternate slang terminology in that manner. They inevitably know plenty of words for bodily functions and as any adult around children experiences, they often glory in trying the full vocabulary out. This is for play or shock value, however, or for the sexual connotations the words carry. During genuine communicative conversation, however, people tend to stick to one preferred word or phrase and typically don't vary.

It was possible that *wee* was the word used with her father and that this was also why it appeared to have additional sexual connotations, whereas *pee* might be her mother's word, and thus, Cassandra was, indeed, expressing two different things with the words. Or perhaps she was accustomed to using two different expressions for the same act, because of the parents using different words. However, it still seemed odd to me that she would alternate so indifferently within the context of the conversation. I thought, it was almost like two different kids talking.

The penny dropped with that thought.

What if these *were* two different kids? As in multiple personalities. What if there was more than one Cassandra in there? What if she was telling the truth and the second girl genuinely hadn't realized that first one wet her pants?

*G*erda was not proving any easier to crack than Cassandra or Drake. Each morning I stopped at the rehabilitation center before work to spend half an hour to forty-five minutes with her. However, she showed no inclination to speak to me spontaneously. Indeed, she showed little interest in speaking at all, as even direct questions produced only the barest of mutterings.

After a few days of wearisome struggles to make conversation, I resorted to reading to her, to demanding nothing from her, no words, no sound, indeed, no response. I just came and I read.

To say there was an actual method to my actions in doing this might have been stretching the term, but I did have a process in mind. My very, very earliest experience with elective mutism and, indeed, with special education itself, had occurred when I was still a college student and took on work as an aide in a preschool program for disadvantaged children. There I'd been given charge of a four-year-old named Mary who did not speak. She spent most of her time hiding under a piano, and I'd started our relationship by lying under there with her and carrying on a long, very one-sided monologue while she just watched me. When finally I ran out of conversation, I started reading to her. It took months to achieve a relationship with her and to get her speaking again, but it did happen and the connection between its happening and the long hours I spent apparently doing no more than reading to Mary was not lost on me.

In fact, during my years as a graduate student in special education I devised a small research project in learning disabilities on one occasion. This was in the 1970s when learning disabilities were the New Big Thing. Tests were popularly used to identify which of a child's learning modalities were strongest and which were weakest as a way of explaining learning problems. For example, a person might be strong in visual memory and thus a good sight learner but might be weak in auditory discrimination and, thus, was poor at learning to read using phonics. All this kind of knowledge was in its infancy in that era and as seems a common human trait when first discovering things, we immediately think we know all about it. Thus, it became hugely fashionable to give these modality tests and then assume we knew precisely why a child wasn't learning—because he or she suffered various visual, auditory, or kinetic weaknesses—and, therefore, all that was necessary to correct the problem would be to switch the child to his or her strengths. Which, of course, sounded really good in theory but isn't quite how it worked out. But we didn't know that then.

I was curious from the onset about more subtle factors that might be influencing successful outcomes. For my graduate project, I designed a small research study in which I divided the children with identified learning disabilities and poor reading performance into three groups. In the first group, the children were paired with a trained tutor who used the most up-to-date learning modality-based methods to help them with their reading; in the second group, the children were paired with an untrained college student who was instructed to read books, magazines, and comic books to them; and the third group was a control group who had no special interventions. The tutors/college students met their children twice a week for half an hour, and the project ran for six months. In the first month, both groups' reading scores improved, although the improvement of the first group was statistically better. However, after six months, this wasn't so. In both groups, the children had made statistically significant improvements in reading, and the first group, with the trained tutors, was still making slightly higher scores. However, it was no longer statistically significant. Both groups improved, whether the children were being actively taught or whether they were simply listening to an adult read.

My conclusion from this was not that we don't need to actively teach children to read nor that we don't need to address reading problems with specialist help but that the significant influence was human interaction, rather than the method used. To me the results of the study spoke of how much it matters to us that someone else is willing to take the time to be with us, that our problems tend to improve simply by being with people who pay positive attention to us.

Consequently, coming along each day to spend half an hour of time reading to Gerda not only didn't seem like a waste to me, it seemed a feasible method of intervention.

I discovered, however, it didn't to a man named Dr. Jamieson.

"And you are *who*, exactly?" he asked, as I came out of Gerda's room Monday morning.

I gave my name and explained briefly that I was there because of a request from Joy Hansen, who had contacted me because of my experience in psychogenic language problems.

"Are you a relative?"

Realizing I must not have been clear, I said no again and proceeded to explain a second time that I had come at Joy Hansen's request because of my experience in psychogenic language problems.

"You're a child psychologist?" This was said in a tone of voice that left nothing to the imagination, and clearly here was not a man for ambiguity, so he added, "And so *what* exactly are you doing here?"

For a third time I explained I was here due to Joy Hansen's asking my advice on Gerda Sharple. *Because* I had experience in psychogenic language problems.

"What's that got to do with anything here?" he asked.

"Because," I said, very slowly, very plainly, and in a tone of voice verging on what I'd use with a small, dull child, "Joy Hansen had questions regarding the nature of Gerda's mutism."

"She isn't mute," he replied and used the same very slow, very plain tone of voice back at me. "She's had a massive hemiplegic stroke. Strokes cause brain damage.

Brain damage affects the center of speech. That's why she's mute."

Odd, I was thinking, how in such a short exchange we'd already decided we hated each other. Sad, too, as it wasn't going to further Gerda's case any.

"Is it all right that I come to see her?" I asked, because I sensed this was actually an issue of territory, not treatment methods.

"There's nothing for you to see," he replied. There was a small heartbeat of a pause and he stepped back slightly, his shoulders relaxing. "I mean, I appreciate what Mrs. Hansen's trying to do, but she's a social worker and that's her job. I appreciate what you're trying to do, too. Which is your job. Realistically, however, there's not much you can do. This is a different part of the continuum than you're accustomed to working with. At your end, everything is newborn. Just starting. Growth. At my end, it's decay and death. So there's a difference of approach to treatment that's significant. Nothing is going to happen in this instance, no matter how much effort you put in. Mrs. Sharple has had a massive stroke. She's eighty-two. She isn't going to be the person she was, no matter who does what."

"Is it all right that I come to see her?" I asked again.

He paused, regarding me. Then finally he nodded. "As you will."

The encounter was depressing. Normally I see narrow-minded people simply as unable to think deeply, creatively, or persistently enough to realize the limits of their views, and this allows me either to ignore them or challenges me to show them alternatives. However, as I passed room after room of decrepit elderly patients, I had to acknowledge the reality in Dr. Jamieson's dead-end thinking. We did come from opposite ends of the spectrum, and yes, my work was about growth. It was about potential, about opening up the possibilities of a lifetime ahead. I was used to thinking that way. I had come, challenged by the possibility of giving Gerda a chance to return to the cottonwoods and the cats that had defined her rural existence.

Was this realistic?

The stink of disinfectant, the moans, the incoherent "hellos" of an unseen Alzheimer's patient followed me down the corridor. Who *was* I to be here? While I wanted to give Gerda a chance, only Pollyanna could deny how slim this chance was. I was no miracle worker. Not only did I not have any precedence in my own experience for successfully treating mutism in the elderly, but regardless of whatever progress Gerda and I might accomplish, decay and, ultimately, death *would* still be waiting in the wings anyway. That was just reality.

It wasn't a cheerful way to start the day.

Opening my box, I took out the bag of M&M's. It was twisted closed, so I carefully undid the twist and poured half a dozen brightly colored M&M's onto the tabletop in the therapy room. "What do you remember from last week?"

Drake quickly signed the word for "candy."

"Yes, that's right." I signed "yes" as I said the word.

Without prompting, Drake signed "tiger-friend" and patted Friend on the head.

I smiled.

"Friend eats candy," Drake signed and mischievously

took a piece of candy and put it against the toy tiger's lips before popping it into his own mouth. He laughed noiselessly.

"Hey, smart! 'Friend eats candy.' That's what you were saying with your hands, wasn't it?"

Grinning, Drake nodded. Indeed, he did it again, signing the sentence quickly and then feeding Friend another M&M.

"You're very good at talking with your hands. I can see you like to talk that way."

He reached down for Friend's paws and attempted to make the toy tiger sign "candy."

"You and Friend like this idea, don't you? Of making signs and getting candy?"

Impishly, he smiled at me.

"But you know what? I think you're so clever because you have a secret. I think you already know signs."

Unexpectedly, his smile faded. Drake put his hands flat against his sides.

"You look concerned when I say that," I said.

He smiled in the beguiling manner I was now coming to recognize as a gesture of appeasement.

"I didn't mean: don't use other signs," I said. "I think it's cool you can do ones I didn't teach you. But know what? No one had told me you knew how to sign. So that makes me curious."

Drake's demeanor had changed entirely. He lowered his head and looked away.

"What's wrong?"

Grabbing hold of Friend, Drake pulled the big tiger close and pressed his face against its fur.

"I see a little boy who's upset," I said. "But I don't know why. Can you tell me what's wrong?"

He shook his head.

"I wasn't angry with you, Drake. Did you think it made me angry that you knew something I hadn't taught you? Or was it when I said the word *secret*? When I said you had a secret? Did that make you upset?"

Raising his right hand, he signed "Crying."

"You feel like crying?"

He made the sign again, then pressed against Friend and wouldn't look at me.

For a few moments longer I coaxed him, but to no avail. Whatever it was that I'd said or done, it had left him anxious and unhappy. Pressuring him further was only going to make the situation worse. So I leaned forward and reached into my box.

"Well, let's do something else for now. Shall we read together?" I lifted out a book of Mother Goose nursery rhymes.

My intentions for that session had been to gently confront Drake with the tape of his speaking to his mother. My hope was that if he realized I knew, and if he heard himself and the familiar voice of his mother, this might be enough get him started. I'd brought the nursery rhyme book along with the idea that perhaps I would then be able to gentle him into speaking in the same way Lucia had on the tape—by reciting the rhymes with me. Given his unexpected upset, however, I could see the moment wasn't right, so instead, I asked him and Friend to come sit on my lap while I read some of the nursery rhymes to him.

Drake listened eagerly to the old familiar verses. I read,

Baa, baa, black sheep, have you any wool?
Yes, sir, yes, sir, three bags full.

"Can you hear the rhythm in that?" I asked. Drake was still on my lap, his back to my chest. Taking hold of his hands, one in each of mine, I clapped them together and said the rhyme again, amplifying the rhythm. "Baa, *baa*, black *sheep*, have you any *wool*? Yes, *sir*, yes, *sir*, three bags *full*."

I stood up. Placing Friend on our vacated chair, I lifted Drake to his feet. Grabbing his hands, I started to do exaggerated motions to the rhythm, pulling him through them like a life-sized puppet. They were just nonsense motions but I wanted to give him a whole-body experience of the sound of the rhyme.

Drake loved this. He began to laugh in his soundless way.

So I went on.

Dance to your daddy, my little babby.
Dance to your daddy, my little lamb.

This was an easier rhyme to act out with the larger-than-life movements I was using. I became more and more physical at I did it. First we jigged, my pulling Drake up by his arms and jiggling him back and forth. Then I folded his arms across his chest, making the motion of a rocking baby. Then dancing again, then I pulled him down until his hands were on the floor in imitation of a four-legged lamb.

"*You shall have a fishy in a little dishy.*"

By this point I was almost singing the words. I'd listened to the rhyme so many times on the tape that it was now more of a song in my mind than a verse. I pulled Drake through the motions.

"You know that song, don't you?" I said. I had been standing behind him all throughout the time I was puppeteering and now I leaned way over so that my face was very close to his. "Dance to your daddy, my little babby," I sang. "You know the song, too."

Drake nodded and smiled.

Turning him around so that he was facing me, I sang the whole song.

"Can you sing it, too?" I asked.

He opened his mouth. For a moment—for the briefest second—I thought, *Ah ha! It's going to happen!* It was going to be simple as that. He'd just start singing.

But not so.

He closed his mouth again.

I whirled him around again so his back was to me and took hold of his hands, puppet-style once more. "Let's sing it to Friend, shall we? Friend wants to hear the song."

So, once again:

> *Dance to your daddy*
> *My little babby.*

No luck. He didn't sing.

"Hey, you too," I said, leaning over him to see his face. "You know the song. Let's try it again. Let's sing it for Friend."

Again, it was only my voice.

I will admit to feeling frustrated at that moment. Thwarted. Why wasn't this kid cooperating? Despite our initial anxious start to the session, Drake had recovered well. He was dancing and laughing. He loved playing with Friend; he knew the song well. The atmosphere was relaxed. He wasn't having to face me. He wasn't even having to start off speaking on his own but rather in a manner he was already familiar with. I had felt quite certain everything was in place to start him speaking and that this would do the trick. So why hadn't it?

Frustrated, I grabbed the tape recorder from the top shelf and put it on the table. "Like this," I said and turned the tape on.

Lucia's voice filled the room.

Drake froze, his eyes going wide.

I smiled warmly. "Who's that?"

No response.

"That's your mama, isn't it? And listen. What's she saying?"

I had broken away from him to get the tape recorder, so he was still at the other end of the small room beside Friend, who was sitting on the floor. Drake remained immobile, his expression one I couldn't read.

"Your mama's saying nursery rhymes, isn't she? Just like we've been doing."

The tape played on. Drake stayed across the room. Staring into the space between us, his eyes unfocused, he clutched Friend to him and listened to the tape.

And then the little voice.

"Who's that?" I said. I said it gently. My frustration had faded, and I did want to ease him into this. I could sense he was finding it hard to listen to the tape.

Eyes still on some unseen point between us, Drake absently fingered Friend's fur and didn't respond.

"Who is that talking? It's Drake, isn't it?"

He shook his head.

"It's Drake. Drake's lovely little voice singing. That's you."

He started to cry.

$\mathcal{I}$ want to talk with you today," I said when Cassandra and I entered the therapy room.

"I don't want to talk to you," she replied. "I want to play pterodactyls."

"Perhaps we will play pterodactyls later, but first I want to talk about some things."

"I want to do that feelings paper. With that bag of colored poker things," Cassandra said. "Where's it at? Where did you put it?"

"Perhaps we will do that later, but first I want to talk."

"Where's it at?" Cassandra pushed past me and went along the shelves. Of course, because I *had* hoped eventually to get to that activity, it was there and she found it. She lifted the papers she had made during the earlier session onto the table and set the bag of poker chips beside it. Then she took the top off my box and found the smaller box containing the marking pens and crayons. She sat down.

"I know you like to be the one who decides things," I said. "I know you like things to go just as you plan. However, right now, we aren't going to do that paper."

"I'm going to do it," she said, unconcerned. "Let's see. 'Baby feeling,' 'flower feeling,' 'pterodactyl feeling.' I've done all those. Now I'm going to do a picture for . . ." She sorted through the papers, looking at the lists of feelings we had enumerated. "Disgusted. I'm going to draw a picture for 'disgusted' and it's going to be puke. 'Puke feeling.' No, dog puke. That's so disgusting, dog puke is. I'm going to draw a picture of dog puke to go with this one. 'Dog puke feeling.' "

The thing about Cassandra was not that she was so manipulative per se, but simply that she could move so fast and switch directions with such ease that it was hard to get in front of her quickly enough to stop her. Literally and figuratively. That itself was a form of manipulation, of course, because speed ensured her control of the situation, but I was surprised at how hard it was for me to keep up with her. At nine she seemed capable of thinking on her feet as quickly I could.

Sitting down opposite at the table, I lay my hand flat across the paper she was preparing to draw on. "No, right now we aren't doing that."

"I'm supposed to do whatever I want in here. That's what I did at Dr. Brown's. That's how I got well."

"I'm not Dr. Brown, Cassandra," I replied.

"You don't know how to make me well."

"This isn't what we are doing right now. We aren't working on the list of feelings. And we aren't talking about Dr. Brown." I looked at her. "We're going to talk about other things instead."

She met my gaze. We were both leaning forward on our arms on the tabletop, eye to eye, like people about to take up arm wrestling.

"You don't know how to make me well," she said again, her tone acerbic and dismissive.

"And you're afraid to let me try," I replied.

Her expression was, if anything, hateful. She kept me locked in her gaze and just glared.

Because her energy was directed at me for just that moment, I took it as an opportunity to whip away the poker chips and the papers containing the list of feelings. Realizing what was happening, she reached to grab the papers as they slid out from under her hand, but I was faster. I put them on the floor beside my chair.

I then quickly grabbed a coloring book out of my box of tricks. It was a basic one, full of simple line drawings, most suitable for a preschool child. Opening it, I laid it in front of her. "Today, we're going to start by coloring."

"*Coloring?* Why *coloring?* You said nothing about coloring. You said we were going to talk. Just now. When we came in. This isn't talking. This is crap for babies! I won't do it!" She was genuinely outraged. With one swift gesture, she knocked it from the table.

I leaned over, picked it up, reopened the coloring book, and put it back in front of her. "Yes, Cassandra, you will. Because that's where we're going to start."

She knocked it off the table again.

I looked at her. "We can, of course, spend the whole time pushing it on the floor and picking it up, which would be pretty boring. But it's going to keep coming back up, because that's where we start."

"You think."

"Yes, that's right. I do think that. Because that's where I have decided we will start. I'm the grown-up here. I'm the person whose job it is to help you. And this is how I am going to start helping."

"You think."

"I know you're scared—"

"I'm *not* scared."

"I know you're scared for me to have control in here instead of you—"

"I'm *not* scared."

"And I know you're scared for me to have control in here instead of you, because it's hard not to worry that maybe something awful will happen. Maybe I will make you do something too frightening. Or maybe you will start to feel feelings you don't want and you won't be able to stop them. I know it's really scary for you to trust me. It's scary even to *want* to trust me. But my job is to help make things better for you. If we're going to change things so that you can leave here and go home, so you can get on with school and having friends and growing up, then we need to start working hard on that trust. And how to start is right here, right now, with this coloring book." I reached down and picked it up off the floor again. I laid it open.

She glared at me, and her teeth were literally gritted. "I'm *not* scared," she hissed in a very low voice. "And I *hate* you." She didn't, however, knock the book off again.

"It's okay to hate me. It's okay to feel strong feelings, because I will never let them get too strong. Even so, you still need to do this." I opened the book to a picture of a rag doll. Then I took out a red crayon from the box. "Today's work is to color this picture. Start by making the doll's skirt red."

"I'm not going to do this." She snapped the crayon in two.

"Well, I'm putting no limits on how long it's going to take us to do this, but we are going to do it, because this is where we are going to start," I replied. "So if you don't want to use a crayon that is so long, here is this part that is now shorter." I handed a broken section of the red crayon back to her.

"I'm *not* going to do this." She refused to pick up the crayon. "And you can't make me."

I suppose if I were a good psychologist, I would have been following someone's well-researched, deeply thought-out theory at that point that said something about good therapy not involving forcing a child to do things. Certainly none of my training had included demanding a child do exactly as I say, but the teacher in me took over at that moment. If I had learned anything as a teacher, it was the importance of setting limits and establishing control before going forward with change, because this defined the safety of the environment. Safety is the most basic task of all. Without a sense of safety, no growth can take place. Without safety, all energy goes to defense.

In a traditional therapeutic setting, there is often no problem with taking whatever time is necessary to win trust. In such a setting, Cassandra might have needed weeks, if not months, to develop the level of trust necessary to allow me to implement change, and this would have been great. I would have loved to have been able to give her that kind of gentle interaction. Unfortunately, here in the hospital, where the cost—both human and financial—of institutionalizing a child over a period of time was high, we needed to march to a faster drummer.

I sat back in my chair.

"I'm not going to do this," she stated.

I said nothing.

"I'm not going to do this."

I sat.

"I'm *not* going to do this! Listen to me, you old hag. I'm NOT going to do this." Cassandra grabbed up the small piece of crayon and threw it at me. Then she shoved the coloring book angrily off the table again.

Picking up the piece of crayon, I put it back on the table. Then I retrieved the coloring book and placed that back in front of her. I opened it to the picture of the rag doll again.

"I'M NOT GOING TO DO THIS!" Cassandra shouted. She pushed the book away again and got up from her chair to leave.

I got up faster. Grabbing her shoulders, I stopped her from going through the door. She struggled fiercely at that point, lashing out angrily. I held on.

At last I maneuvered her back to the table and into her chair. With that, Cassandra started to cry. Indeed, she cried very piteously.

I returned to my seat on the opposite side and sat down.

"*Why* are you doing this to me?" she wailed.

"Because this is where we start."

"But why? Why do I have to do *this*?"

"Because I am here to help you, but I can't do the work all by myself. You have to work, too. And this is the beginning of your work."

"But I don't *want* to," she howled, her voice trailing off into a high-pitched whine. "I want to go home. I want my mom."

I was very aware at just that moment how terrifying this situation must have been for Cassandra, because how was she to know I was any different than her abusers? Or that the enforced hospital stay was any different than her abduction? There was such a thin line here between gaining very crucial control in order to make progress and simply reinforcing trauma. To be honest, at that precise moment, I was feeling pretty terrified, too.

"Cassandra, I want you to color this picture. Here." I put the piece of red crayon in front of her.

"I don't want to," she protested one more time.

"Here."

And finally she picked up the crayon. She scribbled angrily over the picture.

"Okay." I picked out a green crayon from the box. "Now, color the doll's top green."

She snapped the crayon in two.

"I can see you don't like long crayons."

"I don't like YOU!"

"Color the doll's top green, please."

Harshly, she scratched the green crayon across the page.

"Okay." I took out a black crayon. "Color the doll's hair black."

Furiously, she started to scribble with the black crayon.

Indeed, this seemed to give her some pleasure, as she continued scribbling, covering the picture all over in black lines, the crayon held viciously, like a knife.

Oh well, at least she didn't break the black crayon.

I picked a yellow crayon from the box. "Here. Color the doll's shoes yellow." This was a somewhat ludicrous request, as Cassandra had covered the page with so many black lines that the outline of the rag doll had all but vanished.

She took the yellow crayon and scribbled across the bottom of the page in the general vicinity of where the shoes should be.

"Okay," I said. "I think we've colored that page."

"I hate you," she said.

"Now, you may choose what we do next."

"I want to go."

"It isn't time to go. See the clock? Ten more minutes."

"I don't care. I want to go now," she replied.

"All right," I said and sat back. "If that's what you choose, you may go. First we did my activity, now it's your choice. So you can go."

She stared at me. It was an unreadable expression. I couldn't discern whether I'd caught her off guard by acquiescing and she was looking at me in confused surprise, or whether she was sizing me up for the next challenge. Whatever, she didn't rise from the chair.

After a moment, Cassandra's shoulders sagged very slightly and she looked down at the coloring book, still open on the table in front of her. She seemed tired, which was understandable. Certainly I was.

The aura of frisson faded. Cassandra continued to stare at the coloring book. She made no attempt to leave. The silence lingered.

Finally she said, "That's not very good coloring." Her voice was soft and matter-of-fact.

I didn't reply.

"You'd think a little kid had done it. Like maybe a five-year-old. Like maybe that little boy who's here," she said. "People are going to see it and they won't know it's me."

"Inside us we often have parts of us that still feel like little kids," I said. "Even though our bodies are much older."

"I can color much better than that," she replied.

A heartbeat's length of silence.

"When I want to," she added.

"I think maybe that was the five-year-old inside you, coloring that picture. Which is maybe why, when I look at it, it looks like it was colored by someone who felt very scared and angry."

"Or maybe just five," Cassandra said. "Maybe that's just how things look to you when you're five."

"Maybe," I said.

She rose from her chair. "I'm going to go now."

"All right. I'll see you tomorrow. Good-bye."

"Good-bye."

*I*n the afternoon I had a couple of errands to run that involved leaving the hospital for a short while, so I decided to get clearance to take Drake with me. I still worried about the effects of hospitalization on such a young child, and it was now apparent that he wasn't going to go home after a week. I was also concerned about the occasionally stressful atmosphere of our sessions. The chance to take him out, to interact with him in a less pressured way, to do something friendly and fun seemed like a good idea to me.

Drake was delighted. Friend had to come, too, of course, and by this point Friend had his own fan club on the ward. While I helped Drake into his jacket, one of the young aides came and tied a scarf around Friend's neck "to keep the chill off."

Not that there was much chill. It was very late winter, yet nonetheless bright and sunny outside, full of the promise of warmer months to come. In fact, inside the car, it was actually hot.

I strapped Drake into a car booster I'd borrowed from the ward. He loved everything we were doing, waving and gesturing, his head swiveling this and that way in the parking lot. My knowledge of signs for outdoor things was quite limited but I knew "car" and signed that.

Drake observed my sign and then looked up at me. It was an odd little moment, because I was very aware of this "observing" quality. Here was a sign he didn't know. But then he looked at me, made eye contact and, in an equally observing manner, took in my mood.

"You worry about making signs, don't you?"

He regarded me, his expression solemn.

"Has somebody told you it's wrong to sign?" Because suddenly I was thinking of Mason Sloane. Perhaps the staff at the preschool or somewhere else had tried to teach Drake sign language to help him communicate and Drake's family hadn't approved. Had he possibly been punished for signing?

Drake didn't indicate one way or the other, but his sudden seriousness made me fairly certain the answer was yes. Everything then fell into place. This was how he knew signs, but also why he became upset when I had called attention to his using them, even though my comments were not meant to be negative. To him, I was catching him doing something bad.

It then occurred to me how confusing my own behavior must have seemed to the poor little boy. On one hand, I was teaching him signs and, thus, actively indicating that this was okay to do, but then I was also calling attention to the fact that he already knew signs, which he had gotten into trouble for knowing. What a bewildering world he was living in, trying to please all the adults, even when they sent such contradictory messages.

I dropped off some notes at a nearby clinic and picked up some photocopying. Then I went over to another medical facility, where one of our former patients had been transferred, in order to hand in some folders. As a treat, I then stopped at an ice cream shop. Of course, there was no leaving Friend in the car during this visit, so there was much unbuckling and lifting in and out before the three of us finally managed to go into the store.

It was a Baskin-Robbins franchise with all thirty-one flavors, but it was just a small one, the premises long and narrow and not much bigger than the therapy room. Because it was midafternoon on a weekday, no one was in there except us and the girl who was serving.

Enthusiastically, Drake went up and down the counter, looking at the various tubs of ice cream. He kept lifting Friend up to see, too, and pointing at different ones. The girl behind the counter was charmed by his excitement and kept handing over little taster spoons full of the different flavors Drake pointed to.

"Okay, we can't stay forever," I said, "so it's time to choose. Which flavor do you want in your cone?"

Another few minutes were spent going up and down the display. Finally he pointed to a very bright ice cream of green, white, and orange.

"All right. A cone of that," I said to the girl. "Just one scoop, please."

She took down a cone from the display. Suddenly Drake became agitated. He grabbed my arm and tried to gesture something about what the girl was doing. He ran along the counter to where she was, back to me, and gestured again.

"What do you want?" I asked.

He gestured again.

"I'm sorry. I don't understand," I said.

He gestured again, frantically this time.

"This is where words would be helpful," I added, "because I do want to understand you, but I'm afraid I don't, Drake. I'm sorry."

The girl leaned forward to hand him his ice cream cone. "Here you go," she said.

He wouldn't take it. He shook his head.

"What's wrong?" I asked. "Isn't that the flavor you wanted?"

Drake was going to cry. Mouth turning down, he pointed along the counter.

I came down on my knees. "Honey, I'm sorry. I really don't know what's the matter. Is it the wrong flavor? If so, that's okay. I'll take that ice cream cone and you can get the flavor you want. Show me which one you want."

He pointed. It didn't actually seem to be at a different flavor of ice cream. He just pointed in the general direction of where the girl was.

Frustrated, I tried to comfort him. The girl leaned farther over the counter and tried to help, too. She said reassuringly that neither of us had to take the flavor if it was the wrong one, that she could just put it aside.

Steadfastly refusing to take the ice cream cone, Drake screwed up his face. Tears spilled.

I rose up. Not knowing what else to do, I opened my purse, paid the girl for the ice cream cone, and took it myself. But this was hardly satisfactory. Here I was with an ice cream cone I didn't really want and Drake had nothing. The treat had been for him, not me.

I licked the ice cream. It tasted funny. Definitely not a flavor I would have chosen. Quietly, I waited for Drake to regain his composure. The girl stood behind the counter and nervously watched the two of us.

"Okay, sweetie," I said gently when the tears were just snuffles, "can you try again for me? Can you show us what you want?"

He hesitated a moment, assessing, I think, if this were some kind of pressure for speech and how much genuine patience I was likely to have. Then he approached the end of the counter by the cash register again and pointed.

I followed the line of his finger, which was upward, so not really at the ice cream. I looked at the clutter of stuff at the top of the counter—straws, napkins, plastic spoons, small paper tubs—and just behind them, the holder for the cones.

"You want a napkin?" I queried. This much fuss over a napkin seemed obsessively neat for a four-year-old, but I hadn't actually seen Drake at mealtimes, so perhaps he was fastidious in a way I didn't know about.

He shook his head. He kept pointing.

"A straw?" Which seemed even more unlikely, given we were not having drinks.

His mouth was starting to drag down again as I failed to understand.

"A cone? Do you want a different cone than the ordinary one?" I asked. "Is that it? Do you want one of the waffle cones?"

He was teary again.

The girl was going along the top of the counter.

"This?" she tried, tapping the spoons. "This?"—she tapped the napkins. "This?"—she tapped the straws. "This?"—she tapped the little individual-portion tubs, stacked upside down.

And that was it. Drake almost melted with relief. Too near to crying to be able to register any happiness at finally being understood, he just kept nodding.

"A tub? You didn't want it in a cone? You want this kind of ice cream, but in a little tub?" I asked.

He was still nodding frantically.

And so we finally managed success.

I left Baskin-Robbins perplexed and thoughtful. For an otherwise cheerful and reasonably accommodating little boy, he had seemed unusually insistent on the tub. Why not a cone? I hadn't ever come across a little kid who wouldn't accept an ice cream cone.

It also brought home how important it was to get this child communicating effectively with those around him. This had been a surprisingly upsetting episode, not only for Drake but for the girl behind the counter and myself. And truth was, Drake probably had far more important things to communicate even now than whether to have his ice cream in a tub or on a cone.

Perhaps most of all, however, this event made clear how much I had failed with my usual method of intervention for elective mutism. My method relied on being able to intervene as a newcomer who had no previous nonspeaking relationship with the child. That certainly wasn't true now. I too had sacrificed words in preference for understanding. If I had been following my very own rules, I should have left him without the ice cream unless he made some effort at asking for what he wanted. Instead, I too got sucked right into the drama of trying to find out what he meant.

For the first time manipulation crossed my mind. With his merry smile and his charismatic manner, Drake didn't seem like a manipulative child; on the other hand, perhaps this was the perfect method for controlling situations. Beguile everyone. Because who can resist doing what a cute, smiley charmer wants? Could that be possible? Had he managed to dupe me as well?

I had one more stop before returning to the unit. Joy Hansen had asked me for further information on elective mutism. I had intended to drop off some reading material in the morning when I stopped to see Gerda at the rehabilitation center, but I'd forgotten it in my car. As the center was so near the hospital, I thought I'd stop on the way back and drop it off. And since I was there anyway, I thought I'd peek in on Gerda just to see what she was like at a different time of day.

"We're going to make a really quick stop here," I said to Drake, as I unbuckled him from his car seat. "We're going to see a lady who has trouble talking. Just like you. She's very old. She used to talk but now she doesn't. So I come to see her, just the same as I come see you."

Drake was the center of attention from the moment he entered the front lobby of the rehabilitation center. Several elderly people sitting in the chairs called out to him. Given his long hair and cherubic features, they all thought he was a little girl, but Drake being Drake, he still responded good-naturedly, waving to an old woman and old man sitting by the window.

Indeed, in this tabernacle of the old, everyone who

saw us rejoiced in his youth. "Well, look here! Look who we have here!" each person remarked as we passed.

One of the nursing staff paused, as we came down the hall. "Is this your daughter? She's beautiful!" Which, of course, meant I had to delicately explain that not only was he not my daughter, he wasn't even a girl.

An old lady had stopped as I was speaking with the nurse. She bent forward and stroked Drake's cheek. He didn't shy away from the withered hand. Indeed, he smiled beatifically back at her.

"You're so cute, I could just eat you," the old woman said, which to me seemed a rather alarming comment to make to a four-year-old, but Drake just kept smiling.

In her room, Gerda was lying down. She turned her head when we entered, and for the first time I saw her smile.

"This is Drake," I said. "He's one of the children I work with at the hospital. He and I are out for the afternoon. We've just had an ice cream and now we're stopping by to see how you're doing."

Gerda struggled to sit up, so I leaned over and helped her into a sitting position. She reached a hand out toward Drake. It was hard to know exactly what she intended, whether she was wanting to stroke him the way the other old lady had or whether she was gesturing about something. He smiled but was too far from her to touch.

With Drake in the room, Gerda was much more alert and animated than I'd previously seen her. For the first time, she seemed to want to communicate, because she then gestured to me. I didn't immediately understand, but then she stretched back toward the bedside cabinet that was just beyond her reach. Thinking she must be seeking something in the cabinet, I opened the drawer. In there was a small bag of the flat red-and-white swirled peppermint candies that are wrapped individually in cellophane. She nodded fervently, so I lifted it out and gave it to her.

Gerda opened the bag and picked out one. This took considerable effort on her part, making me more aware of the extent of the damage done by the stroke. I was tempted to help but I didn't. We just waited. When she had finally managed it, she held out the candy to Drake.

A winning smile on his face, he took the candy and unwrapped it, popping it in his mouth. There was unexpected poignancy in this moment between silent child and silent adult, both struggling to bridge the gap as best they could.

"Drake finds it hard to speak," I said. I looked down at him. "Can you say 'thank you' with your hands? Like this?" I showed him the sign.

Drake imitated it.

"Now, can you say that to Mrs. Sharple? Can you tell her thank you for the candy?"

Drake signed "thank you" and then "candy." He smiled broadly.

Gerda smiled back.

*H*ow to proceed with Cassandra?

If I looked back over our sessions together, they had been very chaotic. My well-thought-out, coherent plans inevitably ended up in tatters by the end of the session, and Cassandra herself provided very little consistency. In typical therapeutic sessions, activities are either guided by the therapist's experience and knowledge of how to deal with a specific problems or guided by the patient's needs. In our case, the sessions had been a miasma of events that seemed to change randomly from day to day and left me "coping" much more than "guiding." I couldn't tell if this was because there were so many problems fighting to come out in Cassandra's case that no single pattern was yet emerging, or if she was simply so fearful of dealing with deeper problems that she had actively avoided revealing any pattern.

Certainly trust was a major issue and I hadn't achieved it. And forcing a child to color a rag doll according to my wishes wasn't going to have given it to me. I hadn't really been proud of the previous session. The teacher in me had responded to Cassandra's repetitive efforts to control our time together. Once out of the situation, I wasn't convinced it had been appropriate of me to respond that way as a psychologist. Possibly it was a necessary confrontation, particularly in light of the fact that I didn't want her institutionalized any longer than was absolutely necessary, but I did not want to repeat the experience. Nor did I want domination to be what that session was remembered for. I wanted it instead to be seen more as a delineation of our roles, an understanding that she could explore and deal with the traumas of her past, because I was strong enough to keep her safe while doing that.

On the unit, Cassandra was continually in trouble for telling outrageous lies. Most involved graphic sexual abuse and were often so outlandish they would have been laughable if they weren't so sick, or if we on the staff were not so worried that someone might mistake what Cassandra was saying for the truth. As it was, for our own protection, none of us was allowed to be alone with Cassandra. We always had to work in public locations, in pairs, or with a videocamera recording us, and preferably all three.

Then Selma arrived on the unit. She was eight and had very serious problems that included auditory hallucinations and a tenuous grasp on reality. This meant Selma often heard voices telling her things. After a day or two on the unit, Selma became increasingly agitated. All of a sudden, her voices started to say things to her like "Nurse Nancy put her finger in your butthole.

When you were in bed last night, I heard her say she wanted to feel you." This was understandably distressing to Selma, who wasn't always able to discern if such things had really happened or not; and, of course, to us staff it was downright terrifying, because one kid making allegations of sexual abuse was serious enough and now we had two.

We all knew Selma's fretting was being fed by Cassandra, as there had been no sexual content to Selma's hallucinations before she came onto the ward. Moreover, Selma's words were all verbatim the same tales Cassandra had been telling about virtually everyone in authority. Thus far, however, Cassandra had been so covert in priming Selma that no one had caught her at it, until the morning after our coloring book session.

When I came for her, Cassandra was in lockdown. For such a serious offense, it was common to leave the child to serve his or her time in seclusion and reschedule classes or therapy sessions for another time. With her malicious lies and continually provocative behavior, however, Cassandra had become deeply unpopular on the ward, both with staff and other children. As a consequence, they were always desperate for a respite from her. Moreover, I really didn't want to lose a session, which I would do, because I had no time later in the day to reschedule. So it seemed better to take this opportunity to tackle things head-on.

Cassandra was sullen, almost surly, when I said she could come with me. Rising reluctantly, kicking the seclusion room door frame as she left, she did not give much impression of being glad for a reason to go. However, by the time we reached the therapy room, she was her usual self. Indeed, she seemed downright chipper once we were inside.

"I want to draw pictures today," she said.

"Perhaps later. First, can you tell me more about what went on out there?" I said.

"Went on where?"

"Out there. On the ward. I'm interested to hear your side of it."

"I don't remember."

"Cassandra, we just came from lockdown. Why were you in lockdown?" I asked.

She brought her shoulders way up and rolled her eyes in an exaggerated manner.

"Why were you in lockdown?" I asked again.

"Because they hate me." She said this in a matter-of-fact, almost cheery fashion, as if it were the most obvious given.

"The staff told me you had been saying things to Selma that had frightened her and that's why you were to go to time-out. Then you got very upset and so you were put into seclusion."

Cassandra shrugged.

"What's your version?"

"Silly-willy, peedy-poopy, biddily-boddily, ding-dong, nig-nog," she replied and smiled.

Silence.

I looked at her.

She looked back at me, her gaze unflinching.

"Why's this happening?" I asked. "Why, when I ask you something, do you say things like you just did?"

She shrugged. "I don't know."

"Why do you think it's happening?"

"I don't know."

"Okay, maybe you don't know, but why do you think? What's your guess about why you do it?"

Again she drew her shoulders up in the exaggerated shrug. It wasn't so comical this time, but it was off-putting. It gave her an aura of not really caring.

"Cassandra, things are pretty serious right now. You're stuck here in the hospital. You can't go to school. You can't play with your sisters. You don't have any of your belongings here. You can't watch the TV shows you want. You can't play on a computer or stay up late or have special food you like. You can't see your mom or your friends or go places you like going. Life's really messed up. I want to help you out of this. But for me to help you, you need to help me. You need to talk to me. Straight. Not tell lies. Not make up stories. Not say 'I don't know' or 'I don't remember' to everything."

Silence.

"Do you understand what I'm saying?" I asked.

She averted her eyes and nodded slightly.

"So why do you think these things are happening?" I asked.

"What things?"

"*These* things. The things that have put you here. The lying. The silly answers to questions. The trouble on the ward. Any of them. All of them."

"I don't know," she replied.

I looked at her.

She looked back. "I *don't* know."

"I believe you. But do you think about it?" I asked. "Do you wonder why this is happening to you? Do you wonder why you forget so many things?"

A pause. Her gaze went inward, and the pause lengthened. She started to shake her head very, very slightly, but it was hard to know if it was in answer to my question or if she was responding to some inner thought.

"Cassandra," I asked, "do people say you've done things that you really don't think you've done?"

She nodded immediately. Looking up, she met my eyes, and for once it wasn't a challenging look. The silliness, too, was gone. "Yes," she said. "All the time."

"What do you think about that?" I asked.

"I tell them the truth." Her voice was soft. "I tell them I don't remember doing that."

"Sometimes . . . do you know you do things but it feels like maybe it's not exactly you doing them? Like maybe you're looking at yourself doing things? Sort of the way you look at other people doing things?"

She nodded.

"Like when? Could you give me an example of that? Could you tell me the last time you felt that way?"

"Nurse Nancy came in when I was having a shower last night. She put her hand on my body. She was going to feel me up but I pushed her away."

"I don't actually believe that, Cassandra. For one thing, Nurse Nancy doesn't work at the time the kids here are having showers."

"Well, I was wrong. It wasn't Nurse Nancy. It was Lyle, who works on nights."

"Sometimes, when we don't want to think of one thing," I said, "we put something else in our minds instead."

"I don't," Cassandra replied, and she started to say something else but stopped. There was anticipation in the moment. She sat forward in her chair, as if intending to continue. I could feel the expectancy. Then the moment passed. She relaxed back in the chair and was silent.

"Did you want to add more to that idea?"

"No."

Silence.

"Yes."

More silence.

"No."

Silence again. Quietly, I watched her.

"Yes. Yes, I—" She broke off. Narrowing her eyes as if looking at me from a long distance, she said, "Can I tell you something?"

I nodded.

"But don't tell my mom, okay? Don't tell her I told you, because she said never to say it to anyone."

I braced myself to hear another sickening lie.

There was a long hesitation. Cassandra actually opened her mouth to speak, then didn't but stayed that way for several seconds. Finally she closed her mouth. A few moments more passed, and then she tried again. "It makes me sound crazy," she said in quiet voice. "That's why my mom's said never to tell it."

"I'm sure your mom means well, but sometimes people tell us things that aren't helpful. This might be one of them."

"She's trying to protect me. She says they'll take me away if I'm crazy. They'll lock me up."

I didn't point out that that had already happened, so not telling hadn't really worked either.

Perhaps Cassandra was thinking this herself. She gazed at me but not in the brassy, insolent way she normally maintained eye contact. There was an inwardness to it, as if, on one level, she were regarding me, and on another level, she were considering, weighing . . .

A pause.

"What I'm not suppose to tell . . ." she said softly, "is that I've got people talking in my head. Like Selma does. I'm crazy, like Selma, because I hear people saying things to me, too. And I can't always tell when what they're saying is true or not."

"What kind of people?"

"I don't know. Mostly I just hear their voices. I don't see them. Sometimes they're talking to me. Sometimes they talk to each other. Like Minister Snake. That's one of them. That's his name. When I was sitting in seclusion, Minister Snake was saying, 'You gotta pray now. You done something so bad. You sucked his cock and you're so bad.' And Cowboy Snake, he likes that kind of music. You know. That cowboy music that sounds like someone howling. Kind of Ow-ow-ow-ow." She gave a wobbly imitation of the yodeling sound common in some old country music. "And when Minister Snake gets talking, Cowboy Snake sings real loud so that I can't hear what Minister Snake's saying anymore."

"I remember you talking about Cowboy and Minister Snake before. And there were other Snakes, too, weren't there?"

Cassandra nodded. "Fairy Snake. She's little. She's, like, three and she's really pretty. I take care of her. I don't let them hurt her because she's just little."

"And these are voices? You hear them in your head?"

Cassandra nodded.

"Are they pretend, do you think? Part of your imagination?"

"I don't know," she said. A pause. "They're friends. My friends. That are just inside me. But they're real. Well, sort of real. I mean, there's different kinds of real. Most people think there's only one kind of real, but actually, there's more. There's this other kind, too, where you can't touch things because they're in your head. But they're real, too."

I nodded. "Yeah, I know what you mean. I understand that kind of real."

She looked at me. It was a soft look and, for the first time, she seemed unguarded.

"It's useful for me to know about your friends," I said. "I'm glad you told me, because knowing about them lets me find ways to help you."

"My mom said never to tell. I think she'd be mad if you knew."

"I don't think so. Your mom's worried about you. She just doesn't really know what to do."

"She's trying to take care of me the best way she can," Cassandra said solemnly.

I nodded.

There was a small pause and Cassandra pursed her lips. "My mom's not so good at taking care of me. She let my dad get me."

"Sadly, sometimes bad things happen, even when we do our very best. What happened to you was very scary, though, wasn't it?"

Cassandra nodded.

A long silence came then. Cassandra's eyes were unfocused and she appeared lost in thought. The room went deeply quiet, so much so that I could hear the very faint whirring of the video camera beyond the one-way mirror.

At last she let out a long breath. Dropping her head, she said, "I'm tired."

"I understand."

"Can I go back to the unit now? I can't think on this any more."

"Okay."

When Harry Patel came into my office the next day, he was holding a sheaf of papers. Reaching out, he gently pitched them onto my desktop. "Well, make what you will of this," he said.

I craned forward to see it. It was the report on Drake's assessment from the Mayo Clinic.

"It seems thorough. Audiology and Ear, Nose, and Throat. All perfectly normal. Neurology, EEG, MRI. All perfectly normal," Harry said. "So I guess I can understand the family's not wanting us to put the boy through all this again. But . . . it does pass the buck squarely to us."

I looked at him.

"And leaves us with a few difficult questions. Like: Why doesn't the boy talk? What's wrong with him? And why are we making no progress?"

I stared at the papers on the desk.

"They're coming on Monday," Harry said. "We're

going to have to tell them something. Tell them we've found something or tell them we're doing something or . . ." He grimaced. "Or *something*."

After Harry had left, I pulled the papers around in front of me to read them. It was a photocopy of the official evaluation, and it was nothing if not thorough:

> This 3 year 9 month child has been seen for the first time at the Child Development Center by Dr. J. R. Pennell and Dr. D. Beretti. He had been referred by Richard Davis, MD, pediatrician, because of failure to speak.

The report outlined how Drake had been seen not only by the medical team who investigated his hearing but also a pediatric neurological team and a psychiatric evaluation team. In all cases, Drake was judged healthy and at a normal stage of development. Nonverbal intelligence testing indicated he was at the higher end of the "bright normal" ability range, with an IQ of a 130.

I stared at it, trying to take it in. Reading the report made me aware how entrenched my gut feeling was that Drake's lack of speech was due to physical causes. Despite my momentary misgivings about whether or not he was manipulative during our outing to the ice cream store, my overall belief remained: Drake was *not* withholding anything from us. He genuinely couldn't talk. It *so* felt that way to me, even without knowing why.

Yet, here it was in black and white. If all the investigative power of the Mayo Clinic hadn't found a physical reason for lack of speech, it was very unlikely I was going to discover one. So this did point squarely at psychological problems being the cause.

I realized I needed to adjust my attitude. It was arrogant to think that simply because I hadn't seen an elective mute like Drake, he therefore could not be an elective mute. More than that, I had to accept the nasty fact that responsibility for successful intervention did lay squarely with me.

Having read the Mayo report through very thoroughly, I went into my session with Drake armed with determination. I set him and Friend in chairs side by side on one side of the table in the therapy room. I set the tape recorder on the table. I went around and sat down across from him.

"It's time for us to get serious," I said pleasantly but firmly. "Time for us to work really hard. I'm sure you're ready to go home, huh? Your mom and dad are coming on Monday, and we want you ready to leave with them and go home, don't we?"

Drake nodded.

"So let's work really, really hard today, okay? Let's get this big bad problem right out of the way."

He nodded again.

I turned the tape of Lucia and Drake reciting nursery rhymes on.

Drake burst into tears.

"Oops, no. Let's not get upset," I said. "I know this is hard. I know it's scary, but we're going to just get right in there and get this out of the way. And I'm going to help you."

Pulling Friend over, Drake buried his face in the fur.

I rose up and came around to his side of the table.

Standing behind him, I eased him away from Friend. Taking hold of both his arms just above the wrist, I said, "I've made a special version of this tape. I've copied this part over and over so that we can play it and say the rhyme along. You'll hear how I've done it. I'll start the tape playing and we'll all say it. You, me, your mom, and you again. Like there's four of us here. A chorus, hey?"

I had rerecorded the tape Lucia had sent so that the "Hickety, Pickety" nursery rhyme played over and over and over—and I was taking no chances—so, it played over and over for a full thirty minutes.

> *Hickety, pickety, my black hen*
> *She lays eggs for gentlemen . . .*

I started to say the rhyme along with the voices on the tape. Standing behind Drake, holding his hands, I clapped them together to the rhythm of the words.

Drake was crying in his funny, breathy way. He didn't struggle against my moving his hands, but he made no effort to stop crying either.

> *Hickety, pickety, my black hen*
> *She lays eggs for gentlemen . . .*

"You say it, too. Come on. We want to get through this, don't we? Get this awful task out of the way. It's really hard to start, I know. But once the first time happens . . . It'll be easier after that. It's just the first time that's the hardest . . ."

> *Hickety, pickety, my black hen*
> *She lays eggs for gentlemen . . .*

Drake was sobbing.

I didn't want to stop. Indeed, I was quite determined not to stop. Things were much clearer to me now—the degree to which Drake relied on charismatic behavior to get him what he wanted, while using dependent, piteous behavior to stop what he didn't want. Such an uncompromising approach was awful, but we needed to break through this wall of silence.

"I'm sorry you're upset, but we're going to do this. Just like you've done on the tape. Just like you've done with your mama. Because we want you to go home with your mama on Monday. It's very important we get this done."

> *Hickety, pickety, my black hen*
> *She lays eggs for gentlemen . . .*

Drake was starting to struggle. I could tell he wanted Friend, so I lifted the enormous tiger up and set him on Drake's lap.

"Here, Friend can help us, too. You take Friend's hands. You hold his hands to clap along; I'll hold your hands, and we'll all clap along to the rhyme." Which wasn't terribly easy to do when a three-foot-tall tiger was sitting in the lap of a kid who wasn't any taller. Especially when the kid wanted to do nothing more than bury his face in the tiger's back.

> *Hickety, pickety, my black hen*
> *She lays eggs for gentlemen . . .*

Drake wasn't going to cooperate. He continued to cry. I paused. Kneeling down beside the chair, I took a tissue and wiped his face. He had been crying most of the session, so he was soggy and reddened, wisps of his long girlish hair plastered to his cheeks and catching in his mouth.

"Here. Let's take a moment to relax," I said gently. Pulling out another tissue, I continued to mop up. "I know it's hard. I know it's scary. A lot for me to ask of you, isn't it?"

Drake nodded fervently.

"But I also know you can do it. If you really try. Just like you've done with your mama on the tape. I want to hear your voice, too, just like on the tape."

This started him sobbing again.

"No. No, no, no. I know you're upset. It's all right to cry, but we're still going to have to do it. I'll help you. We'll do it together. And you and I, I know we can."

I waited a little longer, helped Drake blow his nose and wipe his eyes, and then we started off again. I continued on as I had, standing behind his chair, clasping my hands over his over Friend's to clap along to the rhythm of the nursery rhyme. This seemed the most feasible way of going about the task because it kept us from having to make eye contact, it kept him close to the security of Friend, and the actions helped displace some of the intensity.

> *Hickety, pickety, my black hen*
> *She lays eggs for gentlemen . . .*

> *Hickety, pickety, my black hen*
> *She lays eggs for gentlemen . . .*

> *Hickety, pickety, my black hen*
> *She lays eggs for gentlemen . . .*

Over and over I did the rhyme, clapping the small hands and tiger hands together, hoping that the rhythm, the movement, the repetitiveness would prove a calming influence as well as an inducement to speak. *Come on,* I was thinking. Pleading, actually. *Come on, come on, come on. You can do it. Come on.*

> *Hickety, pickety, my black hen*
> *She lays eggs for gentlemen . . .*

He was crying again. He hadn't ever completely stopped, but it was in a tired, hopeless way now.

> *Hickety, pickety, my black hen*
> *She lays eggs for gentlemen . . .*

Come on. Join in. SAY it, Drake. Come on. Please.

> *Hickety, pickety, my black hen*
> *She lays eggs for gentlemen . . .*

I heard him gasping, drawing breath in. Was this it? Were we almost there?

> *Hickety, pickety, my black hen*
> *She lays eggs for gentlemen . . .*

Instead, he threw up. He'd eaten canned Spaghetti-Os for lunch, and there they were. All down his front, all over Friend's back, everywhere.

I let go and stepped back.

The tape droned on.

> *Hickety, pickety, my black hen*
> *She lays eggs for gentlemen . . .*

Maddened, I reached across the table and slammed the thing off.

This had not been an edifying session. Once the awful jobs of cleaning Drake up, arranging to get the therapy room cleaned up, and sponging down poor old Friend were over, I returned him to the ward and retreated to my office, where I collapsed into the chair at my desk and covered my eyes with my hand.

Helen was there, and she had no trouble reading my distress. "Want me to look at the tape with you?" she offered.

No. No, I didn't want anyone else looking at the tape. I didn't want to look at the tape myself. I'd gone too far. I'd pushed too hard. I'd overstepped what I should be doing with that little boy and I knew it. I'd known it even as I was doing it, but desperation to get results had allowed me to override common sense. It was going to be a hard tape to watch. I'd be mortified for someone else to see it. So I declined her offer and just sat.

What were we going to do? We couldn't keep Drake for weeks and weeks. He was too young. The separation and, to put it bluntly, the institutionalization inherent in being on the unit would only create greater psychological problems in the long run, to say nothing of the stress of experiences like our session today. Yet it was obvious he did have something serious going on. *What?* How had the mutism become so intractable at such an early age? *Why?* For what reason was he refusing to cooperate now? *How come?*

If I was brutally honest with myself, not only had I made absolutely no progress with Drake, despite intensive daily therapy, but I literally knew no more about what was causing his problems now than when I'd first met him. This was a scary thought, not only in terms of having spent so much time with the boy and yet having learned so little about him, but also for what it said about the focus of the sessions. Out to do a job, confident of how to do it, I'd given the boy very little chance to direct any of the sessions himself. I'd gone into this like a mechanic, setting about repairing a faulty car engine.

And yet . . . it wasn't as calloused as that. I'd done it because I had wanted Drake in and out of the hospital as quickly as possible, because I hadn't wanted to disrupt his life any longer than absolutely necessary, because I'd known that even if he did require long-term therapy, it would need to be carried out somewhere other than here and by someone other than me; so my job was, in fact, largely mechanical. Help him speak so that these other things could happen.

And yet . . .

Very tentatively, I turned my mind back to the one other thing not yet addressed with Drake. If this mutism was so intractable, the odds were high that something seriously wrong was happening in the family. We were going to have to address that. Up until this point, I'd been holding out hope either that Drake would speak and this would make any such questions about child abuse or other serious family dysfunction easier to pur-

sue, or else that some clue as to the nature of the problem would become evident from Drake's behavior on
the unit, and we would then know more which way to
go. As it was, he still didn't speak, and he hadn't been
anything but cheery, cooperative, and sociable on the
unit. So I was stuck with the prospect of figuring out
how to deal with a dysfunctional family when I didn't
know what the trouble was, who was causing it, or in
what manner it was impacting Drake—and they all
lived two hundred miles away.

Chapter

21

$\mathcal{T}$he breakfast tray had already been cleared from Gerda's room by the time I arrived, and she had lain down again, her back to the door. She didn't respond immediately to my presence. My sense was that she had expected it to be one of the rehabilitation center staff and so just ignored the noise, but when I said her name, she then turned her head quite quickly. More laboriously, her body followed.

"Would you like help to sit up?" I asked.

She reached a hand out in a gesture I didn't immediately understand. It looked as if she were patting a nonexistent dog beside the bed. Then she made eye contact with me and patted the air again.

"Ah. The little boy? Are you wondering about the little boy I had with me the other day?"

She nodded.

"He's a patient at the hospital where I work. That was just a treat, taking him out while I ran some errands."

Her brow wrinkled in an expression that said to me, "Tell me more." Or possibly, "Why is he there?"

"He's at the hospital because he doesn't speak. He talks at home but only to his mother. No one else. Not even his father. And, of course, this is causing him problems. So I'm trying to help him."

A pause.

"Unfortunately, I'm not doing such a good job, I'm afraid. He still isn't talking."

Gerda made a sad, sympathetic face.

I was touched to see her so concerned, especially as she had registered almost no emotion during previous visits. I settled into the chair beside the bed.

"I think I told you, his name is Drake. And I feel so sorry for him. He's only four. There are a lot of expectations in his family. They're very prominent in their community. The grandfather is a real patriarch—demanding, domineering, bossing everyone. He gets so distressed thinking something is 'wrong' with Drake. Whereas, if the boy just had a chance to be himself . . ."

Gerda nodded faintly.

A small silence came then. I knew I shouldn't be talking about one client with another client, even if it was very unlikely Gerda would ever pass any of the information on. But it was unethical, so I searched for another direction to take the conversation.

"Twilight child," she said, her voice soft. "Twilight child, twilight child."

Surprised, I looked at her, because here was the elusive spontaneous speech I had been brought in to find.

Unfortunately, poetic as they were, the words didn't make much sense to me. She regarded me intently with her blue, blue eyes, but her expression remained quite unreadable.

I nodded slowly, hoping that was an adequate response.

Gerda looked away. She seemed to study a blank part of the wall beside the bed and then looked back, saying in a very quiet voice, "Tim come west in the boxcar, so he had part thoroughbred in him. Should have been a saddler, but Papa hitched him to the wagon."

I scrambled madly to figure out what we were talking about, how we had gotten from Drake to the topic of boxcars and Tim, whom I took to be a horse.

"Gone down along the breaks to hunt chokecherries. Mama put all the buckets on the wagon and a big picnic lunch. Papa hitched Tim and they all went. Louisa and me, we always got left home. Boys could go. 'No place for girls,' Mama would say. I'd say, 'Mama, boys are no good picking chokecherries. Let me and Louisa come.' Mama says, 'You'll get your dresses dirty down along the breaks.'

"The boys'd come home, their hands, their lips, their tongues, even their teeth stained red with chokecherry juice. Could eat as much as you want of chokecherries because no one can eat many. You get choky in the back of your throat from the juice. Got to have a drink of water. But you always try again."

I was still bewildered by this unexpected burst of speech. Nonetheless, as Gerda spoke, I was transported back to the countryside of my Montana childhood, to the world of sagebrush, buffalo grass, and wild gray-green chokecherry bushes hung heavy in early autumn with fruit. My generation was probably among the last to experience chokecherry picking as a regular autumn event in most people's homes. I recalled well the annual outings with family and friends in warm fall sunshine, the taste, like bitter cherries, and the unexpected choking sensation that followed. How distant that world and those times seemed. It'd been ages since chokecherries had even crossed my mind.

"I went chokecherry picking as a child," I said to Gerda. "My grandmother used to make it into syrup for our pancakes. I liked it better than maple syrup."

"My brother Willie, he went in the cow field once. The bull took after him. He ran right up the apple tree that was by the creek and when he was caught up there, that bull came and stuck his face up and licked Willie right on the cheek. You could hear Willie howling clear in the house. Clear upstairs where Louisa and me were mending. He thought he'd been bit. Said, 'That bull took a taste of me, Mama!' and he was crying. Alfred thought it was funny. When Mama caught me looking through the fence, I got the belt to me. She says, 'No place for girls.' So unfair. Willie's so much littler. And I like cows. I wasn't scared of the bull one bit."

Nothing Gerda said made real sense. Or, rather, it did in its own little universe, but it made no sense there in the rehabilitation center. I assumed she was recounting memories, but they came out haphazardly, and they did not include me in the conversational way most people relate memories. Indeed, if I attempted to join the topic, Gerda didn't respond to me. She kept talking randomly, not as if I weren't there precisely, because I very much had the sense she was talking *to* me; but her words didn't have the give-and-take of a conversation, so I didn't know how to interpret them. Nonetheless, I left the rehabilitation center in good spirits. She *could* speak spontaneously.

I wanted an in-depth meeting with Dave Menotti over Cassandra. Despite the high profile in the media, dissociative disorders—and more specifically, multiple personality disorder—are not well understood, particularly in children. In my early professional years, multiple personality disorder was considered very rare and, indeed, was not believed to occur in children at all, so no child with that diagnosis had ever come my way. Then in the 1980s, multiple personalities suddenly became the plat du jour. Mysterious and fascinating, it was a fashionable, even desirable, diagnosis to have. And, indeed, everyone seemed to have it. While still regarded as uncommon in children, several of the children I had previously worked with who were now adults were rediagnosed as having multiple personalities. Indeed, so were some of my colleagues.

Overexposure eventually dampened the allure. The disorder was wrested back from the popular media. Serious research was undertaken and a body of knowledge was developed based on objective data rather than sensationalized personal stories. It was found to be not as rare as we had believed in the 1970s, but neither was it common. And it remained a complex, enigmatic psychological disorder.

The problem with dissociation as a disorder is that dissociation itself is a continuum behavior from mild on one end to severe on the other, and every single person is on this continuum. Dissociation is normal, and everyone dissociates. Any time we become so absorbed in an activity that we lose track of what's happening around us, that is dissociation. Most adults experience it regularly while driving—they become involved thinking about supper or their job or their family or even something so mundane as what to buy at the grocery store and lose awareness of driving their vehicle. They don't lose control of the vehicle. They just stop seeing the road and the surrounding environment and see instead what is in their heads. They are able to drive perfectly well on "automatic pilot" and will snap out of their thoughts at the first indication of needing to give more attention to the road, but during the time they are "lost in thought," they have no cognitive awareness of the stretch of road they've just driven. This is normal behavior. Everyone does it. And like all behavior, there is a huge variation in "normal." Some people dissociate hardly at all; others dissociate easily and frequently. Both can be effective adults and perfectly normal.

It is also normal to dissociate in stressful situations, to try to subvert pain or a negative situation by "thinking of something else." Indeed, this is generally considered a good thing; self-help books show us ways to do it effectively; parents often encourage children to cope in this manner; and people who show such abilities are often regarded as creative, adaptive, or intelligent. So the question is not, do you dissociate or not? Or even, how much do you dissociate? Rather it is, at what point on the continuum does it move from being resourceful and helpful to maladaptive and damaging? This is a difficult question to answer, not the least because that point isn't in the same place for all people, and not all dissociated states, even on the far end of the spectrum, are bad.

Multiple personality disorder in childhood is an even more complicated issue. As part of normal imaginative play, most children dissociate easily and, indeed, quite

completely, to try out different identities as police offi-
cers, astronauts, cowboys, parents. Likewise, many
healthy, well-adapted children have imaginary compan-
ions who show a different personality from the child.
Some construct whole imaginary worlds, elaborately
detailed and peopled with a diversity of characters.
These creations can last throughout childhood, adolescence, and even adulthood without any implication of
psychological disturbance. On the other hand, there are
completely unrelated organic factors—drugs, allergies,
physical illnesses—that can also cause dramatic behavior changes that mimic dissociation, such as the inabil-
ity to recall recent events, abrupt changes in attention
span, or "cloudy" thinking. So multiple personality disorder isn't a straightforward diagnosis to make.

As a consequence, I very much needed Dave
Menotti's input, because my own background was inadequate for such a diagnosis. He'd been away for
much of the previous week or I probably would have
snagged him to look at the tape at the point when I first
became suspicious of this possibility. Now, after my
most recent session with Cassandra, I definitely needed
his opinion.

Dave watched the tape with great interest. It was a
dreary afternoon, quite late in the day, and darkness
came sooner than it should have because of a heavily
overcast sky and icy rain. Our video cameras filmed in
black and white only, and the tape I'd used to record
this session was an old, much-used one, so it was full
of snow and flickers. This only added to the gritty,
rather bleak ambiance.

Left arm across his belly, right elbow braced on it,
Dave absently twisted his lower lip as he watched. His

brow furrowed as Cassandra began talking about Minister Snake and Cowboy Snake.

"Even when a child has a diagnosis of MPD, it isn't very common to have clearly defined alter egos," Dave said. "That is more of an adult phenomenon. The alters tend to become more complex and significant as the individual matures. I'm not sure why, whether it is simply part of the maturational process and reaching abstract thinking levels, or whether it is because the behavior becomes entrenched. In my experience, however, the alters are quite nebulous in most children. Not really 'personalities' per se. Which makes them harder to track down, harder to recognize. But it also usually makes them easier to reintegrate with the main personality, because they haven't become so detached." He let out a long breath. "But yeah, I certainly get the feeling this is what we are dealing with here."

"There's a very high correlation between MPD and severe trauma, isn't there?" I asked.

Dave nodded. "More than just severe trauma. It usually implies repeated severe trauma. Trauma of the sort the child perceives as life-threatening. And that the kid can't get away from. That keeps happening over and over again with no real opportunity to heal in between. Yeah. I think it's in the nineties—96, 98 percent of kids with MPD have suffered that level of abuse."

He sighed. "So even if she never reveals what happened to her during her abduction, we need to assume Cassandra has been a severely and repeatedly abused girl."

*W*hile these insights into Cassandra's perplexing behavior were a diagnostic breakthrough, they were,
sadly, a breakthrough only in terms of our perceptions
of her, but not in terms of what she was doing. I'd
hoped that she and I had at last started to form a positive relationship, that our quiet conversation and my
deeper comprehension of what was going on would
provide the much-needed connection and we could start
to move forward. Not so. Cassandra remained as challenging and hard to like as before.

As seemed to be the norm these days, she was in lockdown when I came to get her for our session together.
Once again it was over Selma. Selma's vulnerability
made her a magnet for Cassandra, who, on the one
hand, seemed genuinely to like the younger girl, and on
the other hand, seemed completely unable to stop from
bullying her. This wasn't helped any by the fact Selma
wasn't very bright, and, as a consequence, was hope-

lessly gullible, taking everything said to her as literal truth. This gullibility itself simply fascinated Cassandra, who then became even more outrageous in her lies, as if to see just how ridiculous she could become before Selma would call her on it.

Even more fascinating to Cassandra, however, were Selma's hallucinations. I was quite certain Cassandra was identifying with all this—identifying not only Selma's hallucinations as the same kind of voices she herself had with Minister Snake or Cowboy Snake, but also identifying Selma's overtly psychotic behavior as evidence that voices in one's head *did* mean one was crazy. Thus, she too was in this category.

In reality, Selma's hallucinations were of a much different nature. They focused almost exclusively on demons, vampires, ghosts, and other supernatural evils. Being around her was like being trapped in the world of *Buffy the Vampire Slayer*. Selma genuinely saw and heard these things. In addition, the voices continually whispered to her about who among the rest of us were demons or vampires in disguise. As a consequence, Selma had to perform countless rituals to keep the world safe from the activities of all of us secretly evil entities. Indeed, Selma seemed unable to say or do anything that did not revolve around the paranormal. This made her a disconcerting partner in any conversation, because she was inclined to inject complete non sequiturs about vampires or witches into even the most mundane exchanges.

Until meeting Cassandra on the ward, Selma had had no particular sexual content to her vampire obsession. Consequently, it was initially easy to tell what images Cassandra had planted, because Selma simply parroted back Cassandra's tales of abusive and sadistic sexual activity verbatim, except she usually inserted "ghost" or "vampire" for a person's name. Things quickly started getting scarier, however. Perceiving that molestation was a really nasty thing, Selma began to incorporate it into her general concept of ghosts and vampires, even though she seemed to have no real idea what the actual words meant beyond "something scary." Thus now, along with vampires jumping out at you, biting you, and making you undead, they might anally penetrate you or "suck you off" as well. Selma began to say these things earnestly to anyone at any time and in any conversation.

Understandably, Selma's parents were not at all amused by this new development. They felt it was solely our fault Selma had been exposed to this kind of thing. They were also as terrified as the staff that someone who didn't know what was going on would take Selma's comments seriously, feeling there couldn't be smoke without fire, and accuse an innocent adult of sexual abuse.

So the unit was in an uproar. Cassandra was strictly forbidden from interacting with Selma, and efforts were made to keep the two as much apart as possible, so that Cassandra couldn't break this rule. This wasn't easy. The unit wasn't enormous and to enforce this separation, Cassandra's movements had to be very controlled. Because of her endless accusations of sexual assault, we remained on a "paired supervision" order with her, meaning that every interaction required the attention of two adults.

All these restrictions made it virtually impossible to have any kind of normal dealings with Cassandra on the unit. Everything was necessarily defensive. We were containing her more than treating her, and it was difficult to know how else to go about it. It also greatly impeded my efforts to treat her psychological problems. While I now had a conceptual framework—that she was showing signs of early multiple personality disorder—it was still next to impossible to have any kind of continuation between sessions, as each day when I came for her, there was a new crisis to be confronted and resolved, and that took up most, if not all, of our time.

So there we were yet again that morning. Cassandra was back in lockdown, having been caught in Selma's room, and, indeed, having been caught actively bullying Selma.

I paused a minute outside the seclusion room. The door had a small window, and I looked through. Cassandra was sitting cross-legged on the floor with her back to the door. I opened the door and went in.

She didn't turn around.

"It would be more helpful if, when it was time for our session, you were on the ward and not in lockdown."

She sat gloomily and didn't answer.

"I don't like losing our time together, but it isn't really right that every time the staff puts you in lockdown, I then come and take you out."

"It's not my fault," she muttered. "I didn't do anything. I can't even *breathe* around here. I hate it."

"Well, come on."

She got up sullenly and we left.

As with the previous session, however, by the time I closed the door to the therapy room Cassandra had recovered her spirits. "I want to do that feelings thing," she said as cheerily as if nothing had happened out on the unit. "You know that one where we're giving names to the feelings. Do you got that here? Where is it?"

"You seem much happier when you come in here," I said. "On the unit, you always seem very angry. Once we are in here, it looks to me as if you have forgotten all about it."

"Well, yeah. Wouldn't you?" she asked in a condescending voice and went to the shelves to rummage around for the feelings drawings. "It sucks in seclusion. Of course, I'm glad to be out of it."

"I find when I am very angry or upset, I can't make those feelings go away just by walking into another room."

"I can."

"How?" I asked.

She shrugged. "I don't know. I just do."

"What kind of thoughts do you have when you are in the seclusion room?"

She shrugged again. Her back was to me, as she was still poking around in the papers on the shelves, and her shrug was casual and dismissive.

"What kind of thoughts were you having just then?" I asked again.

"I dunno."

"Cassandra, turn around. Come here and sit down."

"I want to do the feelings thing. I can't find it."

"I want to do that, too," I said. "And we will. But first I want you to do this. Turn around, please, and sit down."

"I want to do the feelings thing."

"Okay, that's fine. I've got it here in my box. But sit down first, please."

Immediately she turned around and reached for my box. I put my arm over it. "Sit down, please."

There was a long moment's hesitation, and then she slumped into the chair opposite me in a rather surly manner.

I opened the box and took out the list of feelings she had named and illustrated. As I laid it on the table, I kept my hand on it, as it was clear she intended to run the show herself.

"Okay, I'm going to demonstrate how we actually play this," I said.

"I don't want to play anything. I want to draw. I want to put names on the rest of the feelings. That's what we're supposed to do. That's good psychology, huh?"

Which very nearly made me laugh. Or it would have, had she then not grabbed for the papers and said in an irritated voice, "So give me it."

"No."

"I want to draw."

"No, that's not what we're doing today. We're doing something different. We're using the list today as a list, not as an art project. Remember the poker chips? Here." I spilled a pile of red ones out.

"I *want* to draw."

Why, WHY could we not just do things? I was so tired of fighting her every inch of the way. "Okay, here are the lists of feelings," I said. There were three sheets of paper, each divided into five columns and twelve of the columns contained a feeling word—*anger, love, disgust,* and so on—most of which she had already illustrated and renamed as "baby feeling," "dog puke feeling," and so forth. I laid them out side by side and then pressed my right arm across the top of them so she couldn't move them. "Okay, I'll take my turn first and show you how this is played," I said. "My cousin is coming to visit me. I haven't seen him in a long, long time. In fact, not since he was twelve and I was eleven.

"Now, here is how this game works. I'm going to put poker chips under the different columns that show how I feel about my cousin coming to visit. For instance, I feel happy he's coming, because even though it was a long time ago, he and I had a lot of fun together when I last saw him and I like my cousin. So I'm going to put some poker chips on 'Happy.' Maybe about five. But *also,* I feel worried, because it's been such a long time since we met. Maybe he's changed and I won't like him now. But I'm not *too* worried, so I'm only going to put three poker chips on 'Worried.' "

"What about 'excited'?" Cassandra said. "I bet you feel excited, too, that he's coming, because maybe you'll do something exciting together."

Pleased to see Cassandra clearly understood the exercise and was starting to join in what we were doing, I readily agreed and reached to put chips on "Excited."

"Yeah, 'cause maybe he's going to fuck you," she added and then laughed.

I ignored the comment. "Okay, so now it's your turn. Use this system to show me how you felt just now in seclusion."

Cassandra surveyed the list. "I don't see 'Hate' here."

"No, I don't either. Here." I quickly wrote "Hate" at the head of one of the empty columns.

"Okay, so where are the other chips?" she asked. "Because they're worth more, huh?"

Obviously she did have the concept of this. Indeed, to the point that I wondered if someone else had attempted to use a variation of this exercise with her. I grabbed the bag of blue chips and put them down.

"What about the white chips?" she asked.

"The white chips are worth less, not more."

"Yeah, well, I need them, too."

Yet again I could see this starting to turn into an exercise in control and manipulation. I grabbed the bag of white chips and flung it on the table, my exasperation perhaps not as well disguised as it should have been. "So. There are all the chips. Here are all the feelings. Show me how you were feeling in lockdown just now."

She picked up a handful of blue chips, the ones worth the most, and began stacking them on "Hate."

"A lot of hate," I said.

"Yeah. A lot of hate."

"Anything else?"

"Nope," she said, shaking her head. "That's all."

"Because quite often we actually have lots of feelings at once. One particular feeling might be the most powerful. It might *seem* like the only feeling we have, but quite often there are others, too."

"Nope. Hate. I hate this place. I hate everybody here. I hate 'em so much I want to fuck them up the backside. I want to fuck this whole hospital."

"Okay," I said. "That's clear."

Cassandra reached over and picked up more blue chips, which she added to the pile already on "Hate." The stack was about two inches high by this point.

"Yes, I can see you felt very hateful when you were in lockdown," I said.

"If I had a million of these, it still wouldn't be enough," she replied.

"Yes, I can see that."

My new concern was that she was going to attempt control of the exercise this way now, by stacking the blue chips on the paper, by insisting on stacking *all* the blue chips on the paper. Control, control, control. Whatever we did, a battle for control was always at the center.

"Okay, so *you* felt nothing but hate," I said. "But let's do it again. Let's ask this time: what about Minister Snake? How did Minister Snake feel in lockdown?"

Her eyes narrowed and she looked at me.

"Yesterday you said Minister Snake was talking to you in lockdown. Could you feel Minister Snake when you were in the seclusion room today? Was Minister Snake there, too?"

She hesitated. Her eyes were still narrowed, still gazing at me in what felt like an assessing manner. Assessing what? I wondered. If I understood what was happening to her when she talked about Minister Snake and the others? If I was accepting of their perspective, too? Or was she simply assessing if this was an effective new manipulative technique and she could attack me anew? I had no way of knowing.

"Can you do the same thing for Minister Snake?" I asked. "Put the chips on the feelings Minister Snake was feeling then?"

Very slowly, she nodded. Then she said, "But there's another feeling that's not there. This list isn't very complete."

"That's okay. We can add them as we go along. It's hard to think of them all at once. So which other one is missing."

"Feeling ashamed. Because Minister Snake was feeling ashamed of what I was doing. And mad. And . . ."

There was the sense she was going to add something, but she didn't.

I leaned over and wrote "Ashamed" on one of the papers. Unlike when I'd hastily written "Hate," there wasn't the sense now that she might snatch the paper away and divert the activity by trying to draw pictures or give additional names to the feelings. I was intrigued how, whenever we started to engage these other "friends," these other components of her personality, Cassandra immediately settled down. She ceased her incredibly annoying efforts to control everything and responded much more earnestly to what we were doing.

"So, which chips?" I said. "Which ones for Minister Snake."

She put a blue chip on "Ashamed" and a red chip on "Mad." Then, picking up a white chip, for a long moment she studied the list. Finally she put it down under "Hate." She took up a second white chip and added it to the "Hate" column, below the stack of blue chips. She put a third white chip under "Hate." "That's 'cause he hates me," she said quietly. "He hates me when I act like that."

"What about Cowboy Snake? Can you show me how Cowboy Snake felt in seclusion?"

Cassandra started to sweep away the chips already on the paper, but I put a hand up. "You can leave them there. We can put everybody's feelings on at the same time."

"No, I want to start over."

"All right."

She took up three blue chips and put them under "Worried." Another blue chip went on "Sad." Another one on "Lonely." Two went down under "Scared."

"He has quite a lot of feelings," I said. "And I notice he's got all blue chips. So he feels them quite strongly, doesn't he?"

She nodded. "He's emotional," she replied. This was an intriguing comment to me, not only because it was a oddly mature statement for a nine-year-old, but also because it showed unexpected awareness.

"And what about Fairy Snake?" I asked. "How did she feel in lockdown."

"She wasn't there. She's too little."

"I see."

" 'Cause she'd be scared. That would be her feeling. She'd be really scared, if she had to be in lockdown, because she wouldn't understand what was going on. She's just little. And I take care of her. I don't let anything bad happen to her. So she wasn't there."

I nodded. "Anyone else?" I asked quietly. "Besides you. And Minister Snake and Cowboy Snake and Fairy Snake?"

"There's the Sister Snakes. They're twins. They're thirteen, but they weren't there. They're named Becky and Bicky. But lots of times they're not around. They have to be at school so they graduate."

"I see. So, anyone else?"

"No," she said softly. "That's all of us."

A conference on Drake's progress was held on Monday afternoon. Both his mother and his grandfather attended. Yet again, however, Drake's father was absent. Thus far, none of us had met the man.

This was my first meeting with Lucia and Mason Sloane since that afternoon at the preschool in Quentin. I was dreading it simply because I had made absolutely no progress with Drake and I knew full well Mason Sloane would not be happy about this. For all the worry I'd had about being too hard on Drake, about being too goal oriented in my work with him, Mason Sloane would definitely think I hadn't been goal oriented enough and, truth was, I felt a little afraid of him. This was exacerbated by the fact that I myself had expected to be much more successful with Drake, so even without Sloane's pressure, I already felt like I was letting the side down.

The major difference between this meeting and the

one in Quentin, however, was that I wasn't going to have to go it alone. Indeed, Harry decided to chair the meeting himself, even though I was the one responsible for Drake's therapy. Reckoning that the aggressive behavior was, in part, simply a power play, Harry hoped Sloane would be more cooperative in dealing with someone he perceived of higher rank.

Harry explained all the things we had done with Drake, including assessment tests, an IQ test, and various medical examinations, in addition to my therapy sessions. He said Drake showed every indication of being an intelligent, adaptable, well-balanced child. The only exception was speech.

"This is the big mystery," Harry said. He laid the Mayo Clinic report the Sloanes had sent us on top of the other papers and sat back in his chair. "I want to be able to tell you we have made good progress in treating Drake," he said. "This is really such an extraordinary case. To have such an intractable problem at such a young age, juxtaposed against an otherwise emotionally stable and well-adjusted child . . . I very much want to be able to give you a diagnosis and, even more importantly, a solution to this, but the truth is, at this stage . . ."

Harry lifted the Mayo report up again. "I do have enormous respect for this clinic. They are very good, arguably among the best, if not *the* best in the nation, so I also respect the fact you sought out this level of help for Drake. And I acknowledge that their findings here seem very thorough indeed. But . . . and this is a very big 'but,' what they say here does not add up with what we are seeing. This boy simply is *not* responding in line with these findings. So, before we go any further, I would like to put our own resources, including those of the medical hospital, to work on this case to help find a solution. This will mean replicating some of the Mayo investigations where necessary."

Mason Sloane's reaction was swift and fierce. "All you doctors are the same!" he complained. "Making money. That's all you want to do. Test after test after test, repeating yourselves over and over again! Repeating everything every other doctor's done. Telling us how important it is to do them and then *you never get anywhere*! You never help my grandson!"

And he didn't stop there.

Mason Sloane launched into a red-faced tirade about how he had *told* us there was nothing psychologically wrong with Drake. He *knew* that. Did we think the Sloanes could have accomplished what they had—come west with the pioneers, cross the prairies in covered wagons, established the strongest group of banks in that part of the country, established *Quentin* itself, for God's sake, because Quentin would never have grown into the important regional city it had without the strong blood of the Sloanes? How could we imply their blood was mentally *unsound*? No grandson of his was *mental,* for Christ's sake. He had been class valedictorian. His son had been class valedictorian. Indeed, his son had gone to Harvard business school and graduated in the top of his class. Did we think his son's son was capable of any less?

Harry gave me a little glance as all this was going on. It was just tiny, momentary eye contact. It said volumes.

Being shouted at wasn't enough to deter Harry. Calm and unperturbed, he pointed out in a slow, calm voice, as if speaking to a particularly backward child, that he was casting no aspersion on the mental health of the Sloanes. What he was concerned about were underlying *physical* causes. In an effort to make his point clearer, Harry mentioned that during the previous week I had used American Sign Language with Drake and Drake had responded with remarkable aptitude, both in learning the signs and in using them appropriately to communicate. Harry went on to explain how psychologically based mutism usually inhibited all forms of communication. In contrast, Drake seemed eager to communicate but unable to, and this pointed to physical causation. Consequently, it was crucial we rule out such things as neurologically based expressive disorders; and yes, while it would be most unusual for the Mayo investigation to have missed something like this, it would be far worse to carry on treating Drake for the wrong problem.

One of the advantages of being able to listen to a case presentation of one of my clients, rather than having to give it myself, was that it allowed me a small amount of distance from the case, such that I could examine the situation more objectively. Consequently, what occurred to me as Harry spoke was phobia. Genuine phobia, in its true psychological sense, as opposed to using the word as a casual behavioral description. Could Drake be actually phobic of the sound of his own voice? The sensation of vocalizing? Of saying words? I was well familiar with the connection between trauma, either physical mouth trauma or overwhelming psychological trauma, and elective mutism. Indeed, we commonly referred to types of elective mutism as a "phobic reaction to speech." But could it be a real, *true* phobia that made the physical act of speaking so terrifying Drake couldn't contemplate it but, as long as vocalization wasn't involved, he felt calm enough to communicate in other ways? I had never encountered anything this extreme in my work with other elective mutes, but it seemed possible. I was also aware phobias could form around the most unusual things, and for the individual, they could be absolutely paralyzing.

So my mind took off running with these thoughts to the point that for that moment, I tuned out of the actual conference. I was thinking now in terms of desensitization and other common approaches to treatment of phobias. If this was the issue, how could I go about desensitizing Drake to the sound of his voice? Which, of course, immediately made me think of the tape he had made with his mother.

Hmmm, I was thinking. He had spoken with her. If he was so phobic as to refuse even the smallest sound with the rest of us, why would it be okay to speak at home? That didn't make sense with what I knew of phobias otherwise. With true phobias, no matter how supportive the environment or the people, you can't switch them on and off.

I glanced over at Lucia as I was considering these matters and experienced a small, unexpectedly lucid moment. All of a sudden, I *saw* her, sitting beside Mason Sloane. Sitting in the *shadow* of Mason Sloane in quite a literal sense there in the conference room. Arms wrapped around herself, she was slightly back from the table. The way she was seated gave the impression she was physically behind Mr. Sloane, although she couldn't have been. I looked with more precision and, really, she couldn't have been seated more than twelve or fifteen inches back from the table edge.

Nonetheless, one got this sense of her being physically behind him because he was leaning forward over the table, making his point, whereas she was drawn in upon herself and inclined slightly toward him. I was struck by the fact that she was a genuinely beautiful woman. Her dark hair was shoulder length and cut stylishly. Her eyes were huge and dark. Soulful, doelike eyes, to use the cliché, was an accurate description in this instance because there was also that underlying wariness one always detects in the eyes of wild animals, even when they are at ease.

I was quite certain Lucia was anorexic. She was past being simply thin. Her skin was waxy looking in the fluorescent light, and she had about her that gaunt brittleness one sees in those photographs of prisoners of war crowded around the fence of some nameless camp. Caught off guard, unaware I was watching her, she also had that same kind of vacant desolation on her face as war prisoners had.

I was then jerked from my thoughts because Mason Sloane went nuclear.

"*Sign* language!" he shrieked in a horrified tone that would have made one think Harry had said we were using cocaine or leg irons on Drake with great results. "I will *refuse* permission for that boy to learn sign language. He is *not* deaf. I will not have you make a damned fool of him, learning *miming*. He did *not* come here to be taught how to act like a defective!"

And I thought, *Well, here's the explanation for Drake's fearfulness in using sign language*. I could just imagine Drake coming home from preschool and showing off a few signs, only to have his grandfather explode at seeing his grandson do what "defective" people did.

Sloane's loathing of sign language was only the buildup, however, because what he really wanted to shout about was Harry's implication that Drake was brain damaged. Because that's what "neurologically based expressive disorder" meant, wasn't it? And Mason Sloane wasn't about to tolerate that kind of insult to the revered family name.

There followed a moment of very unpleasant confrontation between the two men, because Harry, mild-mannered as he was, was not a pushover. He pointed out that Drake had been sent to us for evaluation and intervention and in the process of that, it was our task as professionals to do whatever seemed best for Drake. This included evaluating his ability to communicate physiologically as well as psychologically, if that's where the questions were. We'd be negligent otherwise, Harry explained. If a neurological disorder *did* exist, all the psychological intervention in the world was not going to make a difference.

This, of course, was definitely not the kind of directness Mason Sloane expected from, as he called us, "people he hired." So he did what I'd been braced for all along.

Slam! Bang! He knocked all the papers across the table. Standing up, he banged his chair rudely, demanded Lucia follow him, and stormed out.

Harry, I, and the unit staff remained seated at the table. We exchanged exasperated glances.

Then Nancy Anderson shook her head and gave a mirthless little chuckle. "Mom must have been messing around. No kid nice as Drake could be carrying that jerk's genes."

* * *

Worse had happened, however. Our meeting had been held in the conference room, which was up in "Heaven," the same area of the hospital as where the psychiatrists' offices were, on the floor above the unit. When Nancy and I returned to the unit afterward, we found everyone there in an uproar. Mason Sloane had come raging straight down from the conference, stating he was not having his grandson stay a moment longer and insisting that Drake be released to them immediately. Because Drake was a voluntary admission and Lucia was there, Mason Sloane was within his rights to demand this. By the time Nancy and I had arrived, Drake was already gone.

I couldn't believe this. Standing in the middle of the empty dayroom, I groaned in pained frustration. How *could* he? How *could* this happen? There had to be some way we could stop him, that we could demand he continue treatment for Drake. This would be terrible for the boy, locked in his silence, trapped with a man who would not sanction sign language, who would not tolerate imperfection of any kind.

The rest of the staff were as distressed and disappointed as I was, and several of us gathered in the nurses' station, venting our anger, searching desperately for solutions. Slowly, our talk tailed off into sadness. The plain truth was, children belong to their parents. While we might strongly disagree with the Sloanes' decisions regarding treatment for Drake, all we could really do was record that in his case record. We had no rights to see things changed. Drake didn't talk. He was otherwise, however, a well-adjusted child. We'd have a hard case proving he was better off here in an institutional setting, that we were providing him with crucial services that he couldn't receive elsewhere. Indeed, only a short time before I'd been on the other side of this fence, fighting to keep him out of the unit, telling everyone that he did not need such major intervention and was better off at home.

Shit.

My mood was not greatly improved by the time I reached my office. Helen wasn't in that day, so I was alone. Closing the door behind me, I flung my stuff on the desk and flopped into the chair. Staring at the miscellany of things on my bulletin board, I let my mind run.

I *wasn't* ready to stop with Drake. The issue wasn't so much that I had failed in my intervention; it was that I'd failed even to understand what I was intervening with. *Something* was wrong with him. Here was an intelligent, outgoing child, who, according to all the reports, was normal, was physically healthy, was generally well adjusted and *he didn't talk*. That was *not* normal. People didn't do that for no reason at all.

And he *did* talk at home with his mother. So, however well adjusted he may have appeared in Harry's observations and Harry's tests, Drake was doing something that was really very maladaptive. He spoke there. He never spoke here. He never spoke at school. He never even spoke to his father. But he spoke to his mother. Poor cowering, defeated Lucia. He spoke to her. Was this because she was the only one he felt safe with? Were she and he a little island in what was really a very dysfunctional, abusive family and this was the source of his mutism? Knowing Mason Sloane and observing Lucia, it was not difficult to imagine this possibility.

These were not new thoughts. The whole abuse/dysfunctional family issue had occurred to me over and over, because that was a pattern I *was* familiar with, and it really was the only pattern that vaguely seemed to fit in all of this. But because Drake didn't talk, there had been no way to investigate this at all. I had absolutely no proof.

Gloomily, I sat at my desk, knowing Drake was gone, knowing Drake had been returned to whatever was happening behind closed doors, and all this without our ever having established even the smallest thing that might at some point in the future throw him a lifeline.

I lost that little boy," I said. "The little one who was with me the other day."

Gerda's brow wrinkled.

"There is a lot of pressure in his family to be absolutely perfect. He doesn't talk, and they wanted me to flick some kind of switch to make him start and that would be the end of it. They got very upset when we suggested there might be more to it and stormed off with him." I looked over at her and sighed. "I'm really sad about it."

Gerda reached out and patted the air, as if patting an invisible child's head. She made an exaggerated frown.

I nodded. "Yeah. It's awful. Something *is* wrong and no one is listening. No one is asking why he has this problem."

I paused and reconsidered. "Not that I mean that in a nasty way. I don't want to imply they're neglecting his problems, because they've actually gone to quite a lot of trouble for him. Just that they've got their own agenda. Their emphasis is only on how the world sees them; that's what's important. How respectable he is, so that they will present a perfect face to the world. No one seems to be looking from the perspective of why this has happened, how it will impact his life, and what we can do to enable him to deal with it meaningfully."

"I wanted blades for Christmas," she said softly.

I looked over at her.

She was staring at the wall. "For my skates. Left blade was chinked. Fourteen that year. Louisa and I went skating every night. Done our chores. Went in the half-light. Went in the twilight. In the darkness because darkness came so early that time of year. So cold. Creek froze hard. Like a ribbon through the hills. And I put my skates on and I was a bird. So free. Gliding so fast over the ice. Down the creek. Through the hills. Fast as a swallow.

"But my blade had a chink. Left blade. Stopped me going fast. I said, 'I want blades for Christmas.'"

She paused. "Blades aren't expensive," she said softly, quietly in what was almost a meditative tone. "Karl could do a sharp pair for me at the mill. I wanted it *so* much. Couldn't go fast with a chink in the blade or I'd fall. And fourteen that year. Going fast mattered."

Gerda turned her head and met my eyes, held my gaze a moment, and then looked away again.

"Come Christmas and I seen that long narrow package just for me. *Knew* it was blades. Seen it under the tree and I felt so happy. Felt happy for days.

"Then Christmas comes and I open it . . ."

She sighed. A pause intruded. She sighed a second time.

"Perfume. In a fancy bottle. Fancy glass bottle so narrow and this high." She measured with her hands. "With a long pointed glass stopper. Not blades at all. Perfume in a fancy bottle.

"Mama looks right at me. Says, 'You thought it was blades, didn't you?' She *said* that. Then got so angry with me because I wasn't grateful. I spoiled Christmas for everyone. Ruined everyone's happiness, because there was a big fight. Because I cried when I should have been grateful. What's wrong with you, they say. Perfume in a fancy bottle came from the city. It's special. A gift any girl your age would want. And Mama and Papa went to so much trouble to get it."

Gerda paused again

"But why did they get me perfume?" she said, her voice still querying after all these years. "I asked my sister Louisa. Said, if Mama knew I want blades so much, she could see the look in my eye, why'd she get me perfume? Perfume's so much more expensive. Why did they spend so much money on something I never wanted? Why do that, if they knew all along what I did want? Why not give me blades?

"Louisa said I shouldn't have spoiled everyone's Christmas. Mama and Papa made a special effort, getting that. Should be grateful. It's what normal girls want."

One of the most challenging aspects of working with highly manipulative individuals such as Cassandra is the way they make the rest of us feel about ourselves when with them. Most people who go into psychology, psychiatry, and the other helping professions do so at least in part with hopes of alleviating some suffering in the world, of helping those less fortunate find a better life. When the person being helped does not get better, does not respond to efforts of help, it tends to bring up understandably unhappy feelings in the helper, be the helper a therapist, teacher, medical doctor, aid worker, drug counselor, or whomever. You often start to feel a kind of dread about working with the individual, a sort of hopeless, helpless frustration that makes it hard to like the individual and want to be in the situation, but at the same time it also generates an intense worry that if you don't continue, things might get worse. It is easy to envision horrible and realistic scenarios, such as institutionalization, jail, or suicide, happening if you fail, and equally easy to feel if the failure happens, it's your fault.

The manipulative person often feeds into these complex feelings in the helper in a way that creates a feeling of specialness. From what the person does and says, you begin to feel that *only* you can save this person. You are the one there on the front line with the clearest view of how bad things are, and you alone are all that stands between the individual and serious consequences. This specialness can feel almost like a sense of mission sometimes, and it makes it easy to believe that by trying harder you will succeed. And what "trying harder" usually means is crossing boundaries that have previously been in place—boundaries of time, touch, or situational structure, for instance—and if you do these things, this will prove to the person your commitment to help, will show him or her that you want to *be* there in such a meaningful way that this will make all the difference.

You believe that if you only do this one more thing, you will finally connect with the person and he or she will start to get better.

This is actually a normal caring response. It isn't unhealthy in itself, and in relationships with other normal and healthy individuals, these "caring" responses of feeling worried or guilty for not helping, of being willing to go the extra mile, actually *do* make a difference. The person in need responds to them by getting better. And *that's* the important distinction.

The highly manipulative individual has a different reaction. Instead of improving, he or she uses these responses to perpetuate a destructive behavioral cycle and, in fact, actually manipulates people to provoke such reactions from them to feed this cycle. Consequently, the normal caring response has the opposite effect on these mentally ill individuals and actually perpetuates the problem rather than stopping it.

In most instances, this manipulation is not a conscious effort on the part of the mentally ill person. They do not set out purposefully to control other people in this manner. In most instances, they are genuinely trapped in a cycle of re-creating past troubled relationships and are unaware of using their manipulative behavior to make people in their current life feel and respond to them in the same way they experienced in this past relationship.

Because of the tendency for this kind of manipulative behavior to bring up such difficult feelings in the person who is trying to help, a phenomenon that is called "countertransference" in psychiatric terminology, one has to be very aware when working with manipulative individuals, not only of what he or she is doing but also what it is doing inside oneself. This is the only way to avoid getting sucked into these responses and eventually the only way to help the individual recognize what is happening so that the destructive cycle can be broken.

With children, of course, it isn't quite so straightforward. Developmentally, they are still very egocentric, which means they cannot think as objectively about themselves as people in later adolescence and adulthood can. Moreover, in Cassandra's case, the issue of multiple personalities complicated things further. While on the ward or at the start of therapy sessions, she was often very manipulative and controlling, there were other moments when she seemed quite earnest. Were we connecting with a nascent alternate that did not manipulate? Or was it possible the whole multiple personality thing itself was a manipulation? This was unlikely, given Cassandra's age, and would indicate a scary level of pathology; nonetheless, the possibility couldn't be ruled out altogether. So I needed to keep an unusually alert and open mind. The personalities might provide a useful way of reaching Cassandra. At the same time, they might be there to control me.

Cassandra was yet again in lockdown when I came for her. I opened the seclusion room door and went in. I sat down on the padded floor beside Cassandra. She didn't look at me.

"You know, every single time I've come for you recently, you've been here in the seclusion room."

"That's because they hate me," she muttered.

"No, I think it's because you're breaking the rules."

She hit her heel hard against the mat and didn't answer.

"There are certain things the other staff and I can't let you do," I said. "We're sorry you have to spend time in lockdown, but when you break the rules, that's the consequence."

"It's not fair!"

"You think it's not fair," I said.

"No. Because I can't help it," she muttered.

"You don't think you can help acting this way?"

"No. I wouldn't be in here otherwise, would I? So don't be stupid." She kicked the mat again. "I might as well be dead."

"You're really feeling angry."

"I hate you. You're no good. You don't help me any."

"It would be easier to help you if you weren't in lockdown, however. Wouldn't it?"

"Dr. Brown used to help me. When I saw her, she didn't make a bunch of rules like you do. She didn't even have a seclusion room. I got *better* when I was with her."

"You wish I were Dr. Brown. And you wish you could do things your way. But sadly, that can't always happen because we can't allow you to hurt yourself or to hurt other people."

"Yeah, but you always want to do it *your* way. *Everything* has to be your way. And that's not fair," Cassandra said.

"I'm older and more experienced. I've been taught a lot of things to make me smart. So when I ask you to do things my way, it's because I know these are ways to help kids get better," I replied.

"Dr. Brown knew better stuff than you," she said disparagingly.

"Cassandra, I know you liked Dr. Brown—"

"I *didn't* like Dr. Brown. I *had* to go to her. But *she* knew what she was doing."

"Okay. What I'm saying is, it's not helpful to keep bringing Dr. Brown into the conversation. She isn't here. So I'm going to stop talking about her. And when you discuss Dr. Brown from now on, I'm not going to participate."

"I *wish* she was here."

I stood up.

Cassandra swiveled her head and looked up at me.

"So I'm going to go now," I said.

"Huh?"

I started for the door of the seclusion room.

Cassandra leaped to her feet. "Hey, wait. This is my time with you."

"Yes, I know it is. But sadly, you're in lockdown."

"Yeah, but you're supposed to work with me now. This is the time I always go with you," Cassandra cried.

"Yes, I know. But you aren't ready today."

"I'm ready. I didn't say I wasn't ready, did I? Why are you always such a bitch?"

"You aren't ready, because you're in lockdown. And why are you in lockdown?"

Cassandra shrugged. "I don't know."

I looked pointedly at her.

"I don't remember."

"Okay, in that case, I'll help you remember," I said. "One reason is because you were in Selma's bedroom again. A second reason is because you did not come out when a staff member asked you to, even though you know that is not a place you are allowed. A third reason is because you punched and fought with Larry when he tried to remove you. A fourth reason is because you were screaming about Larry touching you sexually when that wasn't happening. Those are the reasons why you are here. Now, when people are put into the seclusion room, they are meant to stay in here until their time is up and they feel more in control of themselves."

"I feel in control," Cassandra said.

"Yes, you say that, but events show differently. Every day for the last four times, you've been in lockdown when it is time for your session with me. Each day I've let you come with me, but then the next morning you are back in lockdown again. That means the same things are happening over and over, instead of your getting more in control of them. When I see you doing the same thing over and over, I get concerned that I'm not helping you by taking you out of here to go for our sessions. So, from today, if you want to come to your sessions with me, you need to be on the ward, not in lockdown. If you're in here, you will stay until it is time for you to come out; and if you miss our session, I will be sorry about that but that is just how it is."

"No fair!" she cried, outraged. Indeed, her face went all red with the intensity of her feelings. "No *fair*! You're just making up rules as you go along! Just to boss me!"

"I'm sorry you feel that way. But my job is to help you get better so that you can go home, and when I see I am doing something that doesn't help, then I change it."

"No *fair*! You hate me! You don't want to help me! You don't *want* me to get well!"

I went out and closed the door behind me.

Cassandra exploded inside the seclusion room.

Shrieking, screaming, howling like an injured animal, she flung herself against the padded walls, against the padded door.

The hardest moment I had thus far had with her was then, when I walked away.

Chapter

25

$\mathcal{L}$osing Drake continued to eat at me. As the hours passed and the next week started, I kept thinking about him, replaying in my mind our therapy sessions, trying to glean from my memory what I had not managed to see in real life.

I could only envision three possible scenarios to explain his mutism. In the first, Drake was as he had appeared to me in observation: an elective mute, who just happened also to be outgoing and otherwise well adjusted. If this was the case, I wasn't too worried about his long-term prognosis. My sense was that he was adaptable and mentally stable. Thus, the mutism would most likely resolve itself as part of the maturational process, whether we burned the house down to roast the pig or not.

In the second scenario, Drake was not speaking because, in fact, he couldn't speak. There was a physical reason for his silence. The audiotape and the Mayo report made it unlikely this was the case, but if so, leaving the problem untreated was going to do nothing but create greater problems in the long term. We were wasting valuable time chasing imaginary problems and not dealing with the real one.

In the third scenario, Drake was a child in real danger. Such severe mutism at such a young age red-flagged a seriously troubled environment. While it was puzzling that he had not given signs of distress in other areas, I had to admit how deft he was at using charm to deflect attention from things he didn't want to deal with. Perhaps he was using the same remarkable control he showed in not speaking to wall off his traumatized feelings. If this was so, then we had really failed him.

Over and over I thought about these different interpretations. All of them were fatally flawed. If he were really all right and this was just a quirky kid thing, why had it not responded to intervention? If it were a physical disability, how could he talk on the tape? Why had nothing shown up in the Mayo exam? If it were the result of trauma, why were there not additional indicators? Why had we not seen his guard slip even the littlest bit during treatment?

The one wild card was Drake's family. Respectable and industrious citizens of Quentin they may have been, but it was not hard to discern dysfunction below the surface. The worst among them, of course, was Mason Sloane. Along with his imperious attitude and his explosive temper, he was a perfectionistic control freak. None of us had had a single chance to speak face-to-face to Drake's parents without his grandfather being present, other than that brief exchange with Lucia I'd had out in

Quentin after Sloane had stormed out. Otherwise, Mason Sloane controlled everything.

I wondered more and more about Lucia's role in all this. Sloane always garnered the attention with his outrageous behavior, but Lucia, in fact, was in a much more influential position with Drake. I had not interacted with her often enough to understand whether marrying into such a difficult family was the source of her problems or whether she was a troubled individual in her own right; however, Lucia oozed anxiety and unhappiness the way an overfull septic tank seeps into the surrounding ground.

And Drake's father? We kept being told Drake had one, that he did, in fact, really exist. None of us, however, had concrete evidence of this. Even the day Drake was brought to the unit, it was by Mason Sloane and Lucia. Even on that occasion, Walter was "working."

Given this group of adults, dysfunction was a rational assumption, but was it enough to conclude serious child abuse? Moreover, assumptions, however logical, are not the same as evidence. This is a very important—and necessary—distinction. It is evidence, not creative deduction, which counts, and this is how it should be. And the flat truth was, we had absolutely no concrete evidence of abuse in Drake's case. Nonetheless, this interpretation of his mutism weighed heavily on my mind, making me so regret losing Drake at this point.

In the end, I couldn't rest comfortably on the case, so I decided to call the Sloanes. This was well within acceptable procedure for the unit. Because we were, in part, a diagnostic unit, this meant long-term care was almost always in the community. Consequently, there was normally extensive follow-up in the period immediately after a child was released in order to continue programs started on the unit. With Drake, this wouldn't be the case, of course, given the manner in which he had been removed from the unit; however, a follow-up call was still within reasonable protocol.

Along with finding out how Drake was doing, I also hoped it would give me a chance to catch Lucia on her own. I timed the call for early afternoon, thinking that not only would Drake probably be taking a nap but most likely so would the old man, wherever he might be.

Lucia answered. She sounded startled when I said who I was. I said how sorry I was that things had ended as they had, and I said I was still concerned about Drake. I explained we usually followed up our work on the unit, so I was phoning to see how he was.

"He's fine," she said and her voice was curiously flat. "He went back to his preschool on Monday. Everyone was so happy to see him. He was glad to be back."

"That's good. And what do you think is going to happen now regarding his mutism?" I asked.

I heard an intake of breath, the sort before one starts to speak, but nothing followed.

"Have you got plans to get further help?"

"Father says there is a program in California," she replied in a mousy little voice.

"By 'Father,' you mean the elder Mr. Sloane?"

There were little noises on the other end of the phone. I could imagine her nodding but she didn't speak.

"So, what program is this? Something especially for treating elective mutism?" The only programs I could think of in California that had gained nationwide attention were for autistic children, so I was dismayed to hear this. I had horrible visions of Mason Sloane, full of unrealistic expectations, trailing Drake around the country from specialist to specialist.

Lucia still hadn't responded. I could hear rustling and bumping on the other end of the phone, as if she were moving around, but she didn't actually say anything.

"Lucia?" I asked.

That's when I realized she was crying.

I hesitated, because I didn't want to embarrass her by calling attention to it, but finally I said, "Is something wrong?"

She wasn't simply wobbly-voiced at this point. She was sobbing and seemed unable to speak.

"Can I help you in some way?" I asked.

"I'm sorry," she managed to choke out.

"No, no, don't be sorry. It's okay. I'm sure this is all very distressing."

"Yes," she wept.

"It's okay. I'm not in any hurry. Take your time."

This seemed to make things worse, rather than better.

"Is there something I can do to help?"

"Noooo." More sobbing.

"Are you sure?"

Nothing but weeping on the other end of the phone.

"Would it help if we got together? Perhaps just you and me? We could go over things. Would that help?"

"It's too far," she sobbed.

"It's a long ways, but it's not too far. I'm happy to come out, if you want. Just you and me. How would that be?"

She made little whimpering noises that I took to be an affirmative.

I pulled over my diary. "I could come out tomorrow. Wednesday afternoon. Would that work?"

"No," in a tiny voice. "It can't be then. It can't be here. He'll be here then." And then more crying. A minute or two passed with her being unable to speak.

"So what date could you make?" I asked.

"Thursday. Thursday afternoon. At Starbucks. On the corner by the mall," she managed to say.

I paused to look at my calendar, my thoughts going frantically to what I could rearrange.

"I have to talk to you," she whimpered, then started to cry again.

"Yes, sure. Of course. That's okay. Thursday will work. Say, 2:30?"

Before I got any kind of confirmation, the phone went dead.

$\mathcal{I}$ returned to the dayroom late in the afternoon to see Cassandra. Given we hadn't had our session that day because I'd left her in the seclusion room, I wanted to thrash a few things out before our next session.

Sprawled over one of the chairs, she was watching TV.

"Hi," I said. "May I talk to you, please?"

"Yeah, sure," she replied cheerfully and leaped up. She was dressed in what looked almost like a dancer's outfit—black leggings, a long-sleeved pink T-shirt with a short-sleeved black T-shirt over it—and it emphasized her lithe, spidery build. For a flashing moment, I thought of a young Audrey Hepburn, what with the graceful movements, those huge dark eyes, and the gamine haircut.

I took us to the far end of the dayroom, which was well away from the TV and the other children. Cassandra scrambled over the back of an orange Naugahyde chair and slid into the seat. "What do you want to talk about?" she asked.

I sat down in the chair next to hers. "I want us to get a few things straight before the next session."

"Like what?" she asked. There was this breezy, bright tone to her voice, as if I were bringing her some totally new information she was keen to hear.

As always happened when I was with Cassandra, my mind raced forward, trying to interpret what was going on, trying to figure her out. Was this casual optimism the dissociation showing itself? Was she acting like a different person now because she literally *was* a different person? Or was this part of her manipulative defense? If she acted as if nothing had happened—"pretended to forget"—did she hope I would, too?

"We're going to start running things a little differently from now on," I said, "because at the moment, the way we're doing it is not getting us very far in our time together."

"You stress a lot over things, don't you?" she said earnestly.

"It'd be helpful, Cassandra, if you just listened to me right now."

"I am listening," she replied, her voice pleasant.

"Here's how it's going to go. If you are in lockdown when it is time for our sessions, you're going to stay in lockdown."

"That won't help me very much. I thought you wanted to make me better," she said.

"This has been our big mistake. It's not about *me* wanting to *make* you better. It's about *you* wanting to *get* better. I can't make you better by myself. More important, that's not my responsibility. It's yours. So if you are in lockdown when I come, I will say to myself, 'Cassandra does not want to work on getting better today,' and I'll go away and do other things."

She regarded me, her demeanor thoughtful but still rather detached. There was about her a palpable self-confidence. She didn't speak.

"And if we get to the therapy room and I say, 'Today we're going to do this,' and you say, 'I won't do that,' or 'I'm going to do something else instead,' or 'I want to do it my way,' or otherwise keep us from doing what we're in there to do, again I will say to myself, 'Cassandra doesn't want to work at getting better today,' and we'll stop work and I'll bring you back to the ward."

"You're saying that wrong," she pointed out. "You should be saying to yourself, 'Cassandra doesn't want to work with *me* at getting better today.' Because maybe I want to work at getting better. I just don't want to do it with you."

"Yes, you're right. That would be another way of saying it. Both of which have the same result. That we aren't working together because you do not want to do the work that day."

"That's okay with me," she said casually. "I'd rather be on the ward than with you. I hate being with you." Her voice remained pleasant.

"Which is your decision. What I'm saying is that rather than my getting all concerned and trying to get you to cooperate when you don't want to, I am going to go with your decision. If you decide to work with me, you can come with me to the therapy room and we will work. If you decide you don't want to work with me, you can sit here in the dayroom for the time you usually spend with me. Or if you are in the seclusion room, you can stay in the seclusion room."

Silence.

We again entered into the territory of aggressive eye contact. In fact, Cassandra leaned forward so as to stare me down even better. "Why are you telling me this?" she asked.

"Because these are the new rules."

She sat back in her seat and flopped her arms out over the metal arms of the chair. She still had her eyes on me. "You hate me, don't you?" she said. She didn't ask it as a question. There was no emotion in her voice. She might have been saying, "You have blue eyes, don't you?"

"No, I don't hate you," I replied. "In fact, I like you. It's just that my job here is to help you and unless you want to work with me, I can't do that."

"Everybody hates me." The same equanimous voice.

"I'm sorry you feel that way," I said.

"It's unfair."

"Life does seem unfair to you, doesn't it?" I said.

She nodded vigorously.

"What are you going to do about it?"

She shrugged in an exaggerated way.

"The truth is, Cassandra, the way things are right now, they're a real mess for you, aren't they?"

She rolled her eyes comically.

"Getting into trouble on the ward, going into lock-down all the time, getting your privileges docked, having problems with me every day, not being able to go home, having to cope with creepy thoughts, trying to get away from them. Things are a mess."

She shrugged.

"You're trying to pretend that's okay," I said. "Right now. You're trying to act as if none of this is serious.

And I can understand that. I'm sure it must feel really, really scary having to deal with your life all the time. These problems are everywhere. They affect everything. They involve everyone. You can't get away from them, even for a minute. So I imagine pretending things aren't serious makes you feel—at least for a moment or two— like they don't hurt so much. I can understand that. I can understand why you keep doing these things."

I seemed to catch Cassandra off guard. For the first time in several minutes, she broke eye contact. She glanced away, glanced up, looked back at me, looked away again. Her brow furrowed. I'd expected her to deny responsibility, to say these things were my fault or the staff's fault for not helping her better, but instead she simply sat, her focus shifting to an unseen place in front of her.

"The real problem you and I are having, however," I said, "is not about things being so scary. I *know* they're scary. I know that makes them serious, and I know deep down you take them seriously. I also know they're so, so hard to deal with. So that's not the problem. The real problem is that you haven't decided whose side you're on.

"The plain truth is, Cassandra, I can't make you better. Your mom can't make you better. Dr. Brown can't make you better. Even taking you away from the bad places, like where you were with your dad, and bringing you back to nice safe places won't make you better. Do you know why that is?" I asked.

Her head was lowered. She didn't respond.

"That's because what's wrong isn't out here where your mom and Dr. Brown and I are. It's in there." I reached over and tapped her chest. "It's there inside you. So wherever you go, your trouble goes with you.

"The problem we're having is this: that troubled place inside you hurts a lot. I *know* that, Cassandra. Some really, really awful things have happened to you. Things children shouldn't have to experience. But you did experience them and they hurt you very much. I do understand this. I also understand that it's natural for us to try and protect something that's gotten badly hurt. I understand that's what you're doing, that you don't really want to be horrible and difficult with everyone. You are just trying to protect that troubled place inside you, because it hurts so much, and you don't want it to get hurt again.

"Unfortunately, there's a really big problem in doing this. And the problem is: you've protected your troubled place so well that you've ended up taking its side. You've ended up saying, 'I'll take care of you, Troubled Place, no matter what. I won't ever let anyone hurt you.' But the difficulty now is that Troubled Place is, in fact, hurting *you,* because it's making you have to do all these bad things to keep it safe.

"We need to change this. In order for us to make things better for you, Cassandra, you need to get on *our* side. On the side that is trying to fix that Troubled Place, so it will heal up and go away and leave you alone.

"We *can* do that. We can beat this. But we can only do it if all of us together are on the same side, because it's too big for one person alone to beat, whether that one person is you or your mom or me or Dr. Brown. We have to learn to fight together like a team, because that's the only way we'll be strong enough to make what happened to you stop hurting you."

Head still down, Cassandra's mouth crumpled. Tears trickled out of the corners of her eyes.

I reached a hand over and laid it on her shoulder.

She leaned forward, way forward, until her forehead rested on her knees. She sobbed.

It was the first time I'd really seen her cry and once she began, Cassandra continued to weep heavily.

It was late afternoon, about four-thirty or quarter of five. Thick cloud cover made it even darker outside than it usually was at this time of year. Everywhere else in the hospital was lit by bright fluorescent lighting, but the dayroom had quirky lighting, mostly small ordinary tungsten bulbs on tracks overhead, in order that the area over by the television could be dimmed without throwing everyone else in the big room into darkness. And it *was* a large room, more like a hall than a living space. Consequently, the kids watching TV were distant from Cassandra and me, as was the nurses' station. The lateness in the day, the weather outside, and the TV brought a nighttime feel to most of the room. The lights were on over the nurses' station and were glaringly bright where we sat, but everything else was in shadows.

For some reason this made a strong impression on me, as did the furniture where we were sitting, a group of chairs with steel armrests and hard-wearing, washable, waterproof Naugahyde seats and backs—institutional furniture—which, perhaps in some misguided effort to make them seem less institutional, were in colors no one could really live with—either bright orange or, alternately, an equally strong turquoise. As Cassandra cried, I sat quietly, not thinking, not doing anything really other than just being, and the lighting and the furniture imprinted itself on me.

* * *

I got up at one point and found a box of tissues at the nurses' station, which I brought over, but otherwise I just sat. I kept my hand on Cassandra's back, rubbing her shoulders occasionally, but mostly just resting it there. We were discouraged from touching the children beyond a hand on the shoulder, both for our own safety in this litigious day and age, and also because most of the children had issues of one sort or another with touch. In the case of a child like Cassandra, it was an absolute necessity to observe these strict boundaries because of her lies. Nonetheless, I still felt it was crucial to touch her now, to cross that gulf of physical space that isolates each of us from the other, and respond with sympathetic, caring, and appropriate touch.

She cried and cried. There were maybe ten minutes or more of really heavy sobbing, her body doubled forward in the chair, her face pressed into her hands, resting against her upper legs. She was consumed by it and isolated by it, showing no awareness that I or anyone else was in the room. Then the physical burden of so much crying began to catch up with her. Her sinuses grew too clogged to remain in that position. Her breath was catching, so she had to sit up to get air.

I pulled out tissues and handed them to Cassandra. She took them, a whole wodge of them, and pressed them against her face. This renewed her crying.

Time passed. I didn't speak. Cassandra continued to cry. Like small snowdrifts, used tissues piled up on her lap and in and around the chair. More time passed.

The other children rose from their places near the TV and left the room to go for dinner. One of the staff came out of the nurses' station and approached us but stopped perhaps ten feet away. He watched us a moment, assessing whether or not Cassandra would be coming for a meal at some point; however, he didn't say anything. Neither did I. We just exchanged looks. I shook my head slightly. Finally, he turned and left. Cassandra and I were alone in the huge shadowy room.

Finally the tears gave way to exhausted hiccupping. She lay slouched over to the right in her chair, her head almost resting on the steel arm. Her face was swollen and red; she could only breathe through her mouth.

"I'm so tired," she murmured at last.

"I'm sure you are."

"I hate to cry."

I nodded.

Then silence. Cassandra continued to lie crumpled to the side of the chair, still dabbing at her inflamed cheeks and drippy nose.

The usual noises native to hospital environments ebbed in around us, most of them metallic sounds: grindings, gratings, clangs, bangs, bumps, buzzes, made vague by walls and corridors, but there were also human voices, always remote, always blended, forming simply a human noise.

Cassandra looked at me. It was a quiet, searching expression, and when I made eye contact with her, she held it only a moment and then looked away.

"Can I tell you about something?" she said at last.

"Yes, of course," I said.

"When I was little," she said, "Uncle Beck used to come in the room where I was sleeping."

I nodded.

"That's when I lived at my dad's. Uncle Beck used to babysit me all the time. I don't know where my daddy went. My daddy wasn't there very much, but Uncle Beck was there all the time."

I sat back in my chair.

"When I was in bed, he would come in and get under the covers with me. He'd feel me up. He'd put his hands all over me."

"I wouldn't like that," I said, "if someone did that to me."

"I couldn't do anything about it. If I tried to tell him to go away, he put his hands over my mouth. One over my mouth and one around my neck. He said, 'I could break your neck like a matchstick, you little bitch.' I think he could, too."

I nodded slightly.

"He couldn't put his prick in my cunt, because he had to hold me that way, with a hand over my mouth and a hand around my neck. So he put his prick in my butthole."

She paused. She wasn't looking at me. Her head was actually turned away from me, her gaze downward toward the floor.

"That hurts so much," she said very softly. "It hurt so much. I wanted to cry and cry and cry."

I nodded.

"I couldn't. He hated me to tell him I didn't like it, say not to do it. He got really mad when I did. He said, 'You little bitch, you want it. You know you do. You keep asking for it. So don't talk shit now.' But he hated it more if I cried. It made him really, really mad at me. Sometimes he'd put a piece of newspaper on the floor and shit on it. Then he'd take the turd and put it in my mouth. He said because I talked shit, there *was* shit and that would shut me up." A pause. "Now when I cry, my mouth always tastes like shit."

Silence.

Cassandra was leaning over the right arm of the chair, her head against her hand, the other hand bracing her elbow. She just sat, her expression distant and inward.

"That sounds horrible, Cassandra. You had a very frightening time when you were with your father. Terrible things happened," I said softly.

She nodded almost imperceptibly.

"I'm really sorry for that. What your Uncle Beck did was very wrong. Those things shouldn't ever happen to a little girl."

A tear trickled from the corner of her eye. She made no effort to wipe it away.

"But those times over now, Cassandra. They're finished. You're with your mom. You're safe again."

"But my mom didn't keep me safe."

"Your mom didn't know then what your dad was going to do, but she does know now. Things are different now. Just because things happened once does not mean they will happen again. You're safe with your mom now. Uncle Beck isn't here anymore."

"Yes, he is," she said very softly and she looked at me then, the eye contact brief but unambiguous.

I regarded her.

"Because what you said's true."

She let out a long breath.

"You said I had a Troubled Place inside me. And I do. And that's where Uncle Beck lives now. It's just exactly like you said. My Troubled Place goes everywhere I go. Even when I don't want to, I can see Uncle Beck. Even here. If it gets too quiet, if I'm not careful, I'll see him. I'll feel him doing that stuff to me."

"Then it's time to get rid of Uncle Beck, Cassandra.

He doesn't belong in your head. That's a private place for just you."

Cassandra looked at me, her great dark eyes searching my face.

"Maybe you're thinking Uncle Beck's too strong," I said. "You've had to live with him all these years. It's probably hard to imagine being able to get rid of him because he's been so powerful."

She nodded faintly.

"But this is what I meant about our needing to be on the same side. If we work together, if you and I and the nurses and the doctors and your mom and your stepdad all band together on the same team, there'll be more of us than him. We *will* be stronger. We *can* beat him then. We can make him go away."

She continued to regard me, her expression unreadable.

"Can you see that? Can you see how it works? All of us on one side together," I said and held up one hand, fingers splayed, "and just Uncle Beck on this side." I held up one finger of my other hand. "Can you see? We'll be stronger, huh? No one person could fight all these."

She nodded.

"But not so strong this way, huh?" I said and held up four fingers on one hand and two on the other. "Because that's you and Uncle Beck together on this side and the rest of us over here. That would be harder."

"I'm not on Uncle Beck's side. I don't want to be on his side."

"Which is why you've got to stop protecting that Troubled Place, because that's where Uncle Beck lives. When you protect that, you're protecting him in there.

You've got to get over on our side so we can get him out of there.

"It's still going be a big fight," I added. "And some of it is going to hurt, because we'll have to get in and look around in that Trouble Place to find where he's at and then beat him out of there. But it *can* be done, Cassandra. We *can* make him go away. Things don't have to be this way."

She didn't react. Still slumped far to the right in the orange Naugahyde chair, her head all but resting on the steel arm, she just stared forward, her gaze vague.

"Does this make sense to you?" I asked.

There was a long pause, then slowly she nodded.

"So shall we try?" I asked.

Again the pause, but this time it grew even longer. She was completely silent, completely still. Her unfocused eyes were so vacant as to be dead. Then at last she brought her gaze into focus and looked over at me. She gave a faint, faint nod. "Okay."

$\mathcal{I}$ found it hard to shift gears back into ordinary life after that conversation with Cassandra, not only because it was so intense, but also because it had occurred so late in the day. The harrowing impact would have been eased if I'd been fresh and if there'd been other people and events coming after that required my attention. As it was, it was the last interaction of my working day. Consequently, it loomed over me, immovable and implacable as a leviathan.

I'd had plans to meet up with a friend after work. We were going to have a bite out in a new, trendy vegetarian restaurant, and afterward I was going to help in her quest for the perfect patio-door curtains. On this evening, however, I just couldn't. I could not go directly from Cassandra to something as frivolous as shopping. I didn't want to spoil my friend's innocent pleasure with bleak insinuations that what she was doing was shallow and meaningless against the tapestry of suffering in the world. At the same time, however, I did not want to demean my own feelings or the horror of Cassandra's life. So I phoned with vague apologies and backed out of the evening's arrangements.

Although I knew a lighthearted girlie evening would not have worked for me, I knew, too, that going home alone to my apartment would probably not be helpful either. I needed space in which to distance the conversation, to put it into objective, realistic proportions. Quiet, respectful space and quiet, respectful distraction. So I stopped to eat at a small independent fast-food diner specializing in ribs and French fries, and afterward I went to the local library.

Our city had an active historical society, and there was a large well-organized database of local history available to the public in the main library. For some time I'd been intending to go in and look up Gerda's family in hopes of giving a more concrete structure to the gauzy fabric of Gerda's stories.

The database, which covered the period from the city's earliest pioneer days in the 1860s to 1960, was in three parts. The first was composed purely of statistics: births, marriages, deaths, land ownership, records of commercial development, and so forth. The second was a collection of local photographs donated from various sources or copied from private collections. The third section was called "Grandma's Stories" and consisted of personal recollections taken from oral accounts, which the members of the historical society had collected over the years by interviewing elderly residents of the area.

I wanted to know the history of Gerda's birth family and didn't actually have her maiden name, so I had anticipated difficulty locating the information I was looking for. As it happened, not so. She and her husband had married locally in the 1930s, so those records were in the database. From the marriage details, I was easily able to trace her maiden name. From there, it was straightforward to her birth family because hers was a distinctive German surname.

There was a curious sensation in seeing the now-familiar names from Gerda's stories—Louisa, Willie, Alfred—recorded in the dispassionate statistics of the database. It was almost as if I had come across Peter Pan's birth certificate or Frodo Baggins's address.

From the records I couldn't tell if Gerda's parents were immigrants themselves or simply second-generation Americans who had been attracted to the area's large ethnic German community, where the German language was still commonly spoken in some public schools right up through the 1950s. Certainly, the couple seemed to have an interesting history. They had been married in Pennsylvania, and soon afterward, they made the long trek west to take up what was described as "donation land," an early form of homesteading, where land was offered by the federal government to individuals who agreed to settle there and become residents. A little farther down the page, I read where her parents lasted only four years on this land and then returned east again.

The story became more curious, because eight years after returning east, they turned around *again* and came back here. This amazed me, because the distance one way would have been close to twenty-five hundred miles and this was in the era of covered wagons. The thought of making three such cross-country journeys in such conditions seemed an astounding undertaking. Why, I wondered, had they not stayed the first time?

I went back to the statistics section to look at the birth dates for Gerda and her siblings. She had been born here on the homestead, as had Louisa, Willie, Alfred, and Karl. They weren't the only children, however. There were five elder children, two of whom had been born in Pennsylvania and three during the first period the family was in the West. All five had died in childhood. Indeed, as I looked carefully at the dates, I realized four of them had died within six weeks of one another.

There was nothing to tell me more than that. Just the statistics. The four children who had died close together were three girls and a boy, aged six, four, three, and one at the time of death. The other was a girl, aged four, who died about the time the family was returning west for the second time.

I looked at the names and the dates. There was no way to know how or why so many children had died close together. Illness? That was the logical conclusion, because if it had been a disastrous accident, one would have expected them to all die about the same time. I suspected it was something like diphtheria, as I knew there had been a couple of catastrophic epidemics in the early history of the community. Or perhaps it was simply the ills of poverty and hardship. No way of knowing.

This couple's story came forth, even with nothing more to go on than dry statistics. A wedding, a new start in the West, no doubt with dreams of wealth and fortune. Land of their own. Land of opportunity. And then devastation. Far from home and their own families, they lost all their children. I looked at the records more closely. Yes. All of them. There was five-year gap between those deaths and the birth of the fifth child to die, a girl named Elfie. So the couple packed up and went home to Pennsylvania. Then what? What drove them to make the long trek back again to the homestead? No money? No work in the East? Or was it something more daring, more romantic? Had they been escaping from the confines of one of the many closed religious communities in Pennsylvania, which were largely ethnic Germans? Or had they perhaps always intended to return all along. Perhaps they just needed to find their feet again, needed the strength to start over. Elfie had been born by the time they started the trek back. Gerda's siblings and she followed in the years soon after they had arrived.

I moved off to another part of the library to confirm what I was already quite certain of, that the small holding where Gerda had been living with her cats and her chickens was, indeed, the same donation land her parents had settled almost a hundred years earlier. And yes, it was.

Spending the evening in the library did prove a successful transition away from the intensity of Cassandra's situation, but it left my head full of other kinds of thoughts. During my Montana childhood my family had frequently gone on outings to nearby ghost towns, and I'd loved walking through the old abandoned cemeteries. They were often sited on hillsides, lonely and windswept, yet with breathtaking panoramic views. The land had long since reverted to buffalo grass, and the overgrown graves were havens to whirring locusts and rattlesnakes nestled midst the fallen headstones. An oddly sweet sadness, almost a kind of longing, would always overtake me in such places, as I tried to bring to life in my imagination the people behind the carved dates, the stone angels, the weathered lambs. So it was this night in the library. I felt the same sort of poignancy, to be reminded how everything that feels so vital and important now will also fade, like shadows into twilight, and be forgotten.

On my way into work the next morning, I called by the rehabilitation center to see Gerda. Armed now with some concrete information on her background, I hoped I could stimulate conversation. Real conversation, the kind with give-and-take.

Pulling the orange plastic chair over, I sat down and told Gerda of my library adventures. She listened carefully as I talked about the procedure I'd gone through to find information on her family and on the farm. I said how interesting it was to me to learn things like this. I mentioned how, in my childhood, I'd explored abandoned homesteads in the area near where I grew up and loved hearing about the people who had lived in the West in that era.

Listening to me, Gerda had a soft, very slight smile, but she didn't speak.

"I saw where your parents came all the way out here from Pennsylvania but then after a few years, they went back to Pennsylvania. Then came back here all over again. I looked it up in the atlas this morning and it's 2,575 miles from there to here."

Gerda's pale eyes were on my face.

"Did you know they did that?" I asked.

She nodded.

"It seems astonishing to me. They would have walked much of the way . . . covered wagons, oxen. Crossing the Rocky Mountains."

Gerda nodded again.

"Did your family ever talk about those journeys?"

Gerda looked away. There was a patient in another room who was calling out. The voice was quivery and frail. "Nurse! Nurse!" she called, only it wasn't quite that urgently said. But it was very plaintive. For a moment it seemed to pull Gerda's attention away from me and she listened to it.

"Laudanum," she said softly, still looking toward the door.

"Pardon?" I asked.

Gerda turned, although she didn't look back at me. Her eyes went to some unseen spot beyond the end of the bed. "She wanted to taste the laudanum. Mama kept it in an earthenware jar with a stopper. Was precious. Laudanum was precious. It took pain away."

I knew laudanum to be an opium-based drug that had been popular with morose romantic poets of the nineteenth century but that was really all. I didn't know how it came to be mentioned here nor who "she" was.

"Most folks didn't have laudanum. Mama brought it with her. She'd made it herself. Kept the basket of poppyheads sitting on that box. On the gun box. Papa's gun box. All withered. Withered poppyheads, looked like nothing, but she'd poke them and sweat them by the fire. Mama said they're precious. They take the pain away."

"Your mother was making laudanum from poppies herself?" I asked.

Gerda looked at me. It was an unexpectedly searching look. She scrutinized my face almost as if she were taking my measure, as if she wanted to know if I was equal to what she had to tell me. On the other hand, there was a faint undercurrent of uncertainty to her expression, as if perhaps she'd simply forgotten for a moment who I was. Then she looked toward the door again.

"She was tired that afternoon. Sleepy. Mama couldn't wake her up," Gerda said. "Then Mama found the laudanum jar. Found she'd gotten into it. Gotten into it for a taste. And because it had sugar in it, she ate it all."

"Who was this?" I asked.

"They couldn't wake her up. Put her by the fire that night, but she was too sound asleep."

"Was this a sister of yours?" I asked.

"She slept for two days. Then she died."

"Who was this? Can you tell me? Was this in your family? One of your sisters?"

"She died. Four years old. And nothing even said she'd been born. Wasn't wrote nowhere. Wasn't wrote she'd been born. Wasn't wrote she died. They had to leave her there. Bury her in the dirt and wasn't no marker. No one to remember. Except Mama."

"And you," I said.

Gerda looked over at me then. There was eye contact and with it Gerda nodded. "Yes, I remember."

"And now me, too."

Chapter

28

$\mathcal{C}$learing my schedule, I made plans to drive to Quentin on Thursday. I was quite worried that once Lucia calmed down after the phone call, she would have second thoughts about meeting me, especially if it risked crossing her father-in-law. This would give her cold feet and she wouldn't show up at Starbucks. Needless to say, the thought of making a seven-hour round-trip for something that might not happen wasn't something I relished.

Harry and I discussed the phone conversation at great length. Clearly something was deeply upsetting to Lucia, both in her emotional behavior and in arranging to meet me in this clandestine manner. The obvious conclusion was that she had important information to share. Harry speculated that she might be planning to leave her husband, no doubt taking Drake with her, and this would cause a huge furor. He talked about how, in strongly male-dominated families in his native India, the wife was often in great danger if she tried to break away, and perhaps this was a similar situation.

My guess was that Lucia was going to reveal the events leading up to Drake's mutism, that she was finally ready to divulge what had happened behind closed doors to affect her son in such an extreme way.

Regardless, we both knew that for the first time we were going to see inside this family, and that, in all likelihood, Lucia was going to disclose either past or present domestic violence or child abuse, possibly both. This, of course, would then leave me with a very sticky situation to deal with right there in Starbucks.

Harry and I talked about the options for handling such revelations. Obviously, her choosing to talk to me in a public place indicated her unwillingness to be at home. Was this because the abuser was likely to come in on us? Because she feared being overheard? Who was involved? Mason Sloane himself? Or was the abuser her husband, Walter? Thus far, Walter had remained a very mysterious figure.

If Lucia did disclose domestic violence, how could I then best support her? Getting her to the police was of paramount importance, but she well might not be willing to make that step straightaway. Unfortunately, Quentin was so far away that neither Harry nor I had any personal contacts in the social service structure there. Was there a rape crisis center? A safe house for abused women? How sensitive were the police in these matters? How completely *had* the Sloanes infiltrated the infrastructure of Quentin? Was it the company town Mason Sloane implied, built on his family's money, and thus, unlikely to provide Lucia any confidentiality or safe haven at all?

Worse, what if she disclosed violence and then didn't want help? Didn't want me to do anything about it, except listen to her? What if she disclosed abuse toward Drake but then said, "Don't tell anyone"? This kind of situation had happened to me before, and it was hell to deal with. Given my position, what were my legal obligations in a situation like this? Did I have to inform her before she started to tell me anything that I would not be able to maintain confidentiality if Drake's welfare was involved? Did I say then that I would have to report abuse, if I were told about it, and risk her not telling me at all? Or did I keep silent and betray her confidence, if need be?

So many gray areas. Harry and I talked and talked and talked, trying to think of all the possibilities, trying to prepare for all eventualities.

It was a long drive out to Quentin and not the carefree journey it had been for me the previous time. On the seat beside me was a sheaf of contact numbers I had compiled, numbers for as many supporting agencies and helplines as I could find, numbers for both Quentin and the city. I also had brochures and leaflets on domestic violence and child abuse and how to handle such things. I'd even included information on separation and divorce and the issues of stalking and harassment, just in case.

When I arrived, I was feeling genuinely nervous, which was something that didn't happen to me often. This had been such a strange case. I'd realized for some time that there had to be more going on than had been made known to us, but the cloak-and-dagger aspect of making this long journey to meet someone in a coffee shop in anticipation of hearing secret details of private lives set me on edge. More than that, however, I was unnerved knowing that at the end of whatever Lucia disclosed, inevitably some kind of difficult decision would be called for, and, ultimately, resolution would lie with me.

I didn't have the nice weather of the first journey. It was cold and overcast. It should have been spring. Or at least thinking of spring, because it was March. Early March was still too close to winter in this part of the world, however. We'd have snow before the day was out.

I found the Starbucks easily enough. Lucia was already there. She'd taken a small table tucked in the corner. I waved, smiled, and then delayed as long as possible by going to the counter to get the biggest, strongest latte I could find.

"Hello, hello," I said perhaps a bit too cheerfully, as I came to the table. I extended a hand.

Lucia shook it limply. She already had tears in the corners of her eyes.

I sat down.

A dreadful silence intruded immediately, that type of horrible, discomforting quiet that is as loud as a shouted obscenity.

"I very much appreciate this chance to meet again," I said in an effort to break it. "I was so sorry for Drake to go like that. I've been worrying about him ever since."

Tears spilled over her cheeks.

I reached into my handbag and took out a small package of tissues, as she didn't seem to have any.

Lucia left them laying there, so I took one out and handed it to her so she'd know I was comfortable with her crying. I said, "It's all right. I know it's hard to talk about things like this."

Too hard, apparently, because before I realized what was happening, Lucia got up and ran for the women's restroom.

Hmm.

I sat a moment, still feeling nervous myself and now a little embarrassed as well, because other people *were* noticing. I got up and went to the women's restroom.

Lucia was vomiting.

I stood outside the stall and waited for her to finish and come out. Which she did eventually, looking drawn. She was still weepy.

"Are you okay?" I asked.

She nodded. Turning on the faucet, she splashed water into her mouth and spit it out. She took a paper towel and wiped her face. "Yes, I'm fine," she said. Which was the baldest lie I'd heard in a long time.

We returned to the table and our now cool coffee.

Again, she started to cry.

"Take your time," I said gently. "I know this must be hard."

She made no effort to speak. Instead, she just wept, going tissue by tissue through the small pack.

Hoping to give Lucia some format with which to articulate her misery, I put the folder of materials I had brought with me onto the table. I opened it. On top was a bright blue, glossy brochure developed by our metropolitan police force for victims of domestic violence. It wasn't too subtle. DOMESTIC ABUSE was emblazoned not once but twice across the front in jagged red graphics, as in-your-face as any rock band logo.

Lucia regarded it tearfully.

"I know these are very hard issues to talk about," I said quietly. "I do understand. And, please, you understand I really am only here to help. I know these are very distressing matters."

Renewed tears.

I maneuvered the blue brochure more directly in front of her. A moment or two passed. I waited patiently.

Still she cried. We'd gone through all the tissues in the pack and were now onto Starbucks napkins. I was past being uncomfortable, past worrying what others in the small café might think I was doing to her, but I wasn't past being horribly aware of our drawing attention to ourselves. If Lucia had wanted this venue because it was more private than at home, she wasn't really making it easy to keep our privacy. I hunched forward, trying to physically enclose us at the small table, but I knew people were staring—quite blatantly in a few instances—and I worried that she was too recognizable in this small city, that too many people would want to eavesdrop just because it was a Sloane talking.

So, once again, I broached the matter with her, hoping to urge the process forward. "I appreciate it's very difficult to talk about these things. And that's okay. I came out here, understanding that. I've had many other parents in situations like yours, so I do understand how hard it is to talk about. I have plenty of time. So don't feel rushed. Don't feel pressured. We'll get it sorted out."

Renewed tears.

I nudged the blue brochure yet closer to her. "Is this what we're talking about?" I asked very gently.

"Noooo," she replied and it came out almost a howl.

"Abuse?"

"Noooo."

I sat back.

She snorted into a napkin, wiped her reddened face. Mascara left a sooty trail in the corner of one eye.

"How so 'no'?" I asked. "Are we talking . . . about Drake? You?"

"Noooo. No, not that. None of that." She pushed the brochure away as if it were a dirty thing.

"Not . . . abuse?"

"Noooo." She lost her composure again.

I didn't really know how to interpret what she was saying. Did she literally mean no, that I was on the wrong track altogether? Or was she saying no defensively, because she wanted to put me off the topic? Or did she mean a specific kind of no, such as, no, it wasn't the kind of abuse you went to the police about, but another kind might still be happening?

I sat, silently watching her cry.

"It isn't that," she said at last. "It isn't anything like that. It's me."

"Can you tell me more?"

"It's *me*."

Puzzled, I regarded her.

"I made it up."

"Made what up?" I asked.

"He *can't* talk." This made her cry harder. Burying her face in a napkin, Lucia bent forward until her head was almost on the table. I sat quietly, feeling the eyes of other Starbucks customers drilling into my back.

When she came up for air, I asked, "Is this Drake we're talking about? Can you tell me more about what you just said?"

"Drake *can't* talk."

"How do you mean? Can't talk?"

"He *can't* talk. I made it up."

"I'm a little confused," I said. "Made what up? In relation to what? When you say Drake can't talk, how do you mean this?"

"That he can't talk," she wailed. "I *made* it up."

"You made up about him talking? How did you do that? I'm still confused, Lucia. Are you meaning he can't talk to anyone else except you? Or do you mean he actually can't say much? Like, for example, when I listened to the tape you made, you were only doing nursery rhymes. Are you trying to say he can't talk beyond that kind of thing?"

"That's not Drake," she wailed. "It's my nephew."

"Where? How do you mean?" I asked, bewildered.

"On the tape. When I was sitting him for my sister-in-law. I made the tape with him. It isn't Drake."

I stared in disbelief.

"Drake has something wrong in his genes. His voice box is not proper." She was sobbing again as she said this, her own voice too agonized to be soft. Everyone else in Starbucks was getting embarrassed by this time, so we were perhaps the most alone we'd thus far been.

"So let me see if I understand this," I said. "You are saying Drake has a genetic problem that has physically affected his ability to speak? That that wasn't him on the tape? That he literally can*not* speak?"

She nodded.

"But . . ." I said, "that report from the Mayo Clinic? It said there was nothing physically wrong with Drake."

"I rewrote it."

"*What?*"

"When it came, I rewrote it. I photocopied the pages

and then wrote new things and pasted them over and photocopied it again, so that it had the letterhead on it. So everyone thought that's what it said when it came. But really it didn't. It said about the genes. About his cords being deformed. And he has other problems. It affects his legs as well."

"Who all knows about this?"

"No one," she said in a tiny, tiny voice.

"What about Drake's father?"

"No. I could not tell him. He has so many worries that *he* is not perfect for his father. How could I tell him I have given him a deformed son? The burden would be too great for him." Then she collapsed into tears yet again.

I got up to get us more napkins, to get myself more coffee, and, for just that moment, to get some breathing space.

When I returned, Lucia was more composed. Head still down, she had her shoulders drawn up around her ears almost as if she expected me to strike her.

"That must have been very hard to tell me," I said, as I sat down. "I appreciate that you did. For Drake's sake, we need to know the truth on this matter."

"It is so important to Father Sloane that everything is perfect," she murmured. "He is so hard on Skip. Skip has nerves because of it. He takes pills every morning. To keep from— He cannot face his father. He cannot even stand in the same room." And she broke down again.

"So all this . . . 'disguising the truth' . . . has happened because of Mr. Sloane? Old Mr. Sloane? You've done this because of . . . what? Pressure? Pressure to . . ."

"How could I say my son was deformed? To *him*? Say I have these bad genes in me to make a defective child? I cannot sleep at night, knowing I have made a son like this, because Father Sloane will be so angry when he finds out. He will disown Drake. He will insist Skip divorces me."

"Surely not," I said. "Those are ideas from another era. Having met Mr. Sloane, I can well imagine how angry he might be, but he wouldn't be able to actually make you and Skip get a divorce, if you didn't want to. Men don't have that kind of power in this country."

"It is not so simple," she replied. "What laws say in a country and what laws say in a family are often different."

Which was true. Abuse comes in many forms. And merely because it is against the law doesn't mean it doesn't happen.

I sat back. All that was in my mind was poor, poor Drake, shouldering a burden that had proved too heavy for both his parents to carry.

We had been in the coffee shop over two hours, and I was growing anxious about the time. I didn't know what kinds of arrangements Lucia had made for Drake or the rest of her life during our meeting, but I was concerned she was not going to be able to stay much longer, and I feared she might suddenly bolt.

Where from here? I looked at the police brochure on domestic violence, still on the table in front of me. That wouldn't do much good. Indeed, none of the things I'd brought with me would be much help. Here, almost two hundred miles from my own support network and too far away to be able to see either Lucia or Drake myself on a regular basis, I was frighteningly aware of having to "think on my feet" here. I felt quite inadequate for the job.

Meanwhile, Lucia, at long last, seemed to be regaining a hold on her composure. The horrible story finally related, she looked exhausted but increasingly relaxed.

"We have a dilemma here," I said. "Time's getting on. I'm concerned you'll need to get back shortly because of Drake. Or because Skip or Mr. Sloane will miss you. I'm thinking also that you're probably feeling very tired by this point."

She nodded in a heartfelt way.

"The dilemma is that we're a long ways apart. If both you and I were in the city, I'd suggest we meet together a few more times so that we could explore the situation more thoroughly and come up with the best way of resolving all of this. Unfortunately, we don't really have that option."

"No," she said.

"But I think we *do* need to resolve it. The way things are now, it's very unfair to Drake. He isn't getting the services he needs, for one thing. Worse, however, is that when he is with people like myself, we are trying to make him do something he genuinely can't do. The whole time he was on the unit, I was working hard with him to get him to talk and my methods would have been acceptable if he were really electively mute. But because he wasn't, I was putting pressure on him to do something he, in fact, couldn't do. That must have made him feel terrible."

Tears sprung to Lucia's eyes again.

I reached across the table and touched her arm. "No, it's okay. I'm not trying to make you feel bad saying that. I know you already feel bad; I know this has had to be so very hard on both you and your husband. People don't do extreme things unless they feel there are no other alternatives. So I know, however badly things may have turned out, you weren't trying to hurt Drake."

Lower lip clenched between her teeth, she shook her head.

"But now that we know what's going on," I said, "the time has come to say things have gone far enough. The time has come to stop supporting the old man's view of the world and start supporting Drake's. We just have to figure out how to do that."

"I don't know how," she said tearfully. "That's the problem. I don't know what to do."

"That's all right. That's why we're both here. We'll do it together. I'm not going to say, 'I'm off now, back to the city. You sort it out.' I'll help you do it. But we need to figure out how to go about it, given that I don't live very close." I smiled at her. "But we *will* figure it out."

Opening another napkin, Lucia wiped her eyes. She nodded.

"What needs to be done, of course, is to tell the old man the truth," I said. "That's going to be the hard part. But eventually we do need to do it."

She grimaced but nodded faintly.

"Perhaps the place to start all this would be by telling Skip. Telling him you altered the Mayo report. And made the tape with your nephew, not Drake."

Lucia didn't respond.

"Do you think you could do that?"

There was a long pause followed by a long sigh. She squirmed slightly. "I do not want to give him more problems. He already takes the pills. They are so he does not try to take his life." A small pause. "Because this happened. Last year. He was in the car in the garage."

"I see."

"So I do not want to give him more problems."

"Yes, I can understand," I said. "And I can understand better why it felt right to you to keep Drake's disability a secret, if your husband has felt under such great pressure from his family himself and has tried to take his own life. But keeping secrets from him might not be a helpful way to deal with all this. My experience is that what is kept from us is often much more destructive to us than what we know."

Lucia nodded.

"So perhaps the place to start is for you to tell Skip. Do you think you can do that?"

Lucia drew in a breath. "I will try."

"Good. Then phone me. When Skip knows, give me a call. We'll make plans of where to go from there," I said. "In the meantime, I'd like to see the original report from the Mayo Clinic. Would that be all right? Would you give me permission to write them and ask them to send me a copy?"

"Yes," she said.

A small silence slipped in, allowing the clink of dishes and silverware, the steamy whoosh of the coffee machines, and the chatter of the other patrons in the coffee shop to loom up around us.

"And, of course, at some point," I said softly, "there's going to be an unpleasant confrontation. No virtue in pretending that isn't going to happen. But it's usually easier to tolerate such things if you have support, if you know that others will care what is happening to you and you can share it with them. It's also usually easier if you know you are doing the right thing. So, whatever the old man says or tries to do, you don't have to bear it alone. None of you does, not you, not Skip, not Drake. If the old Mr. Sloane can't tolerate the fact Drake isn't the perfect grandson he needs, then it may be time to leave him to his views and make a different kind of life for yourselves. The whole world is not here in Quentin. There are many people who will understand and accept Drake and you and Skip, just as you are. As for doing the right thing, have absolutely no doubt this *is* what you are doing in talking to me now. And know you have already done the hardest part, which is to own up to having made a mistake."

"Okay," Lucia said. She let out a long breath and looked at her watch. "I do need to go now. But thank you. Thank you very much."

"Phone me, once you've told Skip."

She nodded and rose from the table. "I will. Good-bye."

I didn't get back to the city from Quentin until almost 8:30 P.M. Over the last hour of the journey I had amused myself planning what I'd do when I got home. After such a grueling afternoon, I wanted only peace and quiet and my own company. So I planned to open a bottle of wine, something I seldom did either on my own or during the week, which made it a real treat; moreover, there was a particularly good bottle of cabernet sauvignon in the wine rack that was calling out to me like a Siren. Then I'd make a creamy, calming plate of pasta with lots and lots of garlic. And before any of this, I'd stop at the video store and pick up something interesting, so once the pasta was made and the wine opened, I could kick back and veg out.

Planning this ideal scenario made the last part of the journey pass quickly, and truth said, it probably gave me as much pleasure as the actual experience would. This was fortunate, because planning it was all the relaxation I got that evening. When I came in the front door, I saw the light on my answer machine blinking. I hit the button.

It was the unit. The caller was one of the nurses, whose name was Carrie. Cassandra had "flipped out," she said. Could I come in?

So the wine stayed in the wine rack, the pasta on the shelf, the garlic in its fine silver skin, hanging in a braid above the butcher block. Never bothering even to take my coat off, I reset the answering machine, switched off the light, locked the door, and headed for the hospital, stopping only long enough to pick up an order of chicken at KFC to eat in the car as I drove.

In an ideal world, not only would we be able to eat pasta and drink wine undisturbed after having put in a hard day's work, but also difficult psychological breakthroughs would result in real, up-front results. In an ideal world, Cassandra, having recognized Uncle Beck for what he was—no longer a real person, but instead a demon inside her—would have had some wonderful, immediate payoff for that very difficult, hard-won insight.

Not so. Not in this world anyway.

In fact, things seemed to go an entirely different way for Cassandra. She had survived the hideous circumstances of her abduction and abuse by walling off things that were just too painful to deal with. In fact, she had walled off whole segments of her personality to the point they were developing separate identities of their own—Minister Snake, who passed judgment on the horrible child who acquiesced to these things; Cowboy Snake, who mourned what was happening, who tried to drown out painful experiences with a howling yodel; and innocent, pure Fairy Snake, kept away from the horrors of what was happening. But so, too, had Uncle Beck been walled up in the process.

It was easy to think that in helping Cassandra recognize her "Troubled Place" and what was going on in there, we would allow her to release those dreadful feelings, to let go of Uncle Beck and all he had done to her. I hoped that would eventually be true; at the moment, however, it wasn't. Recognizing Uncle Beck was with her, was inside her still, was not at all freeing for Cassandra because in tearing down that wall, all the other walls in her mind became unstable. Cassandra, quite literally, fell apart.

Her behavior became very unpredictable in the two days following our talk in the dayroom. She had appeared calm and deep-thinking in the immediate aftermath of the discussion. After I had left, she'd had a meal and had talked openly with several of the other staff about Uncle Beck and about her Troubled Place. This particular terminology really seemed to strike a chord with Cassandra. *Troubled Place* became her byword.

By the next morning, however, her behavior had started to fluctuate. She became very anxious, worried that Uncle Beck might still be about, worried that something might happen to her mother, worried that if she left the hospital someone would abduct her again. Then she grew angry, shouting at the staff, calling them stupid, throwing her tray at breakfast. Then she was crying.

When it was our time together, she was impossible. Everything was a control issue, and we got nothing done. I was able to accept this. As the person who had revealed Uncle Beck and her Troubled Place, I was probably pretty scary to be around, because what else might I get into? So trying to control me was an understandable and possibly necessary reaction. Just very frustrating.

The rest of her day had been no more tranquil. She cycled repeatedly through anxiety, anger, manipulation, and sheer desolation, stressing the staff and distressing herself. Indeed, it continued well into the night, as every time Cassandra settled into bed, she was plagued by visions of Uncle Beck. In the end, she was given a sedative to help her sleep.

And then, of course, I couldn't be there for our next session together, as I had to be in Quentin.

When I arrived at the hospital, Carrie filled me in on what had happened.

At dinnertime one of the boys had come to the nurses' station to say that Cassandra had managed to get into a utility closet off the dining room. In this closet was a small window perhaps only about twenty-four by eighteen inches wide. It had the same safety features as did all the windows in the hospital, which meant it could not open very wide and there was a screen on the outside, but it did not have a metal grid over it as did all the other windows in the psychiatric units. The boy said Cassandra was trying to break the window because she was going to jump out.

When staff went to investigate, they found Cassandra pounding on the window with a metal dish from the dining room. She was in a very distressed state and required three staff to get her out of the utility room and take the dish from her. She was put into the seclusion room until she calmed down. This was about 6:30 in the evening.

Carrie said they'd then let her out of lockdown because she did appear in control again and because Carrie knew one of Cassandra's favorite television programs was coming on. Carrie hoped watching a show she enjoyed would help Cassandra to relax and calm herself.

When Carrie next looked, Cassandra was not among the children in the chairs in front of the TV. Going to investigate, Carrie found her in her bedroom, a chair pulled over into the middle of the room. Cassandra was standing on the seat of the chair, using her shoe to try and break the bulb in the light fitting in the ceiling with the intention of cutting her wrists with the broken glass. There was a metal grid over the fitting and the fitting itself was of sturdy safety glass, but Cassandra was nonetheless making a very concerted effort.

Two suicide attempts by a nine-year-old in as many hours; Carrie knew it was "time for the big guns," as she put it. So she phoned both Dave Menotti and me. Dave phoned back with a prescription for greater sedation, which was administered. And by 9 P.M., I was there.

Cassandra was in the seclusion room when I arrived. Dressed in her pajamas, she had a bathrobe over them, but as is the practice with suicidal patients, she wore no shoes and had no tie to keep the bathrobe closed. I opened the door and came in. There was a soft snick as a staff member locked it behind me.

"Hi," I said.

Cassandra was standing on the far side of the small

room. Her eyes were red in the way of someone who is very tired. They had a vague, rather haunted expression. She didn't say anything back.

"Come here." I held out an arm.

She crossed over to me. I put my arm around her and drew her close.

"I understand you're having a very bad day," I said.

She nodded.

"Can you tell me about it?"

At that moment she pressed in against me, pushing her face into my sweater. She didn't speak.

"Here, let's sit down."

I made myself as comfortable as is possible in a padded cell, which is a soft but very sterile sort of place and is lit far too brightly. Cassandra sat with me, close against my side. I kept my arm around her.

"So, what's happening?"

A long silence followed.

Cassandra picked at the edge of her robe, pulling little threads out of the terrycloth. "You weren't here today," she finally said in a tiny voice.

"No, I'm sorry for that. I had to be away today. I mentioned that yesterday. Do you remember? But I'm sorry. I can see you've had a hard day."

She nodded.

Again silence. I listened into it. There wasn't much to hear in the little room. The ventilation system, mostly. And Cassandra's breathing, which was a bit noisy.

"Can you tell me what's happening?" I asked again, very gently.

"I want to die."

"Yes. I can tell that. Why?"

"My head's too confusing."

"How do you mean? Can you tell me more about that?"

She shook her head.

"Okay."

Two or three moments of just sitting together.

"I'm too tired," she said.

"Yes, the medicine will make you feel sleepy. When you get really sleepy, we'll go in your room."

"I don't want to go in my room."

"I see."

"Everything in my head's confusing. It's like it's arguing in my head."

"Different voices?" I asked.

"I don't know."

A small pause.

"Like voices. But not voices. Like everybody is talking at once. Arguing at once." She snuffled. "I don't want to be like this. It hurts too much."

"Yeah. I can understand that," I said.

"I just want it to go away. I want it to be like it was before."

"Before when?" I asked.

She shrugged. "Just before. Before now. Before today. Or yesterday. Before I started thinking about all this."

"Yeah," I said. "I can see where thinking about all this must hurt."

Cassandra nodded and pressed closer yet to me.

A silence came then, deep and a little sleepy. I was aware of a faint saline scent as I sat there. I think it was embedded in the padding of the cell and not coming from Cassandra herself. It was a profoundly human scent. Of tears, I think.

"I'm going to do something," I said. I twisted around

enough to fish in the right pocket of my jeans because I knew I'd stuffed a felt-tip pen in earlier when I was with Lucia. Taking it out, I uncapped it.

All the movement had meant I'd had to shift away from Cassandra, who had been leaning against my left side. She crooked her head to see what I was doing.

"These thoughts you've got in your head," I said. "I want you to give them to me for tonight. So you can go to sleep."

She looked at me, her expression quizzical.

"What are they? Let's make a list of them." I looked at her. "I want you to go inside your head. Listen to what all this arguing is about in there and tell me about it. What's one thing you hear being said?"

"I don't understand what you're doing," Cassandra replied.

"We're going to make a list of those things you keep hearing so that I can take them home with me. I'll take care of them for tonight. Then you won't have to think about them anymore, because I'll have them safe. That way you can sleep."

"We don't have any paper to make a list."

"We don't need paper. You just tell me what you hear inside your head. Everybody's arguing. What are they arguing about? Tell one of the things."

"They're not arguing. It's just mean voices. Scary voices. I dunno."

"Okay, but what are they saying?" I asked. "Tell me one thing."

"I don't understand what we're doing."

I smiled gently. "Everything feels really confusing to you right now, doesn't it?"

Cassandra nodded.

"You know the bulletin board out by the nurses' station?"

"Yes."

"You've seen it. It's got, like, a million pieces of paper stuck up on it, doesn't it? And everything stuck up there is stuff people want to remember. Like what the menu for the week ahead is. Or when events are or which people want to go on special outings. Or when someone has an appointment to go somewhere off the unit. Yes? Do you understand that?"

Cassandra nodded.

"Well, in your Troubled Place, you've got a bulletin board, too. Stuck up on that one are all sorts of different really yucky, nasty thoughts. And because nobody wants to keep seeing yucky, nasty things, it's understandable you've tried never to go in there to look at that bulletin board. But what's happened is that we've opened up the Troubled Place now by talking about Uncle Beck, and you can't miss seeing all these scary thoughts are tacked up in there."

"Yeah," Cassandra said.

"So what I want you to do is take them down and give them to me for tonight, so that I can take care of them and you don't have to keep looking at them. Someday, further down the line, we're going to throw all those nasty, scary thoughts away, and how we do that is by getting all of them out and looking at them and talking about them until they get really boring and aren't a big deal anymore. When something isn't a big deal anymore, then it's easy to throw it away. So that's what's *going* to happen in the future to all that yucky stuff, but we're not quite there yet. Everything still feels like a big deal. It's still scary. So, for now, I just want you to give these yucky thoughts that are bothering you to me. I'll take them home with me, because they can't hurt me. I'm a grown-up. I'm really strong. And if I have them, then they can't hurt you."

Cassandra's brow furrowed. "I don't understand how to do that."

"That's okay. I'll help. And we'll go one at a time. One yucky thought at a time. So you listen right now to all that arguing in your head. And tell me one yucky thing you hear. Just one thing."

An inward expression came to her face and she cocked her head, as if listening. She shrugged slightly, as if in response to something, and then, without moving her head, she looked at me. "Uncle Beck is going to come get me."

"Okay, good. That's one scary, yucky thought, isn't it? I bet it's been hanging around on the bulletin board in your Troubled Place for a long time, huh?"

Cassandra nodded.

"So," I said, "here's what I do: 'Uncle Beck is going to come get me.'" I took the felt-tip and wrote that on the palm of my right hand.

"Wow!" Cassandra said in amazement. "You're writing on yourself!"

"Yes. Because *I'm* going to take these thoughts away with me when I go. So there's one. Take down another one from the bulletin board in your Troubled Place and give it to me."

"That Uncle Beck's going to put a turd in my mouth."

"Okay. I'll write that here." I wrote the words along the inside of my middle finger.

The novelty of seeing me write on my own hand captivated Cassandra. She leaned over to examine my finger. "Look! You wrote 'turd' on yourself. You really did."

"Yup, because I'm going to take it away with me."

She was almost her old self in that moment, grinning up at me with rather lascivious pleasure at the dirty word.

Part of me was glad to see the old tricky Cassandra still there. On the other hand, I didn't want what I was trying to do to get derailed, so I said, "Okay, can you get something else from the bulletin board?"

"I want my mom to know how I'm doing," she said.

She said it so convincingly that I thought for a moment she meant now. I thought she wanted her mother to know she was in seclusion and feeling so bad she was suicidal. I looked over, catching her dark eyes and searching them.

Cassandra shook her head in answer to my unasked question. "That's something from my bulletin board. What I mean is, I wanted my mom to know. When I was with my dad. I wanted her to know how scared I was. I wanted . . ." Her words floated off.

I nodded. "Okay." I wrote "I want my mom to know how I'm doing" on the underside my ring finger.

"And another one is: 'I'm really scared.' "

I wrote that on the underside of my small finger.

" 'Cause that was how it always was. I was always really scared and so that's in my Troubled Place. On the bulletin board. Because maybe I'm going to be that scared again. And I'm scared of *that*. Scared of feeling like that again."

I nodded.

"And I'm scared to go to sleep. That's different. Put that on that finger, but that's not the same as that one."

She pointed to the words on my little finger. "If I go to sleep, I'm scared I'm going to hear the voices. That's now. That scares me now. But then, back then, I was scared to go to sleep because maybe Uncle Beck would come in. Or maybe Daddy would forget to come home and a burglar or something might come in. Maybe a burglar would abduct me. 'Cause that happens. And I thought it might happen to me and then no one would ever, ever find me. So put that on that finger, because, really, that is a big, big thing stuck on my bulletin board."

And so we continued on, listing more and more worries. The final few were probably a bit of a stretch. I suspect Cassandra had gotten caught up in wanting to see my hand completely covered in ink, but it involved her and, in the end, relaxed her enough that she was chatting playfully and giggling about the state of my hand.

"Okay," I said at last. "That's it. Here, help me roll my fingers up." I reached out and took her hand and together we folded the index finger of my right hand in on the palm. I then let her fold each of the other fingers over. Then I made a tight fist of the hand. "There. All the yucky stuff off your bulletin board, huh? All right here."

Cassandra nodded and smiled.

I rose to my feet. "And I'm going to take them home with me. They won't hurt me. I'm too strong. And now because I've got all those messages, you won't have to read them anymore. All right?"

"All right."

"Eventually you're going to be strong, too. Eventually they won't mean anything at all. One day they'll just be garbage, and we'll throw them away."

She nodded.

I rapped on the window to get one of the aides to come and let us out. "Think perhaps you can sleep now?" I asked, while we waited.

Cassandra nodded again. "Yeah, I'm really, really tired. I feel like I got glass in my eyes."

The door opened.

"Okay. Good night, then."

"Good night," she said. "And see you tomorrow."

"Yup. See you tomorrow."

When it was time for Cassandra's session with me the next morning, the first thing she wanted was to see my hand. I'd made no special effort to remove the words; however, normal activities such as showering and washing my hands had caused most of them to fade. Nonetheless, they were still largely readable.

"Look at that," Cassandra said with satisfaction. "Look, you still got all of that written on your hand."

"I sure do."

"It's lots of stuff. Your hand looks really dirty."

"Yes, it does."

"People are going to see it. They're going to ask what you got all that writing on your hand for!"

"And what shall I tell them?" I asked.

Cassandra grinned. "You'll have to tell them why you got 'turd' written on your hand!"

"I think you get an excited feeling when you consider that," I replied.

"Yeah, I do," she acknowledged.

"And you know what? That's normal. There are certain things the body does, certain words we use to describe those things that make everybody feel sort of excited when they hear about them. Interested feelings. That's just the way we're wired up. Everyone is."

"It's dirty."

"Well, see, that's the problem. One part of us feels it's dirty to think about things that are sexy or have to do with stuff that comes out of our bodies, like pee and poop. So seeing a word like *turd* written on my hand makes it seem like I'm doing something dirty that I should be ashamed of. But another part of us finds it kind of exciting to think about things like this. It makes us feel all tingly and interested. So seeing a word like that written on my hand is sort of thrilling, too. What I'm saying is that everybody feels that way. Not just you. That's because they are normal feelings."

When I'd first started to talk about this, Cassandra was squirming in a rather aroused way but this seemed to pass. She sat back, well away from my hand laid open on the tabletop.

"You remember when we were doing the exercise with the feelings and the poker chips?" I asked. "That was the point of that. Almost everything we do has got several feelings attached, not just one. And sometimes they are even opposite feelings. If you see 'turd' written on my hand, it can make you feel excited and interested, but it can also make you feel ashamed or guilty. You can get both feelings at the same time. Maybe it's going to make you feel scared as well. That's why we wrote 'turd' here last night, wasn't it? Because it was one of your scary thoughts. So seeing 'turd' written on my hand might remind you of what Uncle Beck did and then you'd feel scared. Or maybe the word would make you feel dirty, because getting something on you that belongs in the toilet makes most people feel like they need to wash.

"That's why I wanted to do that poker chip exercise. To help make it clear how we often have several feelings at once, because lots of times we don't realize that. We don't know it's normal to have lots of different feelings at the same time, that this happens to everyone, not just to people with problems. It's important to understand that it isn't weird or wrong to feel a bit excited about something that might also make you feel ashamed. It's just the way people are."

I reached behind me to the shelves and pulled over a couple pieces of blank paper. I uncapped a felt-tip pen. "Here, I'm going to show you something. Show you what happens sometimes."

At the top of the paper, I wrote "turd" and drew a little picture of a turd, which amused Cassandra to no end. She laughed and laughed.

"Okay, so there's a turd. Now, what feelings did I say that a turd caused us to feel?"

"Silly," Cassandra said, still laughing.

"Yeah, silly." So I wrote that. "And excited." So I wrote that word next to "silly." "What else? What else did I just say?"

"Sexy," she replied in a hoarse, rather excited voice.

"Yup, sexy." I wrote that next to "excited." I then drew lines down connecting these words to the drawing of the turd. "What else?"

"Scared."

"Okay, good. What else?"

"Ashamed."

"Good. Any others?"

"Mad." She looked up at me. "Mad? I mean, maybe, like, if somebody made you eat a turd, you'd feel mad at them, too. 'Cause they shouldn't do that to you."

"That's right. So there's another feeling. So when we see this turd, we get all these different feelings—silly, sexy, scared, ashamed, mad—and sometimes we feel them all at once. Can you think of any more?"

"Glad," she said. "Like you'd be glad if you got that turd out of you. If you really had to go. If you were holding it in and no one would let you go."

"Okay. 'Glad.'" I wrote that.

"And hurt. Because that's happened to me. When Uncle Beck would fuck me in my butthole, then afterward, sometimes it would really hurt to poop. Really hurt. *Really* hurt. Once, this one time, I was just crying and crying and blood was coming out. I didn't want to poop at all. My dad made me take a laxative."

"Okay. 'Hurt.'" I put that down. As with the other words, I drew a line connecting it to the drawing of the turd at the top of the paper.

Cassandra was no longer laughing. She'd sat way back again, almost shied away from the paper, the table, and me. She'd also gone pale and expressionless.

"Now I'm going to show you something interesting," I said. I drew three stick figures underneath the words. "See these? These little people?"

Cassandra nodded.

"It's hard to have all these feelings we have written up here at one time. Having so many feelings makes us feel full and confused. Because if you feel, for instance, excited and ashamed and scared all at once, it's hard to know exactly what you *do* feel, isn't it? They are all very big feelings. The kind that shout to get noticed. So if they're all shouting at once, it's hard to know how many there are or which one is which."

"Yeah," Cassandra said in a heartfelt way, but she still stayed well back from the table.

"Sometimes when our feelings get too much for us to cope with, we start making different people inside us to hold the different feelings. Like, for example, I knew this one girl. She was about your age. Her name was Susan, and she'd been in a very bad car accident when she was five. Her little sister was killed and her mom had been really badly hurt and had to stay in the hospital a long time. Later, lots later, when her mother was completely better and things were back to normal, Susan found it really hard to get angry with her mom, because she kept remembering that she had almost lost her mom. Even though things were just fine, she kept feeling scared that something might happen to her mom again. She also worried that her mom was unhappy because her sister got killed. Susan felt scared that maybe her mom wished it had been Susan who was killed instead. Things like that. So she didn't dare get angry in case it made her mom not want her or it made her mom go away. What Susan did instead was make a person inside her to hold her angry feelings. This person was named Mrs. Jones. And Mrs. Jones always felt really, really angry. She always did awful, spiteful things around the house that Susan was afraid to do herself. You know what started happening?"

Cassandra shook her head.

"It became a big problem, because pretty soon Mrs. Jones had *all* the angry feelings. So when something bad happened and the mom would get mad, Susan would say, 'I didn't do that. Mrs. Jones did.' But Susan's mom couldn't see Mrs. Jones, since Mrs. Jones was inside Susan. This made her mom just get madder and madder with Susan, because her mom thought Susan was lying. But because Mrs. Jones took care of all the angry feelings, to Susan it didn't feel like those *were* her feelings. So she didn't really think she was lying."

"Did Susan know she just made up Mrs. Jones?" Cassandra asked.

"Susan knew Mrs. Jones was in there, inside her, but mostly it just felt like it was someone else having those feelings, not her. Those were such scary feelings that she couldn't bear to feel them. So she let Mrs. Jones have them. But, of course, this got her in lots of trouble, because no one else understood about Mrs. Jones and so they blamed Susan for the things Mrs. Jones did."

Cassandra sat quietly, not looking at me.

"And I'm thinking maybe something like this has also happened to you," I said. "Now that we've started talking about it, you can remember the things Uncle Beck did, but you've got a lot of really big feelings about what happened. I'm thinking maybe when you were little and you couldn't do anything about what was happening to you, it just got too hard to live like that, and so you needed to make some other people inside you to help you cope with those feelings."

Tears started to slide over Cassandra's cheeks. She was sitting absolutely still, frozen even, all her muscles tensed.

"It was okay you did that, Cassandra. You were taking care of yourself. Sometimes when we are in difficult situations, we have to do things that we wouldn't do otherwise, and that's what was happening with you. You were strong and brave to do something to keep yourself safe. But now it's time to stop doing these things. Those difficult times are over and those ways you kept yourself safe aren't helpful in the life you lead now. So it's time to see that Uncle Beck is just like this turd here. He doesn't belong inside you. Now it's time to flush him down the toilet."

Cassandra's needs had been so pressing that I didn't get a chance to meet properly with Harry Patel and have the kind of discussion I'd wanted regarding my trip to Quentin. All I had managed was to catch him briefly in the hospital corridor that morning and pass on the shocking news that Lucia had been faking Drake's ability to speak. Harry registered wide-eyed surprise, and then we were off in opposite directions.

Lucia phoned in the middle of the afternoon.

She was crying.

"No, no, that's okay," I said. "You're not bothering me. No, of course, it's okay to phone."

"I cannot do it," she sobbed.

My heart sank.

"I can't tell Skip. He's going to be so upset. His father's going to . . . I'm sorry. I cannot do it."

I let out a long breath of air. At least she'd phoned.

"I do not know what to do," she said in a long, low moan. She was weeping noisily.

"Well, let's look at the possibilities."

"There are no possibilities. I do not know what to do."

"Well, we sort of have to take a 'where there's life, there's hope' view, Lucia. There *will* be something we can do," I said with a whole lot more optimism than I was feeling.

And so the conversation went. I talked with Lucia for almost an hour. She sobbed through most of it, her voice little more than a whimper when she did manage to speak.

It was obvious she was in enormous distress. Although she did not say outright that she was suicidal, it was not hard to imagine that. Nor was it hard to imagine the impact such distress might be having on Drake's father, whom I now knew to be depressed and suicidal himself. What a situation.

And what to do about it? Truth was, I didn't see any more options than Lucia did. The only difference was that I couldn't say that. So I listened. I tried to keep my voice calm and reassuring. Over and over I said the same things—that there *was* a way through this, that I knew it was very hard for her but she could do it and, ultimately, that it would have to involve revealing the truth about Drake to more people.

I asked if it would be better if I talked to Skip or if Skip came to the city with her, and we all had a meeting here. No, she said. No. No. No. To everything.

So we just kept talking. Or rather I did, while she cried.

Slowly, we worked our way back around to the point where we had left off in Quentin. Lucia couldn't cope with the idea of my telling Skip, so, in the end, she once again came to where she thought perhaps she could. Emotion spent, she talked, her voice quiet and flat. Yes. She'd try. And that's where we finished up.

As soon as I got off the phone, I went in search of Harry Patel. He was in a session and, indeed, was booked right through five o'clock. So I asked his secretary to find out if he'd be willing to stay late and have a word with me then.

When I returned to the seventh floor to see Harry after five, I found him in the little kitchen area behind the secretarial office. The floor was empty and the office staff had already gone home.

"Kitchen area" was a sophisticated name for what was simply a small room behind the reception area that contained a table and chairs, a half-sized sink, some counter space, a coffeemaker, and a microwave. Harry had a minuscule teapot out—barely big enough to hold one large mug's worth—and he was heating a Pyrex bowl full of water in the microwave.

"Very difficult to make tea around this place," he muttered, peering into the microwave. "Too many coffee drinkers."

"Couldn't you just do it in the coffeemaker?" I asked. That's what we did downstairs, if we wanted tea. Put a teabag into the coffee carafe and let the hot water drip through.

Harry made a face of exaggerated disgust, the sort of look you'd expect on the face of a wine connoisseur if you'd just suggested he might enjoy some of that nice boxed wine you'd opened two months ago and kept in the cupboard above the stove.

"I want *tea*," he replied. He lifted a small canister off the counter. "Here. Like this. My sister sends it to me. This is proper tea."

The canister was made from woven wickerlike material, but I couldn't tell what it was called, as most of the writing was in Bengali. The microwave dinged. Harry poured the water into his tiny teapot.

And then at last we sat down at the table to talk.

I told Harry all the details of the meeting out in Quentin. I told him, too, about the phone call earlier in the afternoon. And I admitted the one thing I didn't understand about myself in all this: the degree of shock I felt at this case. I was accustomed to dealing with both the victims and the perpetrators of child abuse. Indeed, I could listen to Cassandra telling about the hideous experiences with Uncle Beck, and while I was horrified for her sake, I was not shocked myself. Yet, this case did shock me. This was the boy's *mother*, and she had willingly sacrificed her own child to protect herself and her husband. She was willing to hurt a *four-year-old* to keep adults safe. I just kept thinking of what Drake had been needlessly subjected to—medical examinations, psychological interventions, the time here on the unit—and I was shocked.

I wanted to run my feelings by Harry to get his opinion, not only because I was perplexed about why this should affect me so strongly when I could accept much worse abuse cases as part of a day's work, but also because I feared it would interfere with my ability to work with Lucia, if I didn't pay attention to it. Intellectually, I was all right. Intellectually I could recognize the degree of fear and confusion Lucia must have felt to do what she had done, and I could respond in a rational way. However, if I wanted to be genuinely compassionate toward her, I needed to appreciate why it brought up such subjective feelings in me.

So we talked over that issue a little while. Harry, as always, was slow and meditative in his words, taking long pauses to stare into his cup of tea, as if to read information from the pattern of the tea leaves. He talked about the psychiatric perception of motherhood, about Jungian archetypes, about how we connected all these things with our own experiences, and from there he digressed into a discussion of how mothers were portrayed in mythology. I don't know if he ever really answered my concerns specifically, and truth was, the theories that underpinned Harry's perspective as a psychiatrist were to me just that—theories—which made them no more substantial to me than the myths he was recounting. Nonetheless, it was a helpful conversation. I think what I'd really needed was simply to acknowledge those feelings aloud, to express my concerns about responding appropriately to this case, because once I had, I felt better about it, even without answers.

At last the conversation came specifically to Lucia and the problem at hand. Harry and I explored the things she had done to cover up Drake's disability. We also discussed Drake himself and what could be done to help him. I had contacted the Mayo Clinic for a new report, but still had not received it, so we didn't know the full extent of his physical problems, but it was obvious that for him to prosper, he was going to need special support to acquire a nonverbal method of communication, and he had already lost a crucial four years of doing this.

Harry's brow furrowed in a thoughtful expression. "The more I think on all this, the more I'm wondering if Lucia isn't suffering a kind of Munchausen's by proxy," he said.

Munchausen syndrome by proxy is a strange and complex psychiatric disorder whereby people seek attention through the suffering of someone else. A carer—usually a parent or a medical worker—does things that harm the individual in his or her care, including fabricating, exaggerating, or inducing symptoms. This is done to get attention, sometimes just straightforward attention from people the carer perceives as powerful and authoritative, such as the medical community. Other times it is done more elaborately, so that the carer him- or herself appears valiant or important. In such instances, an affected individual may set fires in order to rescue the people inside a building or in some other way endanger people with the intent of garnering attention for being heroic in saving them.

I hadn't considered that possibility with Lucia—that she might, in fact, be purposefully avoiding appropriate intervention for Drake in an effort to get continued attention for his "specialness"—and I have to admit, the possibility of that made what was happening seem even more odious to me.

Leaving the seventh floor that night, I felt worse than when I'd arrived. That Lucia and her husband were so weak that, rather than stand up to Mason Sloane, they would make their son suffer for them was bad enough. The thought she could be doing it for attention was literally nauseating to me.

The staff at the rehabilitation center where Gerda was held assessment meetings on patient progress every two weeks to establish if goals were being met and if changes were necessary. The patient was included in the meetings where possible, as were immediate relatives. Joy Hansen phoned Monday morning to ask if I would come to the assessment meeting being held that afternoon for Gerda.

When I arrived in the conference room at the nursing home, a man I didn't recognize was sitting at the far end of the table. Tall and big-boned, with thinning mousy-colored hair, he looked to be in his mid-fifties. While he wasn't precisely what I'd describe as elegant, his well-cut, expensive clothes and his groomed appearance gave him a refined air.

I glanced questioningly at Joy, as I sat down beside her. "Son," she scrawled on the edge of her notebook.

A few minutes later, Gerda was brought into the

room by wheelchair. She was wearing a short pink
fleece robe and had a fresh, well-scrubbed look to her to
a point that her skin looked vaguely translucent, like
that of a Madame Tussaud's waxwork. Her long, yel-
lowed hair had been brushed out to flow over her shoulders, which made her look quite beautiful in a faded
way, although it occurred to me at that moment that
this was not a usual style for an eighty-two-year-old,
and Gerda herself would probably never choose to wear
her hair like that. Unable to manage her hair herself and
unable to communicate to any of the staff how she preferred to wear it, she might actually be finding her appearance embarrassing and we would never realize it.

"Hello, Gerda, we're here for your review," said the
staff nurse. Then they started off around the table, each
one of them who worked with Gerda—the nurses, the
physiotherapist, the occupational therapist, and so on—
giving their reports.

These were crucial meetings, and from the perspective
of a professional, I knew the value of the patient's presence. Not only did it enable the patient to participate, it
also protected important patient rights to information.
Nonetheless, I found it uncomfortable sitting through
the meeting with Gerda present. Despite the concept of
giving her access to the decision process, it was, in reality, lip service. She couldn't speak in a communicative
way. Simple as that. So her future was being decided
right in front of her, and however much she might not
want the outcome, it was unlikely she could do anything about it. Being present only allowed her to see it
happening. It didn't allow her to change it.

Unfortunately, there was no realistic alternative. No
one present was being calloused or uncaring. The sim-

ple truth was that we weren't in control either. Her circumstances themselves—age, health, income, support network—would decide everything.

Including Gerda, however, lent an aspect of humiliation to the proceedings that I was uncomfortable with. She was reduced to the status of a child in front of us. Inadvertently people slipped into the third person during the discussion, talking about her in front of her, not as a means of exclusion but simply because she was not of decision-making status. And I was left thinking how sad this was. Perhaps there was no other choice. I was realistic and experienced enough to appreciate that. It was sad, nonetheless, and it would be wrong to lose awareness of that.

Joy presented her findings, and then it was my turn. Only Joy had thought to include me; to the other staff I was still someone of indeterminate status. Which was fair, given I was not being paid and gerontology was not my field of specialization. And even more fair, given I really had nothing to add to the official assessment. While Gerda was now speaking spontaneously to me on a regular basis, it remained coded in memories. She *was* communicating. Indeed, it surprised me how much could be conveyed through this odd, symbolic form of speech. I knew now not only about her homestead childhood; I knew also the emotional territory of a lonely, marginalized child. And I knew as well, from her interactions with Drake, of her interest in other lonely, marginalized children, of her ability to recognize them, of her efforts to reach across the great gulf of age and disability to respond to them, to want to know what was happening to them. Yet there was nothing I could add to an official report on her rehabilitation. Gerda communicated in this way simply because the stroke had left her unable to communicate in the way the rest of us do, and while it *was* communication, she still could not make a telephone call or speak to a doctor or notify someone of an emergency situation.

I said my piece. Gerda's eyes were on me as I spoke, and if there exists telepathy in this world, it was happening then. I could hear her silent pleading. I could feel her desperation not to go down the road she was headed on. Her desolate sorrow echoed in my head. Nonetheless, I had to say what I had to say.

When the meeting ended, the decision was made. Gerda would move on to full nursing home care.

Afterward, when Gerda had been wheeled back to her room and most of the staff had returned to their duties, her son, Edward, came around the table to where I was sitting with a cup of coffee.

"I want to thank you for your efforts," he said. "I've been told you've been coming specially to see my mother."

I nodded. "You're welcome. I've enjoyed it."

"I wish we could have come up with something else for her," he said. "I know she won't like it."

"No," I replied.

Edward gave a faint shrug of his shoulders. "But she's always been difficult."

"In what way?" I asked.

"Mother is very passive-aggressive."

This seemed an extraordinary thing to say, so I asked, "How so?"

"She's always been one of those people who never does anything with her own life, but she also resents anyone else trying to do anything with theirs."

"Did you find this?" I asked.

"Yes, definitely. We all did. You should have met my father. He was extraordinary. Quite a go-getter." Edward smiled and sat down in the chair next to mine. "Funny how families are. How, if you look at them. You know. When you get older. When maturity gives you a more distant perspective. You do wonder at the workings of them. At how things ever turned out as they did."

I nodded.

"My father was, in his own way, very sophisticated. At least for those times. He was from Philadelphia, which was a long ways from here. In more ways than one. His family wasn't rich, but they'd still managed to help him get a good education. He was cultured, was my dad. Well versed in things like Greek mythology and botany. Music and art. Loved his art, did my father. And opera. He *knew* opera, can you believe that? Out *here*? My mother, on the other hand, never went past eighth grade. They met—it was during the Depression, so nobody had jobs—my father was unemployed and working piecemeal at whatever he could find and he got a temporary job at the sawmill and that's how he met her, because her father worked at the sawmill as well. He rented a room at their house and that's how they started courting. And know what? My dad married her, and then he spent the whole rest of his life as a manual laborer. I mean, here was a guy with two years of college. He could tell you about all the great artists living in Florence during the Renaissance and explain how all that creativity came about because of the Medici family's money, and then he'd tell you what all those pictures they painted meant. Yet he just stayed out on that ratty little farm they had, raising pigs and chickens to supplement the pittance he got paid at the mill. He had a strong personality, my father did. Influenced both Anna and me. Gave us such a love of culture." He grinned in a rather admiring way.

"Whereas my mother never bothered to learn anything. If she told us things, it was stuff like how they had to scrape grease from the frying pan to put across their bread when she was little because they didn't have enough money for butter, or how she raised a bum lamb once; it followed her everywhere, just like in the nursery rhyme. That was all she knew about, that very inward-looking down-home stuff. Yet she controlled my father. He refused to move off the farm. He refused to go anywhere, even into town. Kept saying it would kill her. Kill her to live somewhere else than here, just because she was born and raised here. But in the end, it killed him. Had a heart attack two days before he was supposed to retire. Just too much hard work."

"He must have loved her very much to do that," I said.

Edward gave a half shrug and twitched up the corner of his mouth. "I suppose they did love each other. In a way. But it was love without respect. One of those marriages of the kind they had in those days, when people had to stay together for economic reasons. I mean, how could my father respect someone who didn't want to do anything with herself but live out in the sticks with a bunch of animals? My mother is just plain stubborn. She acts so meek and mild, but she controlled us all that way. Not by doing things, but by not doing things."

"Yes, families can be challenging, can't they?" I said.

"It's not that I don't care about her," Edward replied.

"I do. But she *is* just plain stubborn. She wants things all her own way. The number of times I've said to her, 'Mother, you need to move into town. Why don't we sell this place and you can get one of those nice apartments in a retirement community.' We have a couple of them near us, where we live in Detroit, and that would have been ideal. I *could* take care of her then. So I *have* offered to help. But what does my mother say? She says, 'What about my cats?' I told her, 'Well, they're not going to take dozens of cats, are they? But then nobody *needs* dozens of cats.' I said, 'Get it down to one. Maybe we can find a place that would take one.' But, of course, she'd rather have cats than people. Which goes to show what her mind is like. And it always was like that. She always preferred cats. I used to shoot them when we got too many. I learned to use a .22 that way, shooting those blamed cats, because half of them were wild anyway. But Mother is just like her sister, my aunt Louisa. Both of them loved to be miserable and gloomy."

As he talked, I just sat, staring into my empty Styrofoam cup. There was nothing I could say.

I didn't want to go in to see Gerda afterward. I didn't want to look into her eyes after this meeting. On some level it felt as if I had betrayed her. I hadn't, of course. Things had been no more in my control than hers. Being there as a professional, however, being there among the decision makers, I nonetheless felt guilt by association.

But then, what choice was there? How could the decision have gone any other way? Unable to walk, to talk, to stand, to bathe herself, to use the toilet alone, she couldn't live alone. As she was, she wouldn't yet even be able to cope with assisted living. So it had been a fair, reasonable, and inevitable decision. Sadly, just not the way life should have to be.

After another cup of coffee to fortify myself, I did go in to see her, walking the long, narrow corridor of the rehabilitation center to her door, second to last on the right. Sitting up in the chair beside the bed, she was alone in the room.

I pulled up the orange plastic visitor's chair. "I'm sorry about the way things have gone. Sorry you aren't getting to go home."

She gazed at me. Something in the damage the stroke had done seemed to make it difficult for her to communicate straightforwardly, even with gestures, so she seldom even nodded or shook her head in response to conversation.

"Perhaps further down the line," I said. "Perhaps if you keep working hard. Because you have improved a lot since the stroke."

She continued to gaze at me a moment or two longer, her blue, blue eyes on my face. I gazed back, studying their blueness, seeing the cloudiness of age and wondering vaguely if blue eyes went bluer in old people, because it seemed that way to me.

"Sitting in the twilight," Gerda said.

I smiled at her.

Her eyes drifted away from me to some unseen point beyond.

"Fire in the haystack that autumn," she said softly. "We didn't have no hay for the winter. Mama says sell the horse, can't feed the horse and us, too. Papa says, 'No money in that horse, except for the glue factory. Won't no one buy that horse for anything else.' "

Gerda paused.

"Sitting outside in the twilight," she continued quietly. "A cold night. Frost is coming. Moon's coming up. Autumn moon, laying on the hill. Tim's in the corral. Munching. I say, 'Don't eat so much, boy. Please, don't eat so much.' I say, 'I'll take care of you.' I'm going to work. I tell Papa this. Papa says 'You're useless, girl.' "

"How old were you?" I asked. Gerda didn't seem to be able to answer direct questions when she was expressing one of these memories. Any time I asked, she went on as if I had said nothing. But I kept trying.

She just sat.

When she didn't answer, I said, "That must have been hard for you, your parents threatening to sell Tim."

"Mama had too many mouths to feed. Sitting outside on the step, no one notices. Twilight's come. No one notices."

"It's awful when you're little and you can't make anyone hear you. Especially when you've got feelings about something and no one realizes," I said. "I remember when I was small, we had this mother cat who kept having kittens and my family were always getting rid of them. I always tried to stop them, but lots of times I couldn't. It upset me so much."

"Sitting on the porch steps in the twilight," Gerda said. "Not day nor night. Nothing. No one can see what's in the twilight. Might as well be nothing. Papa can't see I was there. Says we'll sell Tim. Didn't matter what I wanted. Can't see I was there."

For once, when I arrived for my session with Cassandra, she wasn't in the seclusion room. Indeed, she wasn't even in the dayroom, where she usually waited for me. She was in the unit classroom with the other children, who were all sitting around a big table, doing work in the individual folders sent in from their various schools.

This unexpectedly ordinary scene startled me, making me aware of how seldom I had seen Cassandra in any context that might be deemed "normal." It pleased me as well. Chaotic and traumatic as the last week had been, clearly we were making progress.

Cheerfully Cassandra came with me. She was dressed in her dancer's clothes again—black leggings and long-sleeved T-shirt with a brightly colored short-sleeved T-shirt over top—and for some reason had only socks on and not shoes. She sprinted ahead of me and turned not one but three cartwheels in a row down in the corridor.

"You're very lively today!" I said.

"Yeah, I know." She turned a fourth cartwheel.

My first inclination was to correct her, to point out that the corridor was not really a place for turning cartwheels, that the floor was hard and that wearing only socks meant she might slip and hurt herself, that there were doors all along the corridor and someone might come out and bump into her; however, I held my tongue. Cartwheels weren't an ideal thing to do there, but they were a whole lot more acceptable for an energetic child than being a pterodactyl or throwing oneself against the walls of a padded cell. So I smiled instead and put my arm out when we arrived at the therapy room.

"Come here. Here's our room."

Cassandra bounded in past me.

"We're going to do something different today," I said. I turned out the lights and closed the door. As it was overcast outside and the room faced north, we fell into murky daytime darkness.

Cassandra had meanwhile leaped up onto the table. She ran from one end to the other and jumped down.

Going over to a small cassette recorder on the shelf, I turned it on. Soft, slow classical music started playing.

"Hey, cool!" Cassandra cried and leaped back up on the table. She shot to the other end again and leaped off.

"I can see you have lots of energy today. In fact, I'm a little concerned you might hurt yourself doing that. Come over here. We're going to do something different. See these pillows on the floor over here? We're going to sit on them. We're going to lie back and get *really* relaxed."

"How come?"

"Because we're going to talk today. And I want us to feel lazy and relaxed."

"Why are we going to talk? What are we going to

talk about?" Cassandra asked. She started to climb on the table again. "I don't want to talk. I want to draw."

"Yes, I'm sure you do. But today we're going to do this." Coming to the table, I grabbed hold of her as she prepared to charge off. I didn't want it to appear I was restraining her, so I made a big playful show of wrapping her in a bear hug, which, of course, was around her thighs, as she was on the table. Grabbing her tightly, I lifted her right off the table.

"Wow! You're strong!" she cried as I started to carry her over to the pillows. "Wow! Do that again! Catch me again off the table!"

"No. We're going to sit down here and do this." I was still holding her tightly around the thighs. I didn't set her down. "All right?"

Cassandra drummed playfully on the top of my head.

"All right?" I asked again, keeping my tight grasp.

"All right," she said in a somewhat deflated voice.

I let her down. After a moment's hesitation, she did sit with me on the pillows.

"So what's so important to talk about?" she asked.

"We're going to relax first. Get really comfy. Listen to how soft the music is. Take deep breaths so we feel really good. Then I want you to tell about what happened to you when you were with your dad."

"Why do you keep making me talk about that?"

"Because the way we get rid of your Troubled Place is by opening it up and cleaning it out, so there is nothing in it anymore."

"Dr. Brown never made me talk about it."

"I'm not Dr. Brown," I said.

"Dr. Brown'd tell you not to do that."

"Not to do what?" I asked.

"Make me talk about my dad taking me. Dr. Brown said to my mom, 'Don't ever make her talk about it. She'll get psychological damage.' " Cassandra looked at me in a pointed way.

I raised an eyebrow.

"She *did* say that. I heard her. I was in the other room, but I was sat really, really close to the door. And she said that."

Silence.

Cassandra was watching me in that intent, unflinching manner she had. Indeed, she'd sat bolt upright again to fix me more firmly in her gaze.

"Know what?" I replied. "If I heard someone say that about an experience I'd had, it would make me feel scared."

Cassandra's expression was one of confident superiority. She even had a little smile on her lips. "*I'm* not scared. Dr. Brown was just trying to take care of me. She was a better doctor than you."

"To me," I replied, "Dr. Brown saying that makes it sound like talking about your abduction would be a very dangerous thing to do. Doesn't it? If it were me in your shoes, I'd think 'Wow, that experience must be really powerful. Even just *talking* about it can hurt. And *I* actually had to live through it, so I must be really damaged already.' If I were in your shoes, I'd probably even think, 'I better *never* say anything to anyone about what happened. Then I'd get more damaged. Even worse, if I talk about it, maybe I will damage the people I tell it to as well. Maybe I will hurt my mom and people I love if I tell them about this. I better lock it up good and tight inside me, so no one gets hurt.' "

Cassandra was no longer smiling, but she didn't take

her eyes from my face. The energetic silliness had vanished. She sat very still.

"You're a very clever girl, Cassandra. You pay careful attention to many things. And that's good. But I'm going to tell you an important secret now. Something you really need to know. And it's this: not everything you hear is right. And in this instance, that *thing* wasn't right."

"But Dr. Brown said it. She said it to my mom. I heard it."

"Yes, I believe you. But it still doesn't make what you heard true. There's several possible reasons why you heard Dr. Brown say that. One possibility is simply that Dr. Brown was wrong. Just because people are grown up or well educated or important doesn't mean they are always right. Perhaps she didn't understand the matter herself quite correctly, so she *thought* she was saying something that was true, but it wasn't. Another possibility is that Dr. Brown said something *like* that but you didn't quite hear it right, because sometimes it's hard for kids to understand what adults say. Another possibility is that Dr. Brown was answering some very specific question your mother asked and for that specific thing, it was best not to talk about it more, or for that specific period in time it was best not to talk about it more, but Dr. Brown didn't mean forever. Or another possibility is simply that Dr. Brown and I do things differently, that we will arrive at the same point eventually but we have different ideas of how to get there. And because you are working with me now, we will go my way, because I know it best. And my way says that that is untrue. Talking about what happened will not hurt you. And it is an important part of getting well."

Cassandra grimaced.

"It's also important for me to say here that I'm never

going to *make* you talk about these things," I said. "I've told you this before, but it is worth reminding you of it. If at any time any of this is too scary or too hard, all you have to say to me is 'Stop' and we'll stop. We'll do something else for a while, until you feel more ready. I promise that. But simply talking about your abduction, talking about how it happened, what happened, who was involved, all those things—they *are* important to talk about. Know why?"

"Unh-unh," she said and shook her head.

"Because then they aren't secret anymore. Then you will not have to keep a Troubled Place inside you to hide all these things in.

"Our minds are kind of funny things. When something really big happens to us, it tends to stay really big in our minds and won't become a proper memory unless we talk about it. Our minds, on their own, don't seem to be able to get big events sorted out enough to squish them down into a size to fit with our other memories. We need to talk about it. Talking helps our minds to organize what happened—helps us understand how it occurred and how we felt and what we did. Sort of like you have a big laundry basket full of clean washing, sitting in the middle of your bedroom floor. It takes up lots of room. You see it every time you come in your room and maybe you'll trip over it, if you aren't watching out. But if you organize it—fold all the towels, roll up the socks—then you can put everything away neatly. Talking does that for our thoughts. It lets us put away things that have happened to us, so that they aren't in the way every time we are thinking.

"This isn't just true of bad things. It's true for anything big, even really good things. If you won a million dollars, for example, the first thing you'd want to do is tell everyone, wouldn't you? You'd want to talk about it and relive it and remember every little detail until you got used to the idea of yourself as someone who won a great prize. It's the same way if something bad happens. If, for example, you have a bad fall from your bike. You want to tell people about it, don't you? You want to tell them what it felt like, where you were hurt, exactly how the accident happened. That's how we cope with big things. We talk about them until our mind gets organized about what happened. Then they're not such a big deal anymore. Finally they start to feel more like ordinary memories and we can stop thinking about them all the time. We don't forget them. We never forget that we won that prize or we fell off our bike, but they've become just ordinary memories. They stop taking up all our thinking, just like the clothes in the laundry basket stop taking up all the space on our bedroom floor once the clothes are put away in the drawers. Then we can get on with what's happening now in our lives and not worry any more about it.

"But just the opposite happens if we have to keep something big a secret. First of all, we have to create a special place in our heads to keep it, and this is what the Troubled Place is. The Troubled Place is chock-full of stuff you can't tell. Usually this is bad stuff. Scary stuff. And you have to do a special kind of trick with your mind to get the door shut on a Troubled Place so that all this bad, scary stuff doesn't slip out into all your other thoughts. You have to lock it up really tight, so even you can't get in there very easily. If you don't, then you don't have any room in your mind for other thinking.

"When you first do it, first create a Troubled Place and manage to get it locked up, it's easy to think you've made it go away. But, in fact, this is the weird thing about Troubled Places. Just the opposite is true. A Troubled Place works just like a freezer does. Everything you put in there, it keeps really fresh, like it's just happened. So if you accidentally crack open the door on the Troubled Place and look at anything that's in there, that thing will hurt horribly all over again."

Cassandra had lain back on the pillows as I was talking. She was no longer looking at me, and she didn't speak.

"If you heard Dr. Brown say no one must talk to you about what happened, that must have been scary for you. I think if I'd heard someone say that, I would have felt what happened to me must be so awful that even the grown-ups around me were scared of it," I said. "I'd be really frightened then because I'd think I needed to really keep my Troubled Place locked up tight. I mean, what would happen if I didn't? What if it got out? What if I *did* say something, even accidentally, and it did lots of damage?"

Tears had formed in the corners of Cassandra's eyes. She was on her back on the pillows and the tears escaped, one running down either side of her temples.

I looked over at her.

Very briefly she glanced at me, then looked away. She nodded.

"If someone said that, I think it would just be putting words to what I already felt—that I must be a bad person because this happened to me, that things like this don't happen to good people and I'm dirty and dangerous to know because of it."

Again she nodded.

Silence then.

I didn't speak again. The music playing on the tape was Mahler's Adagietto from his Fifth Symphony, in my opinion a nondescript piece of music, the kind meant to be background music in a bookstore or in humdrum parts of films that is so subtle you never realize it's there. Now I listened to it carefully.

Cassandra looked at me when I didn't speak, her expression searching.

"I was waiting a moment there," I said, "because I wanted you to have the chance to think about what I just said, before I want to add something else to it. This is very important, so I wanted to wait until all your thoughts were focused on this. And here's what I want to say to you, Cassandra." I looked over at her. "That isn't true, what I just said about your being a bad person or a dirty person or a dangerous person to know because of what happened to you. I know it *feels* true, but feelings often aren't very accurate things. It's easy to fool our feelings, so it's important to learn not to pay too much attention to what they tell you, because lots of times, they're wrong.

"What happened to you is simply something that happened. It didn't happen because you are a bad person. It didn't make you a bad person because it happened. It just happened. And now it's time for it to be over. It's time to open up the door on the Troubled Place and clean all that junk out. Not to throw it away, because those are part of your memories, part of what makes you 'you.' But it's time to make them ordinary. To talk about them until you understand how you felt, what you did, what other people did. To talk about them until there aren't any secrets left in your Troubled Place to stay fresh and scary, to talk until you're bored with them. That will turn them into just ordinary memories, like all the rest of the memories of your life."

"The thing is," Cassandra said, "I don't really remember what happened."

She was lying back on the pillows. I had the overhead lights off, so we were in soft daylight darkness. We had done deep-breathing exercises to relax. I started the music cassette over again.

"That's okay," I said. "Mostly we'll just talk about little parts of it. Sometimes, I will say, 'Tell me one memory,' and it can be anything you want. Other days, I will say, 'What do you remember about this specific thing?' Some days you might remember something yourself that you want to tell. And that will be just a part of our time together. There will be other things we'll do as well."

"Like that feelings thing with the poker chips," Cassandra said.

"Yes, like that."

"Good," she said, "because I like doing that. And

maybe other things, too, huh? Like maybe we'll play some games? Dr. Brown did that with me. She played checkers with me lots of times."

"Except that it's important to remember I'm not Dr. Brown," I said.

"Yes, I know."

"And that we are here to work."

"Yes, I know."

Silence then. I listened into it, hearing beyond the soft music the everyday noises of the hospital.

Oddly, what I was reminded of, as we lay there on the pillows on the floor of the therapy room, was camping. I'd often taken the children in my special ed classes camping and there'd always been those moments, lying on our backs under the stars. There was the same ambiance now in the pale gloom.

"But for today, I'm going to ask you to tell me the story of your abduction," I said. "This is the only time I'm going to ask you outright to tell me the whole story. Other times we'll just talk about parts of it. And it's okay if you don't remember all of it. But I want to know how you remember it happening."

Cassandra didn't respond. We had the pillows out quite flat, so that we were lying almost prone on the floor. She was at an angle to me, and not that close physically. Our heads were, but that was all.

I heard her draw in a deep breath. She held it, then let it out slowly. Still she didn't speak. I listened to the music. I didn't actually recognize what was playing. Schubert, I think, but I couldn't be sure.

Cassandra brought her hand up and held it with the lower part of her thumb against her lips. After a few moments, she slipped her thumb in her mouth. I'd not previously seen her suck her thumb, but she did then, the sound very soft against the music. Still she didn't speak.

"What do you remember?" I said in little more than a whisper.

"I was at the school. We were doing finger painting. I remember that. I did this picture with blue finger paint and went around and around and around, and this kid next to me had red on his paper. I wanted another color. I wanted red. So when the teacher came around with the red pot, I said, 'Could I have some?' and she put this splodge on my paper and it made it go purple. I was just little. I didn't know red and blue make purple and I thought that was so cool. And I lifted it up to show the teacher and a bunch of paint dropped off. I remember that. I remember it falling onto my painting shirt and on the table and I got upset. I'd wanted to show the painting to my mom . . ."

She paused.

"I remember that . . . I remember that . . . it was right before I left to go home. That's when painting time was. I remember the teacher putting them on the radiator to dry. And then I went out. I had on this brown coat. I remember that coat. And my dad was there. He was driving this little red car. I didn't remember him having a red car. I hadn't seen my dad in a long time, so I didn't know it was him. But he said my name. He said, 'Do you still like Barbie dolls, Cass?" I said yes. He said, 'I got some of your old ones. Would you like to have them again, because they're really nice?'

"I couldn't remember having Barbie dolls I didn't know about, but he was my dad. So I went and looked but he didn't have any Barbie dolls in his car. He said,

'They're at home. There's too many to put in the car. Get in and I'll take you over.' "

Cassandra fell silent. The music tape had ended. I didn't want to get up and restart it for fear of breaking the spell, so I just lay quietly.

"I got in the car," she said, and there was in her voice all the regret of that decision.

Again the silence.

"I was going to wait for Magdalena, because she was just about to come out. That was what I was supposed to do. I was in kindergarten and we got out before the third grade did, and so I was supposed to wait for Maggie and then we would walk home. But I got in the car, because he was my dad and I thought he knew about my Barbies.

"And then he shut the door. He let me sit in the front and my mama never let me, so I was feeling sort of excited. And he fastened my seat belt and started to drive. I didn't know where his house was, but it was far away, because he kept driving. And I said, 'How much longer till we get there?' and he said, 'Not long,' and then I said it again, and he said 'Not long' again. And then I said I had to go to the bathroom and he said that was okay because we were going to stop and have a hamburger because it was dinnertime. So we did, and he bought me one of those soft ice cream cones, too, even though I didn't eat all my hamburger, and then we got back in the car again and I was sort of getting worried because it was getting kind of dark out. I said, 'I think I better go home,' because I thought my mom was going to get mad at me. He said, 'Don't worry. She knows you're with me. It's all right.'

"And we started driving again. And it was a really

long ways, because I fell asleep and when I woke up, we were still driving. And I said, 'How much longer?' and he said, 'Not long,' and I said, 'I don't think I want to go to your house,' and he said, 'Well, we're almost there.' But I was getting sick of it by then. I wanted to go home. I didn't want to go to his house. So I sort of started crying . . ."

She fell silent again. The thumb came up. She sucked softly for perhaps a minute or two.

"I was crying. I don't remember what I was saying but I remember asking to go home, because that's what I wanted, and my dad said to me . . . my dad said to me . . . 'I hate to tell you this, Cassandra, but your mom doesn't want you anymore.' He said, 'She phoned me up and told me to come get you and that's why I was at the school.' I started crying really hard then. I couldn't believe that was true. I thought my mom would have kind of let me know about something like that and she never had. But he said it was true. He said, 'Now your mom has a new baby. She doesn't want you anymore. She said three children were too many. She wanted to keep Magdalena, so she told me to come get you because she was going to give you to me. She said I could give you a better life.'"

Cassandra started to cry.

"What a horrible thing to hear."

She nodded.

"And it *wasn't* true," I said. "You know that, don't you? Your mom would never have given you away. She loves you so much and she was so worried when you disappeared. She searched and searched for you. Your dad was just saying that to get you to come with him."

"Stop," Cassandra said.

I looked over at her.

"Stop. I said, 'Stop.'" She had her hand over her eyes. "You said if it got too hard, all I had to say was 'Stop'..."

"Yes, that's right. We'll stop."

She started to cry in earnest then, rolling away from me. I sat up. "Cassandra, come here." I reached out to her. Rising up on all fours, she crawled over to me and I wrapped my arms around her.

She sobbed heavily.

"Thank you," I said. "I know it's very hard when you first start to crack open the door on your Troubled Place, but I really appreciate that you did. I understand much better now. You've worked very hard today."

She was still crying. Several moments passed.

When at last she could gasp for air, she said, "And what was awful, what was *really* awful, was that when I got to his house finally, *finally,* after all that time, there weren't *any* Barbies. Not even one. He'd lied to me. He didn't really have any toys at all."

$\mathcal{T}$he duplicate—and correct—copy of Drake's assessment arrived from the Mayo Clinic on Tuesday morning. When I had finished my morning sessions, I sat down and read carefully through it.

Drake had a complex set of congenital medical problems that included atrophied vocal cords and mild ataxia, which refers to a lack of coordination in certain muscles. This apparently accounted for the faint jerkiness I'd noticed in his movements. I hadn't really been aware he was uncoordinated for his age. Most of my experience was not with preschool children and there is, at four, such a huge variation in motor skills that I hadn't been looking for it. As I read the report, however, I thought back on his refusal to blow bubbles and, indeed, on his insistence on having a cup for his ice cream instead of a cone and realized then that these things probably resulted from lack of coordination in the muscles of his mouth.

The report highlighted that this particular group of problems occasionally appeared as part of a rare degenerative syndrome but that Drake was missing a usual marker for the syndrome in his blood. However, it was still possible he had it and, thus, it would be important for him to have regular retesting to rule this prospect out.

The recommendations at the end of the report emphasized the importance of teaching Drake alternate ways of expressing himself so as not to impair his communication skills. Given that he had no hearing problems and a high IQ, Drake stood a good chance of living an entirely normal life in spite of his disability. It was crucial, however, to give him the tools to do this as soon as possible, in order that he not miss, as the report writer put it, "the window of opportunity" to acquire language that is present in all young children but that tends to decrease as the child becomes school-aged. It was also suggested that Drake might be a good candidate for a voice synthesizer as he grew older.

Reading the report, I was again overcome with a sense of revulsion toward the Sloanes—toward Mason Sloane for being such an imperious, dominating old fart that he could control those around him so successfully, toward Skip Sloane for his weakness in not being able to stand up to his father and separate from him, if necessary, and for his self-absorption in not seeing something *had* to be going on with his son and not doing anything about it. Most of all, however, I felt it toward Lucia. *She* was the perpetrator. The others had let natural personality traits overrun them, showing little awareness or control, but *she* had actively sought to deceive. She had chosen to fake data, to set up an elaborate hoax to absolve her husband and herself, and had done so willingly at the expense of an innocent child. This report stated straightforwardly not only how to help her son, but also how important it was that her son be helped immediately, and it was already eighteen months old. The most valuable time for Drake to acquire language skills was in the preschool years, and with her deception, she has wasted at least a quarter of it. *Knowingly.* It went against everything I felt a mother should be to her child, and it just disgusted me to think anyone would do that.

When I realized I was thinking like that, I was again brought up short by the strength of my own feelings over the matter. It wasn't so much a matter of why I felt so strongly. "Why" would be a factor of my own personality and my own experiences and would be for me to understand as an exercise in self-awareness. The real question was much more basic than that. It was: how was I logistically going to keep such strong personal feelings from interfering?

And it was important that they didn't interfere. Although Harry Patel and I now had insight into what was going on with Drake, we had not yet managed to secure him the help he needed. Moreover, the only way we could help Drake, since he was no longer our client, was by helping his parents. So, to make effective changes, I had to convince Lucia and Skip to help Drake. And that wouldn't happen if I in any way conveyed they repulsed me.

So I thought deeply that morning about why people do what they do, and also about our responsibility as those who intervene in situations like this. It would be a simpler world if life were black and white, if it were only a matter of rewarding the good guys and punishing the bad, if it were only about giving help to those who deserved it. But not so. It's all grays. We're all evil in parts and good in others, undeserving and deserving. And our struggles mainly come down to how aware we are of that.

In the process of trying to understand others' difficult behavior, I've found it is very helpful to realize that no one chooses to be unhappy. If someone is unhappy, they will be so because they genuinely cannot see how to do otherwise. This I've found to be true even in those situations where, from a more objective perspective, it is very obvious what their mistakes are.

So, in the end, I was able to get myself around to the place where I recognized that Lucia must have made the decisions she did because she simply couldn't see alternatives to them; and as a consequence, I was better off not wasting emotion on wanting her to be what she wasn't able to be. Better instead just to get on with the task of helping her find those alternatives.

It was good I had this think in the morning, because in the afternoon, I had to put theory into practice. Lucia phoned again. Indeed, this became a pattern. She phoned three afternoons in a row. Each time she was in tears. Each time she was ready to back out. She simply could not face the prospect of telling her husband the truth about Drake and what she had done.

I took it to be a good sign Lucia was phoning me. If she were genuinely unwilling to make these changes, no contact would have been a more logical response. Thus, I took the fact that she continued to reach out, even though we weren't making any noticeable progress, as an indication she was still considering it.

Nonetheless, the calls were tedious. Over and over and over we covered the same territory. I talked about how important it was to make these changes; how Lucia's and Skip's first responsibility was to Drake, not to Mason Sloane; how Mason Sloane did not have authority to ruin their lives. Repeatedly, I listened to her story, reassured her I was okay with her tears, sympathized with how hard it was to face up to such difficult matters, rallied her on, told her I just knew she and Skip did have the strength to make these necessary changes. At the same time, however, I also tried to be unambiguously open about the fact these changes *had* to take place and, if they didn't, that I would eventually involve Social Services or some other outside body. I explained as gently as possible that while her behavior toward Drake did not constitute child abuse in the traditional sense of the word, it *was* abusive, because it was seriously harmful to Drake. Thus, it couldn't continue. I said I was particularly concerned to learn that Drake required continuing medical intervention to make certain his problems weren't of a degenerative nature. And I continued to express my worry that we were compromising Drake's chances of functioning normally in the future by every day we missed of not providing special language support now.

It was a tightwire act. Even as I got past my own difficult feelings toward Lucia's actions and was able to relate to her without thoughts of revulsion at what she'd done, I still found it hard not to want to scream down the phone at her: *Get on with it!* I could appreciate she needed someone to listen to her, that she had undoubtedly been stifled and silent at least as long as Drake. I could appreciate, too, that Lucia was no doubt in as much need of sympathy and compassion as her son.

And, of course, I was very grateful that she'd found the strength to come forward at all, because otherwise Drake would have vanished from our radar, and that would have been that. We would never have known what became of him. Nonetheless, I could not continue compromising Drake's welfare to support Lucia. For his sake, we *had* to stop this charade.

During each phone call, we went over different ways of telling Skip and Mason Sloane the truth. Lucia seemed to forget these various ideas between calls. It was as if they just dropped out of her head when she hung up the phone, because each day when I mentioned them, she reacted as if they were all new to her.

So I tried a different tactic. Instead of suggesting ideas, I asked her to come up with them. What did she think would be a good way to go about it? What would work from her perspective? By this point she had heard my suggestions three or four times, so I hoped if I gave good enough prompts, she would be able to produce her own versions. Not so. Talking with Lucia was maddeningly similar to conversations with Cassandra. "I don't know" and "I don't remember" were her two favorite phrases.

I suggested that perhaps giving Skip the correct version of the Mayo report and letting him read it for himself might be one good way of introducing the subject, if she couldn't talk about it directly. I also suggested perhaps she write a letter to Skip, because sometimes it was easier to say things in writing than in person. Indeed, I even suggested e-mail. Could they have an e-mail dialogue, if a face-to-face one was too hard? Or what about a nice romantic dinner with a good bottle of wine to relax them?

Yes, maybe. That was Lucia's answer to everything. "Yes, maybe. I maybe could do that." But then when she next phoned, she hadn't done it. She had forgotten. It sounded all new to her when I suggested it again.

I then asked if it would help if *I* told Skip. Lucia's immediate response was no. She was accustomed to protecting Skip from a great number of life's woes and leaving him to my mercy was further than she was willing to go. After these suggestions in various permutations failed for a fourth and fifth time, I finally said, what if the three of us got together? I was trying to avoid another day lost to the rest of my clients by going out to Quentin again, especially as Drake was not officially still on our books, so I suggested Saturday. Then Skip would be available, too.

No. A flat, out-and-out no from Lucia. When I asked why not, she first said it was because Drake would be there. I replied that was okay. Indeed, I felt it was time for Drake to be included, for him too to learn the truth. So then Lucia said no, Saturdays were dangerous. Why was that? I asked. Mason Sloane was likely to be around, she said. He would stop by unexpectedly. He would expect Skip to do things with him. He would want to spend time with Drake. And he'd very definitely want to know why I was there.

I suggested meeting away from the house, perhaps in Starbucks again, but that suggestion was also met with a no. Mason Sloane would find Skip wherever he went. Lucia talked with such certainty it was almost spooky, this sense there were eyes and ears everywhere, that there was no way of escaping Mason Sloane.

So I suggested meeting well outside Quentin. This wasn't a new suggestion. None of my suggestions were new by this point. Previously she had objected, citing being unable to get away. What if it were a Saturday? I asked. Couldn't it just be a shopping trip? Was Sloane that suspicious of them? Couldn't they leave early enough before Mason Sloane came around? I reminded her that sooner or later Mason Sloane was going to have to be confronted over this anyway, so wouldn't this be a good start? Just to simply leave without telling him where they were going? To have a family day out that did not include making plans with her father-in-law?

Lucia hesitated.

It was a long enough hesitation that I could discern she was actually considering what I was saying, so I pounced on it. What about Melville Crossing? I suggested. This was a small town about halfway between the city and Quentin, so it would be a good couple hours' drive for both of us. There was a McDonald's there, quite a large one with an indoor play area. I knew, because we'd stopped there before when taking kids on outings from the unit. So Drake could amuse himself in the play area while we got through the heavy talking.

There was a long pause. Then Lucia said, "If Drake comes, you will tell him . . . you will tell him . . . the truth?"

"Yes."

She started to cry. "You will tell him I didn't mean it?"

$\mathscr{I}$ wasn't able to continue working with Gerda after she was moved from the rehabilitation center. The nursing home she went to was almost ten miles away from the hospital, and, indeed, it seemed this would be only a temporary placement. In the end, Edward decided that once her property had been sold and other affairs put in order, he would move his mother to Detroit and place her in a nursing home there.

As well as logistical reasons for not continuing, there were no longer professional reasons either. Gerda's language problems were, indeed, a facet of the stroke, and, as I had no training or experience in this area, there was little expertise for me to offer. Originally having seen Gerda as a favor for Joy, I wasn't being paid for what I was doing beyond my travel expenses. Consequently, once she left the rehabilitation center, I was no longer going to be working with her.

Nonetheless, I did want to see Gerda one last time to

say good-bye personally, rather than just disappear, because I genuinely had come to enjoy the old woman's company. I had intended to go see her one last time before she moved out to the nursing home, but I didn't manage it. Between Lucia and Cassandra absorbing all my extra time, plus my usual caseload, I was simply too busy in the week following the conference over Gerda's future to get over there. And the rehabilitation center, always short on beds, wasted no time in moving Gerda out, once the decision had been made. So when I rang Joy on Thursday afternoon, she told me Gerda had already been transferred.

I still wanted to stop by and see her. This wasn't going to be easy, simply because the nursing home was so distant from the hospital; however, when I made the plans to go meet Lucia and Skip on Saturday at Melville Crossing, I decided that if I left early enough, I could stop to see Gerda en route. The nursing home wasn't exactly on the way, but it wouldn't be a big detour to stop then. I penciled the address into my diary.

That was Thursday. That evening, Joy rang me at home. Gerda had had a massive stroke and was now in the intensive care unit of the hospital. Friday morning when I arrived for work, I stopped on the ICU floor to see how she was. Gerda had died in the night.

The nurse asked me if I wanted to view the body. This struck me as an extraordinary question before I realized that she had mistaken me for a relative and assumed I was there about mortuary arrangements. I said no, explained who I was, and told her about Edward, whom I assumed they had details for. And yes, she said, Edward had been contacted and was en route from Detroit. She knew there was also a daughter. Somehow she had assumed this was who I was. No, I said and suddenly found myself explaining the intimate, disconnected workings of this family I hardly knew. Then I excused myself and went on up to the unit.

Gerda's death affected me deeply. In part, it was simply the shock one always feels over an unexpected death and being confronted by death's irrevocable ability to terminate even the brightest spark of life. There had been such a vitality to Gerda when we had talked. When she spoke of her past as a strange, symbolic representation of her present, it had transformed historic memory into current events. The young girl, the boxcar horse, and the immigrant homestead had become as alive to me as the room in the rehabilitation center. Now suddenly it had all gone silent again. In a matter of hours, these things had reverted back to history, to things that would fade and pass away and eventually be forgotten, and, indeed, now Gerda with them.

It affected me also in terms of connection and disconnection. How had so many people in Gerda's life missed seeing who she was? Missed understanding her? In many ways, this was one of those "probably for the best" kinds of death. Probably better this than life in a nursing home in Detroit, because everything about Gerda had so pointed to that being a life she wouldn't want to live. Indeed, perhaps it was the distress of that change that had precipitated the second stroke.

I could see all this and appreciate it rationally, but in my mind was still the question "Why?" Why had there been all these missed connections? Why did Edward know so little about his mother? Where was Anna in all of this? How was it that Gerda had failed to communicate with her children? Why does this happen to people? And how sad that now the opportunity to change these things was over.

The sessions with Cassandra were harrowing as she began recounting her experiences during the abduction. She didn't remember much, so there wasn't really a continuous story. Rather, what she recalled was episodic— a huge amount of detail around a single incident and then blanks—but this, if anything, made the sessions even more grueling because those small moments then became breathtakingly real with their detail-by-detail clarity.

Once involved in the task, however, Cassandra showed a hungry desperation to continue. She *wanted* to tell me these things and often spent much of her time between the sessions thinking of what next she wanted to recount. Frequently, she would start the story the moment we met in the dayroom, well before we'd made it to the therapy room.

Indeed, the need to relate her experiences started spilling over into her relationships on the unit. She was now telling Nancy and the other staff about what happened. Even in the unit classroom, doing such simple things as a math workbook, her mind was on the past.

Many of these memories were just little snatches; if she was allowed to recount them, she would then return to the task at hand. For example, on the occasion of the math workbook, she seemed to be dithering over what to do, so the teacher had stopped by her seat to give her help. Cassandra said, "I was dreaming once. I used to have this one dream all the time. Back then. Back when I was with my dad. We were in this boat, going across a big lake. My dad was in the boat. But so was my mom and my sister. Then, when we were in the middle of the lake with no land around, the boat tipped over and we fell in the water. In the dream my mom saved my sister, because my sister couldn't swim. And my dad swam to shore. But nobody saved me. I was going to drown. And then next, I was in this coffin and it was in the front room of our old house. But I was really alive. Nobody knew it. They thought I'd drowned and, because I was in a coffin, I was dead. And I kept trying to say, 'No, I'm alive!' But something kept me paralyzed. So no one believed me. No one thought I was alive and they put the lid down on the coffin and they were going bury me."

"Wow," her teacher said. "That was a scary dream."

"Yeah," Cassandra replied. Then she pulled over her math workbook and started working.

As these stories proliferated, Cassandra's tendency to make up fantastic tales accusing people of outrageous or sexually perverted acts dropped off precipitously. My sense was that Cassandra's lying had worked both as a preventative—keeping people distant so that they couldn't do those things to her again—and also as a way of releasing internal tension, because the cost of keeping her experiences sufficiently suppressed to allow her to function in the everyday world was so hideously high. Those dreadful lies had simply been pus, discharged to ease the pressure of festering secrets.

Our time in therapy now inevitably belonged to Cassandra, who arrived each morning bursting with what she wanted to tell me. Often the desperation outstripped her ability to articulate these things. In other words, she arrived with very strong feelings but little real memory to attach them to. I tended to let her recount what was on her mind and go from there.

For instance, one morning she started by saying, "My daddy gave me a toy bunny."

We were sitting comfortably on the pillows on the floor, as this had become our special place for talking.

That was all she said, but she looked over, her expression expectant.

"When was that?" I said.

"I don't know. I don't remember."

I nodded.

A pause.

"I think it was in the beginning. Because I didn't have any toys."

"And what was your bunny like?"

"It was brown and had a white tummy. And it was really squishy soft."

"That sounds like a nice bunny."

Cassandra nodded.

Since she had come into the therapy room wanting to talk about the toy rabbit, I assumed it had significance for her, that it played some part in the destruction of her childhood. My challenge then involved helping to open the doors on these memories without putting words in her mouth or pressure on her lack of memory.

I usually started by gently questioning, but also allowing plenty of time in between for her to explore her memory.

"What do you remember about your bunny? Did it have a name?"

"Bunny. I think it was just Bunny." She fell very silent, her brow bunching up in an expression of concentration. A minute or two went by, which is a sizable amount of silence in an active conversation.

I listened to the music. Throughout this I had continued playing these tapes of slow, soft classical music. In part I did it to create a tranquil mood and aid relaxation, but I also did it to enhance association between the sound of the music and meaningful discussion, because I had discovered pairing certain activities with certain pieces of music tended to make it easier to elicit these same behaviors again. And beyond that, I found the music to be an invaluable place to put my own mind during these long silences. By listening to the music instead of hanging on to the end of the last sentence, I could keep that expectant impatience that often occurs during silences in conversations from developing.

"Foo-Foo," she said at last. "Maybe the bunny's name was Foo-Foo. You know, like in the song. 'Little Bunny Foo-Foo, hopping through the forest.' Maybe that was it." A pause. "Or maybe not. Maybe that's just the song coming into my head. I don't know."

During this period when Cassandra started talking about her experiences of the abduction, I had not lost track of the fact she had coped with much of the trauma by dissociation—that is, she had hidden experiences that felt too overpowering behind amnesic walls or had protected valuable parts of herself by disowning them.

There still hadn't been sufficient time to explore these matters in-depth. I wanted to lay the groundwork first of recognizing and recounting the abduction so that it would not hold such frightening power. However, I did try to acknowledge these other parts of Cassandra, to continue drawing them into our conversations. It was now clear to me that in our earlier sessions together Cassandra had "switched" on several occasions, and I did not know if these were conscious or unconscious alterations. However, as we talked about "the others"—predominantly Minister Snake, Cowboy Snake, and Fairy Snake, but also Bicky and Becky, a couple other Snake family members and a more amorphous personality simply referred to as the "Naughty One," whom Cassandra maintained was not her at all—I was aware she could access these personalities at will.

This was all quite confusing to me on the outside, because it was hard to discern when she could control things and when she couldn't; and it wasn't helped any by the fact that the literature on multiple personality disorder was scant and my own experience almost nonexistent. I found, however, if I asked Cassandra directly about one of the alters, she could usually access the information, although she would relay it to me as if it came from someone else, rather than "switching" to that personality herself.

Because our eventual goal would be to reintegrate these different personalities back into one, I felt it was important to encourage Cassandra to access these alters for additional information about the abduction. This was both a way to keep the alters part of her conscious mind and to express my acceptance not only of these variously diverse parts of her but also of the secret information these alters held. Once again, the overriding message had to be that nothing was really going to be too overwhelming, too frightening, or too sordid that I couldn't cope with it.

As a consequence, as we lay there on the pillows discussing—or, rather, *not* discussing her toy rabbit—I said, "Who else might know about your bunny?"

Cassandra looked over.

"Does Cowboy Snake know anything about Bunny?" I asked.

"Ow-ow-ow-owww," she howled softly in a haunting tone that I'd come to recognize as Cowboy Snake's signature tune. It was, indeed, a proper yodel, this sound, which I found a surprising noise to come from a young girl's throat, so it always startled me slightly when she did it.

"Ow-ow-ow-owww," she went again, mournful as a coyote. "Ow-ow-ow-owww." Then she shook her head.

"Who, then?" I asked. "Who knows about your toy rabbit?"

"Fairy Snake," she said.

"Can Fairy Snake tell us, then?"

"Little Bunny's soft." Her voice was soft and high, like a small child's. "My daddy gave him to me. He bought him at Toys 'R' Us, 'cause there's a Toys 'R' Us near where my daddy works. My daddy bought it. For me. And Bunny's soft. And I take him to bed." She smiled at me.

"That sounds nice."

She nodded. "It's 'cause I'm a good girl. Daddy bought him for me because I'm a good girl. And Daddy says he and me can go to Toys 'R' Us one day and he'll take a shopping cart and we'll *fill* it with toys!"

"Hey, lucky you."

Cassandra grinned. "And once, *once*, guess what?"

"What's that?" I asked.

"My daddy bought these clothes. Doll clothes. For a Cabbage Patch doll. But I don't got one of those. But he said he bought them for Bunny and I put them on and Bunny had a dress on!" Her voice went up in the squeally, high-pitched manner of an excited child.

"Your daddy did some nice things, didn't he?"

She nodded vigorously.

"Your daddy showed how much he loved you, didn't he?"

She nodded again.

A small pause then.

Cassandra was still watching me. "My daddy loved me a lot," she said, her voice much softer. Another pause. "My daddy loved me." It was almost a whisper.

Silence intruded then. I looked away. Listened to the music. Tried to identify it. Massenet's "Méditation" from *Thaïs*.

"It's confusing, isn't it?" I said, "when we have many different feelings about the same thing. When we feel hate and love and fear and happiness and excitement all at once."

Cassandra nodded. Tears had formed in her eyes. She was no longer looking at me.

"But you know what?"

She shook her head.

"It's okay to feel like that. Everyone feels like that. Everyone has times when they hate someone and love them at the same time. When they're scared of them but they want them there, too. When they have lots of different and even opposite feelings about the same things. It's all right to be that way, because that's how we're made."

The tears rolled over her cheeks. She raised her left hand and caught the tears one by one with her index finger, wiping them on her shirt. "What I want to know," she said very softly, "is why. Why, if my dad loved me, did he let those things happen to me?"

Because the recounting of her experiences was so emotionally draining, I tried to break the sessions into parts to allow us some other activities besides the tale itself, not only because I wanted to give Cassandra a chance to recover before returning to the unit but also because I wanted to model ways she could master herself for regaining equilibrium after dealing with overwhelming feelings and events.

So, this discussion of Bunny, which I saw as an exploration of her father's relationship with her, of trying to understand him as a man who loved her as well as abused her, segued nicely into doing the poker chip exercise.

We got out the feelings papers, and I asked Cassandra to put chips into the columns listing the various feelings. First I suggested she show all the different feelings that thinking about Bunny made her feel.

"It makes me feel good to think about Bunny," she said and looked across the sheets. "And you know what? We don't have that one. Don't have just simply 'feeling good.' "

"Would 'happy' be the right one?" I asked.

"No, that's too big a feeling. Just 'good.' "

"Warm?" I suggested.

"Yeah, 'warm.' That'd do. A warm feeling. A nice feeling. We don't have anything of those." Cassandra jumped up and got the box of markers out. She drew a new line down the last paper to section off the column and then wrote "Good" at the top. "There. Now we have that one."

She paused. She looked along the table at the other sheets of paper, laying side by side. "Look at all those. Remember when I was drawing pictures and putting these names on the feelings? Like here is 'dog puke feeling.' And 'baby feeling.' "

I smiled and nodded.

"I don't know why I wanted to do that," she said. "but I really did. It seems sort of silly now. And my drawings are crap. Look at them." She giggled.

I smiled again. "Things are changing, aren't they?"

Cassandra nodded.

There was a small pause.

"I'm getting better, aren't I?" she said softly.

"Yes, I think so."

Again there was a pause. Cassandra reached across the table for the poker chips and poured a small amount out. She carefully stacked one, two, three blue chips on the column under "Good." She added two more.

"Know what Dr. Menotti said to me?" she asked.

"What's that?"

"If I can go ten days without being in lockdown once, I can go home."

"Hey, that's good, isn't it?"

She nodded. "And guess what else?"

"What's that?" I asked.

"I've already gone seven days."

Chapter

37

*S*aturday morning I started the long drive to Melville Crossing. It was a windy, gray day, one of those where the sky is a dreary unbroken pane of color, dull as a gunship. It wasn't raining and wasn't predicted to rain, although I would have preferred rain, I think, just to give movement and, thus, perhaps a sense of life to the still winter-brown landscape.

When I arrived at the McDonald's in Melville Crossing, it was empty except for staff, and so brightly lit in contrast to the overcast day that it was jarring to come inside. And noisy, too. Some teeth-gnashingly cheery music was being played too loudly through the speakers, and the staff were doing something enthusiastically back in the cooking area, which sounded like it involved throwing pans.

No Sloanes, however.

I bought a Dr Pepper and took a seat in a large booth near the play area. I waited.

I checked my watch. We had agreed to meet at lunchtime and because of the distance we were each covering, we'd agreed to meet at noon for lunch at 12:30 P.M. I arrived at 11:50. Noon came and went. 12:30 came and went.

As families began to fill the place up over the lunch hour, I felt self-conscious sitting in one of the big booths all by myself. It was a good-sized establishment, aimed at attracting trade from the nearby highway, but not that large. A woman with a rowdy group of five children glared at me. I was especially self-conscious because I had nothing more than a drink in front of me. I would have gotten up to get a hamburger but knew if I moved, I'd lose the booth. So I sat tight and glared back.

12:45. How long should I wait? I reminded myself that there were any number of legitimate reasons for a delay, given the distance. In the back of my mind, however, was the fear that they weren't coming at all. Lucia had chickened out yet again.

Where would we go from here? I wondered, as I watched the clock edge past one o'clock. Would Lucia phone again? Would we keep having to have these afternoon pep talks to the point we'd try this meeting again and hope it worked? How long, realistically, could I be expected to do this? Where did my responsibility in this situation leave off, allowing me to pass the baton to someone else who lived closer to Quentin? Who would it be? How? The only thing I could think, if Lucia refused to follow through, would be to involve Social Services, and this would mean filing some kind of formal child abuse report. If I did this, up came the specter of court action and the involvement of lawyers and social workers and so much more trauma than should be needed to get Drake the help he deserved.

Frustrated and unhappy, I sat until the lunchtime crowds thinned. It was 1:20 by that point. I got up, went to the counter, and ordered a Quarter Pounder and some fries.

And then there they were. Skip, Lucia, and Drake climbing out of a dark blue SUV in the parking lot as I was sitting down at the table again. It was 1:30.

I saw Lucia turn and scan the crowd inside the restaurant until our eyes met. She raised a hand in a half wave.

What had she been doing? I wondered. Taking all this time to work up the courage? Having trouble getting Skip on the road because she hadn't actually told him why they were coming here? Or had she been hoping that by being so late, I wouldn't be there, that she could legitimately say, "I came," without having to confront the issues?

Drake spotted me as soon as they came through the door. His parents went to the counter to order lunch, but he and Friend came running across the room to me.

"Hi! And hi, Friend, too!" I said and I signed "Hello" as well.

He grinned from ear to ear and clambered up into the seat opposite me.

"Isn't this exciting? Did you know you were coming to see me?" I asked.

Drake nodded enthusiastically.

"And I'm so glad to see you!" I said. "Did your parents tell you why you've come?"

He shook his head.

"Well, good news! You're here because I understand now about how you can't make words. We're meeting so I can help your mom and dad learn about it. That way we'll discover new ways to talk. Like with our hands." I signed "I love you" to him.

Drake's cheery expression faded as I spoke. He searched my eyes.

"We *do* understand now," I said. "No more of this awful 'Drake must speak,' because now we know why you can't do it. We know it isn't you being naughty. It's not your fault. From now on, I'm going to try and help your mom and dad—*and* your granddad, too—understand that it isn't 'Drake must talk like we do' but instead 'Drake has his own special ways of talking.'" I smiled at him.

Tentatively, he smiled back.

Lucia and Skip arrived at the table. One look at Lucia stayed my urge to inquire about their delay in arriving at Melville Crossing. She was pale and haggard.

"This is my husband, Walter," she said, as he put the tray on the table.

"Just Skip, please," he said and extended his hand. I shook it.

He wasn't what I'd expected. Physically, Mason Sloane was a sturdily built man, and this had lent to his powerful presence in the room every time I'd met him. In contrast, Skip was tall and gangly thin, almost as if at thirty-five he were still trapped in adolescence. His hair was pale, his skin an unhealthy, almost grayish color. He was, nonetheless, strikingly good-looking because of bone structure so suave and chiseled it belonged in a James Bond movie. What let Skip down, however, were his eyes. He met mine only briefly then looked away, down, over to Drake, down again. Shifty eyes, as my grandmother would say.

Skip and Lucia sat down. There was a long, acutely uncomfortable silence as everyone unwrapped their food. Lucia leaned over to help Drake open his Happy Meal. The toy was a little Lego something and Drake held it up joyfully. Both his parents smiled at him. Then Lucia used the handle of a plastic fork to cut Drake's hamburger in half. She handed one piece to him.

I sat quietly, waiting. Praying. Bracing myself.

I think it was at that moment, more than any other time, that I became aware of the extent of Drake's disability. Not because of anything he did but just because of the eerie transposition of a completely silent child against the raucous noise of a fast-food restaurant, of the clatter in the food preparation area, of the music, the chatter, other children whooping and shouting in the play area.

Abruptly, Lucia rose. She was in the middle, between Drake and Skip, but she jumped up. Skip stood to let her out of the booth and then sat back down again.

I turned to see where she was going.

Skip said, "She needs to be sick."

I looked back.

He shrugged without meeting my eyes. "She's upset. It's hard for her to keep her food down then."

We ate in uneasy silence.

Skip reached over to his son. "You finished, buddy? Do you want to go play?"

Drake accepted this invitation readily. He slid down onto the floor and wriggled out under the table, then ran off, leaving Skip and me alone.

Silence.

"I know," Skip said in a very soft voice.

More silence.

"Lucy told me night before last. She'd said something about coming out here today and I couldn't understand why. Couldn't figure out what she was getting at . . . So, she told me."

I nodded.

"I probably knew," he continued. "I probably knew all the time . . ." Which I pretty much imagined.

"Can you see that for Drake's sake, we need to change things?" I asked.

Skip nodded.

"Have you seen the Mayo report?"

"No. Not yet."

"I'll send it to you, if you wish, because I've received the unadulterated version. It speaks in there of the need to reassess Drake in case there is more to this than they were able to ascertain. It's very rare to have a child unable to make any speech at all, so it needs further investigation. There are degenerative conditions . . . other problems . . . and for Drake's safety, he needs to be seen by a specialist again to address these possibilities."

Skip had his head down. He drew in a long breath, and I realized he had become tearful. Raising a hand, he wiped the corner of his right eye. I glanced in Drake's direction, hoping he would continue to play.

"I'm so sorry for this," Skip said softly.

"No, it's all right. I understand how upsetting this must be."

"You have to understand about Lucy. She's a good person. Really she is. And a good mother. She never meant Drake any harm."

"No, I'm sure she didn't. Sometimes things happen that we don't mean. They get out of control before we realize it, and then they just run away with us. I'm sure that's the case here. I'm sure no one meant in any way to hurt Drake. But now it's time to put things straight, because Drake doesn't deserve this."

His head still down, Skip wiped his eyes again. Lucia remained sequestered in the McDonald's toilets.

"Do you think you're going to be able to do that?" I asked. "Take Drake back to the doctors? Get him reassessed?"

Very slowly, Skip nodded.

"As well as getting him reassessed, we also need to set up plans to help him communicate. He's a lovely boy, Skip. A really lovely, intelligent little boy. One of the nicest kids I've ever worked with. He deserves to be able to share more of his thoughts with the rest of us. Whether this is by learning sign language or by investigating surgery and a voice synthesizer or whatever, he needs to start now or it'll be a real handicap for him."

Skip grimaced. Lifting his hand, he pressed it over his eyes.

I paused to give him a moment to compose himself. My earlier difficult emotions over Lucia and her role in all this had largely passed, and, indeed, there was a part of me that actually liked this couple. They did so clearly love each other and Drake, too, in spite of how he'd been treated. I was well aware they *wanted* to do right. Nonetheless, I had to acknowledge that they were one of the most difficult sets of parents I had ever dealt with, because both of them were so timid, weak, and emotionally unstable. I had no doubt that Mason Sloane was a nasty bully of a man, but as is so often the case between bullies and their victims, the victim's behavior plays as big a part in perpetuating the torment as does the bully's.

"We need to start tackling this matter right away," I said again when the silence threatened to overpower us.

Skip nodded.

"Do you feel you can deal with this yourselves?" I asked. "Or would you like help in locating specialists? And in talking to the school? Because, while it's a great distance and I'd need to turn all this over to someone local fairly soon, I'm more than happy to get you started with it."

He shook his head.

"You'd rather do it yourselves?" I asked. There was something in that shake of the head I couldn't read, which made me think perhaps it was a gesture of hopelessness and not a response to my comments. "Or you can't manage it? Is that what you mean?"

He shook his head again.

A long pause then. I sighed, wishing I could shake him. I shifted in my seat. Sighed again.

"We need to move," Skip said at last. Finally he lifted his head and for a brief moment met my eyes. "We can't stay in Quentin. Our life is over there."

"I understand how upset your father is going to be. I can imagine the scene. But this is his only grandson. While he's been difficult to deal with, it's also been clear that he loves Drake dearly. In spite of his rather . . . shall we say, 'strong' manner, he's done it all for the boy. He's going to be upset, but I'm sure he'll come around. I'm sure he'll accept Drake. Won't he?"

"I—I—I just can't stay there. I don't want to go back. Not tonight. Not ever. We're this far. I just want to keep driving."

I looked at him.

Skip had his arms crossed in front of him on the table,

and he was hunched forward over them, his shoulders up around his ears. He stared at the plastic tabletop. "So that's what Lucy and I did this morning. Put what stuff we needed in the car. I stopped at the bank and withdrew as much as I thought I could call my own and we're just going. Just going to keep going from here."

Shocked, I stared at him. I had in no way anticipated this extreme reaction, and I now felt both alarm and guilt, because I'd pretty much brought it about. I didn't know quite what to say.

It was at that point Lucia returned to the table. Skip slid over, and she sat down beside him. She looked at me with great, wary eyes.

"I've told her," Skip said, his head down again.

Lucia nodded.

"I'll confess, I'm a little . . . concerned," I said. "Surprised. Because this seems a very big response. I've got to admit I'm a little worried when you tell me this."

"We'll take care of Drake," Skip said. "I promise you that."

"Yes, but . . . you're just *leaving*? Don't you have a house in Quentin? Belongings? A job? How can you just . . . *leave*?"

Skip shrugged and for the first time he sat up properly in the booth. "Some things you work out with people. Some things never work out. We talked about it these last couple of days, Lucy and me. Didn't we?" He turned to her. "And we know we're not going to work this one out. So I've made the preparations. I've transferred the accounts to my name only. I've shut off the utilities. We've notified the school. So, yes, we're leaving. We'll come back at some other point and sell the house, pick up the rest of it. At some other point."

I still couldn't believe this, and my incredulity must have shown because Skip then said, "You may think this is taking the weak way out, that we're running away, like kids. But not so. Not really. If my dad's taught me anything, it's that when you see a bad deal, you cut your losses and get out of there."

I nodded. Reaching out, I snagged an unused napkin lying beside the remains of Drake's Happy Meal. "Here," I said, and I wrote my name and address on the napkin. "When you get settled, send me a card, would you? Let me know how things have turned out."

Taking the napkin, Skip folded it and put it in his shirt pocket. "Okay," he said, and for the first time I saw him smile.

When I arrived in the dayroom for Cassandra's session, she wasn't there. I looked around, bewildered, and then went to the nurses' station to inquire. Nancy tipped her head toward the corridor. "She's already down in the therapy room."

This surprised me, as children were not allowed unaccompanied in certain parts of the unit, the therapy room being one.

Nancy grinned. "I know. A bit irregular. But it *is* her last day. And she has something special for you."

I walked down the corridor to the therapy room. The door was closed. I knocked gently.

"Come in!" a voice called.

I opened it.

"Surprise!" Cassandra cried, jumping up and down.

"Wow!" I said.

The room was festooned with paper chains, the kind kids make at school by gluing construction paper strips into rings. These, however, appeared to have been made from every sort of paper—magazine pages, envelopes, newspaper, cards.

"Wow!" I said again. "When did you make all these?"

"I made most of them in my room. I was making them before in the schoolroom, 'cause Joe said that was a good thing to do to relax, and he always made us do chains if we got upset. There are different lengths you got to do, depending how bad you are. Which is kind of stupid really. But anyway, when Dr. Menotti said I could go home if I stayed out of lockdown, I asked Joe if I could have the ones I'd made. And then I started making more for in here. To make it look nice, like we're having a party."

"Well, that is really cool, Cassandra. Because there's so *many*! You've worked really hard," I said.

"And look. Come here and look, because I've made you a card." She bounced over to the table and held it up. "And wait till you see what it does when you open it!"

It was a pretty amazing card. When I opened it, there was a pop-up part in the middle, which did stand right up out of the card. It was an abstract design and written across it was: "Good-bye. I Love You."

"This is *really* good. How did you learn to do this?" I examined the card carefully.

Cassandra was hopping excitedly from one foot to the other beside me. "I can do lots of stuff you don't know about," she said in an amicable voice. "You really only know one thing about me, and that's that my dad took me. But I got lots else to me, too."

"True," I said. "Very, very true. And a very, very good point."

*　　*　　*

Because it was her last day on the unit, I'd told Cassandra we'd play games of her choice during her usual time with me, if she wanted. It was always a challenge to terminate a therapeutic relationship, because while hospitalization was over, there was almost always still much work to be done. I'd found, however, if we marked the end in a celebratory way, not only was it less likely we'd get into conversations over issues that couldn't be followed through, but it also emphasized the child's gains over the time he or she was on the unit. The other thing I liked about playing games was the way they provided a safe parallel structure in which to hide while saying those last few meaningful things to each other, including good-bye.

Cassandra had chosen checkers for her game, and she set about it lustily. I hadn't played any games with Cassandra before, so I didn't know how competitive she was. Cutthroat, as it turned out. And unexpectedly astute at checkers, which wasn't a game I was terribly good at. She beat me fairly and squarely first game out.

We played two or three games and during them chatted affably about not much of anything. Cassandra gossiped about one of the boys on the unit, saying he liked one of the other girls and he'd been trying to kiss her when the staff weren't looking. Then she talked about some music CDs that one of the staff members had brought in and how some of the children had danced to them in the dayroom the night before. Finally she fell silent and appeared to be concentrating on her next move.

After a period of quiet, she said, "I'm not going to see you anymore, when I'm gone."

"Well, you *will* see me for a while," I replied. "After you go back to school, I'll be coming once a week to see how you're getting on. We'll spend some time together each time I come."

"Yeah, but you're not going to be my therapist anymore."

"No, you're right," I said. "You're going to be seeing Dr. Ruiz. She's really nice. I've worked with her lots. And you'll still see Dr. Menotti once a month."

"How come you're not going to do it?"

I smiled gently. "I'd like to, but I only do therapy here at the hospital. When kids go back home, my job is called 'liaising.' That's because I used to be a teacher, so I understand how schools work. For that reason my job outside the hospital is to go around to kids' schools and make sure they're still doing okay and they can tell me if they're not."

"I wish we were still going to be working together," Cassandra said.

"Yes, I do, too. I've liked working with you. But you'll like Dr. Ruiz. She's easy to talk to, and she knows how to handle tricky things. She knows a lot about kids having Troubled Places."

"Is she going to know about me?"

"Yes. All about you. Dr. Ruiz will be ready for you, when you go to see her. She'll be like seeing a friend that you've known for a long time."

Silence came then, and we played on for several minutes without speaking.

"You know something?" Cassandra said.

"What's that?"

"You know when I was talking about Dr. Brown?"

"Yes."

"Well, I didn't really like her. I was just saying that."

"Okay."

"I was just pretending," she said.

"Right."

A pause.

"She always kept saying to me, 'Do what you feel like,' which was okay, because she had some cool junk. Like she had all this art stuff. Like clay and paints and stuff. And a real easel. But . . . but I knew I wasn't there to do art. I felt funny there."

"How do you mean?" I asked.

"Well, like I was thinking, 'Why do I have to go here?' Because it wasn't a school and it wasn't a church and it wasn't Brownies or anything. And I wanted to know why I had to go. My mom kept saying, 'You're going there to get better from what your dad did.' So I thought, 'Okay. But what's that? What's she going to do to me?' I kept waiting for something to happen. I kept getting really nervous, you know? Like when you're waiting for something? Because I thought, maybe she's going to ask me junk. I didn't know what she was going to ask. So when she kept saying, 'Do what you feel like,' it felt like she was trying to trick me. Or . . . I dunno. It's hard to say, but I didn't like it. Because, if she was going to make me better, how come nothing was happening? How come she was waiting?"

"That must have been frustrating," I said.

"It was just confusing."

Cassandra took one of her checkers, hopped over two of mine, and reached my side of the board. Taking a spare checker, she turned her player into a king.

"Anyway, I wanted you to know that," she said.

"Thank you," I said.

"I mean, not that I liked coming here either . . ." Looking up briefly, she grinned. "But I wanted you to know I was just saying that about Dr. Brown."

* * *

Cassandra won that game. We spent a few moments discussing if we should play another or if we should switch and play cards. This sidetracked us into discussing possible card games. Cassandra began to tell me at great length about a game called "Booby," which I'd never heard of and which sounded unusually complicated. Then she remembered it required at least four players. In the end, we returned to checkers.

As Cassandra made her first move, she said, "What's it going to be like?"

"What's what going to be like?" I asked.

"That doctor. The one I'm going to see when I leave here. What's she like?"

"That's what I told you a little earlier. Do you remember?"

A pause.

"Well . . ." she said slowly, "*part* of me remembers. Part of me doesn't, I guess."

"Her name is Dr. Ruiz. And she's very nice. She's very easy to talk to and she's worked with a lot of kids who've had experiences like you've had. That's why Dr. Menotti chose her."

"Will she be like you?"

I smiled. "She'll be like her. But she'll be just as interested in helping as I am. She'll care just as much about what happens to you."

Cassandra nodded.

There was a long pause then. Cassandra sat back. Her eyes were still on the checkerboard and the playing pieces, as if she were considering her next move, but she never made it.

Finally, she looked up. "Can I have your phone number?"

I met her eyes.

She tipped her head to the right. "Just in case I need it."

I smiled. "Yes, of course." I pushed back my chair. "I'll get a piece of paper and write it down for you."

"No, here." Cassandra leaped up and grabbed a felt-tip from the box on the shelf. She came around to my side of the table. "Here. Write it on my hand." She smiled at me. "So I can take it with me."

So I wrote the telephone number of my office across the palm of her hand.

Cassandra closed her hand for a moment. Then she picked up the felt-tip herself. "Here. Give me your hand. I'm going to write something now."

I opened my hand flat.

In careful letters she wrote, "Cassandra," then drew a heart beside it. She colored it in. "There," she said and grinned at me. She folded my fingers in over my palm. "There. Now you take that with you."

Epilogue

$\mathcal{I}$ received a Christmas card at my office address from Drake's parents. It was the first time I'd heard from them since we'd parted at McDonald's that gloomy, overcast Saturday afternoon in early spring.

The card came from a large city almost a thousand miles away. It didn't say much of anything about either Skip or Lucia, nor about their new life. I had to assume new jobs and a new house. There was, however, plenty of news of Drake.

Over the summer, Drake had been reassessed by a large university hospital in the city where they were living. It was determined that his disability was not part of a progressive degenerative illness, but rather a rare congenital deformity.

During August Drake had had the first of what would be several reconstructive surgeries aimed at making his vocal cords more functional, and even now, Lucia said, he was starting to make some sounds. This wasn't going to replace sign language, however, as it was unlikely he would ever be able to speak effectively. Thus, Lucia wrote, both she and Skip had been taking signing classes. Drake, though, was so much faster at it!

He had entered kindergarten in the fall in the neighborhood school and was loving it. A full-time classroom aide was helping him make the transition into the speaking world. Drake was already proving to be an able student academically, and it was thought he soon would not need so much support. As ever, he was popular, the other children clamoring to spend time with him and learn how to "speak in code."

And the very special news, Lucia said, was that Drake was going to be a big brother in April.

This was the only contact I had with the family after they left our area. And I never heard again from or about Mason Sloane.

Cassandra was given an official diagnosis of dissociative disorder in recognition of her "multiple identities." She remained under the care of Dr. Ruiz, a specialist in treatment of childhood trauma, for almost three years, by which point it was felt she had "reintegrated" these parts of her personality. I followed Cassandra's progress closely during this time, seeing her once a week during the first year after her release from the hospital unit and once a month thereafter.

Cassandra's natural father was already serving a prison sentence for abduction and other offenses, mostly drug related. Following Cassandra's allegations, "Uncle Beck" was also arrested. He too is now in prison.

Cassandra's journey to recovery has been a long road,

however, and troubles have persisted. Lying, in particular, has remained a huge problem for her, and in times of stress, she is still inclined to revert to sexualized lies. When she was twelve, her claims that a male teacher had abused her resulted in a very unfortunate court case, after which Cassandra was taken into care.

Things have changed for the better since this time, however. At fourteen, Cassandra became a member of the local youth theater and in this medium finally found a channel for her very active and creative mind. She has enjoyed playwriting, acting, and the backstage world of theater. The year she was seventeen, she not only wrote but also organized and acted in three one-act plays on teenage subjects. These were acclaimed locally, and her small troupe was asked to perform the plays in several high schools. This resulted in a scholarship to study drama at college. Cassandra is still writing plays today.

I've never heard from or about Gerda's family again and can only assume they continue to live their far-flung lives. I myself think of Gerda often, particularly when I am home in Montana. Particularly when the chokecherries are in bloom.

Enter the World of Torey Hayden

ONE CHILD

"Hayden is a fine storyteller, recounting the touching bonds that form among children and between Hayden and her students."
The Washington Post

Six-year-old Sheila never spoke, she never cried, and her eyes were filled with hate. Abandoned on a highway by her mother, abused by her alcoholic father, Sheila was placed in a class for the hopelessly retarded after she committed an atrocious act of violence against another child.

Everyone said Sheila was lost forever—everyone except teacher Torey Hayden.

Torey fought to reach Sheila, to bring the accused child back from her secret nightmare, because beneath the autistic rage Torey saw in Sheila the spark of genius. And together they embarked on a wondrous journey—a journey gleaming with a child's joy at discovering a world filled with love and a journey sustained by a young teacher's inspiring bravery and devotion.

"Page after page proves again the power of love and the resiliency of life."
The Los Angeles Times

SOMEBODY ELSE'S KIDS

"A heartwarming book full of tenderness."
Library Journal

A small seven-year-old boy who couldn't speak except to repeat weather forecasts and other people's words . . . A beautiful little girl of seven who had been brain damaged by terrible parental beatings and was so ashamed because she couldn't learn to read . . . A violently angry ten-year-old who had seen his stepmother murder his father and had been sent from one foster home to another . . . A shy twelve-year-old from a Catholic school which put her out when she became pregnant . . .

They were four problem children, put in Torey Hayden's class because no one else knew what to do with them. Together, with the help of a remarkable teacher who cared too much to ever give up, they became almost a family, able to give each other love and understanding they had found nowhere else.

"Hayden is a fine storyteller."
The Washington Post

MURPHY'S BOY

"The world needs more like Torey Hayden."
The Boston Globe

When Torey Hayden first met fifteen-year-old Kevin he was barricaded under a table, desperately afraid of everything around him. He had not spoken in eight years. Torey Hayden refused to call any child a hopeless case, but to help Kevin they needed a miracle.

When at last she penetrated Kevin's silence, she discovered a violent past and a dreadful secret that a cold bureaucracy had simply filed away and forgotten. It would take all of Torey Hayden's devotion to rescue this "lost case." But with a gentle, patient love Torey Hayden made that miracle happen.

"A story rich in reasons for hope."
Publishers Weekly

JUST ANOTHER KID

"Another fine account by Hayden . . . an invaluable
model for parents of emotionally dysfunctioning
children and for educators of all stripes."
Kirkus

Torey Hayden faced six emotionally troubled kids no
other teacher could handle—three recent arrivals from
battle-torn Northern Ireland, badly traumatized by the
horrors of war; eleven-year-old Dirkie, who knew of
life inside an institution; excitable Mariana, aggressive
and sexually precocious at the age of eight; and seven-
year-old Leslie, perhaps the most hopeless of all, unre-
sponsive and unable to speak.

But Torey's most daunting challenge turns out to be
Leslie's mother, Ladbrooke, a stunning young doctor
who soon discovers that she needs Torey's love and
help just as much as the children. As Torey's aide in
the classroom Ladbrooke reveals her dark and troubled
life, and Torey must try and rescue the beautiful and
sophisticated parent who had become just another kid.

"*Just Another Kid* is a beautiful illustration
of nurturing concern, not only for a few
emotionally disturbed children, but for
one woman facing a personal battle."
South Bend Tribune

GHOST GIRL

"A testament to the powers of
caring and commitment."
Publishers Weekly

Jadie never spoke. She never laughed, or cried, or ut-
tered any sound. Despite efforts to reach her, Jadie remained locked in her own troubled world—until one
remarkable teacher persuaded her to break her self-
imposed silence. Nothing in all of Torey Hayden's experience could have prepared her for the shock of what
Jadie told her—a story too horrendous for Torey's professional colleagues to acknowledge. Yet a little girl
was living a nightmare, and Torey Hayden responded
in the only way she knew how—with courage, compassion, and dedication—demonstrating once again
the tremendous power of love and the resilience of the
human spirit.

"An amazing story."
The Washington Post

THE TIGER'S CHILD

"A deeply moving sequel . . . resonates with drama."
Library Journal

Whatever became of Sheila? When special education teacher Torey Hayden wrote her first book, *One Child,* almost two decades ago, she created an international bestseller. Her intensely moving true story of Sheila, a silent, profoundly disturbed little six-year-old girl touched millions. From every corner of the world came letters from readers wanting to know more about the troubled child who had come into Torey Hayden's class as a "hopeless case" and emerged as the very symbol of eternal hope within the human spirit.

Now, for all those who have never forgotten this endearing child and her remarkable relationship with her teacher, here is the surprising story of Sheila, the young woman.

"The characters will haunt you."
Indianapolis News

BEAUTIFUL CHILD

"Moving . . . persuades us that even the most
withdrawn and troubled child can be reached if
someone takes the time, pays attention, and
sincerely, deeply cares."
O Magazine

Seven-year-old Venus Fox was a complex and con-
flicted child. She wouldn't speak, listen, or even acknowledge the presence of another human being in
the room with her. Yet an accidental playground bump
would release a rage frightening to behold. Torey's interactions with Venus would be some of the most trying, complex, and ultimately rewarding of her career,
as she struggled to reach a silent child in obvious pain.
Truly terrible revelations were followed by encouraging
breakthroughs, as a dedicated teacher remained committed to helping a "hopeless" girl—patiently and lov-
ingly leading her toward the light of day.